Chicken Soup for the Soul

GET OUT OF YOUR COMFORT ZONE

T0023525

Chicken Soup for the Soul: Get Out of Your Comfort Zone
101 Stories about Trying New Things, Overcoming Fear and Broadening Your World
Amy Newmark

Published by Chicken Soup for the Soul, LLC www.chickensoup.com
Copyright ©2023 by Chicken Soup for the Soul, LLC. All Rights Reserved.

The publisher gratefully acknowledges the many publishers and individuals who granted Chicken Soup for the Soul permission to reprint the cited material.

Front cover photo courtesy of shutterstock.com (©Vitalii Matokha)
Back cover and interior photo of clipboard courtesy of iStockphoto.com (©hudiemm)
Photo of Amy Newmark courtesy of Susan Morrow at SwickPix

Cover and Interior by Daniel Zaccari

Publisher's Cataloging-in-Publication data

Names: Newmark, Amy, editor.
Title: Chicken soup for the soul : get out of your comfort zone : 101 stories about
    trying new things , overcoming fear and broadening your world / Amy Newmark.
Description: Cos Cob, CT: Chicken Soup for the Soul, LLC, 2023.
Identifiers: | ISBN: 978-1-61159-103-3 (print) | 978-1-61159-340-2 (ebook)
Subjects: LCSH Self-actualization (Psychology)--Anecdotes. | Thought and thinking
    Anecdotes. | Success--Anecdotes. | Self help. | BISAC SELF-HELP / Motivational and
    Inspirational | SELF-HELP / Personal Growth / Happiness | SELF-HELP / Personal
    Growth / Success
Classification: LCC BF637.S4 .C36 2023 | DDC 158--dc23

Library of Congress Control Number: 2023936209

PRINTED IN THE UNITED STATES OF AMERICA
on acid∞free paper

30 29 28 27 26 25 24 23   01 02 03 04 05 06 07 08 09

GET OUT OF YOUR COMFORT ZONE

101 Stories about Trying New Things, Overcoming Fear and Broadening Your World

Amy Newmark

Chicken Soup for the Soul, LLC
Cos Cob, CT

Changing your world one story at a time®
www.chickensoup.com

Table of Contents

❸

~Believe in Yourself~

❹

~Challenge Yourself~

❺

~Try Something New~

❻

~Be Daring~

❼

~Follow Your Dreams~

8

~Go Far Away~

9

~Just Say Yes~

10

~Put Yourself Out There~

⑪

~Reach Out and Connect~

Introduction

A ship in harbor is safe, but that is not
what ships are built for.
~John A. Shedd

I can't tell you how many times I've heard people say they are making a concerted effort to step outside their comfort zones and try new things. It's one of the most prevalent themes in our books, even the ones that are about completely different topics.

So that's why we decided it was time for another book from us about saying yes to the new, broadening horizons, and doing things that scare us or make us uncomfortable. When you do that — get out of your comfort zone — you are invariably proud of yourself. You feel energized and empowered, and ready to try even more new things. It builds on itself and before you know it, you're that fun, adventurous person who's always up for a challenge.

I know it has worked for my husband and me. We've taken some of the big steps outside our comfort zones — paragliding, ziplining, snorkeling, vacationing in the Middle East — and we've taken small steps — trying a new food, shopping at a different grocery store, playing a new game. They all contribute to our general feeling of wellbeing, and they keep us actively involved in the world instead of existing in one with boundaries that are gradually shrinking.

In this new collection you'll read about skydiving and trying oysters, traveling solo in foreign lands and talking to someone new at a party, starting a new career and trying a new hairstyle. The big things and the little things. They all matter.

I'm sure you'll be motivated to step outside your own comfort zone after you read a few of these stories. They're organized into chapters whose names alone will provide you with positive direction:

1. Reinvent Yourself
2. Face Your Fears
3. Believe in Yourself
4. Challenge Yourself
5. Try Something New
6. Be Daring
7. Follow Your Dreams
8. Go Far Away
9. Just Say Yes
10. Put Yourself Out There
11. Reach Out and Connect

So go forth! Try new things, overcome your fears, and broaden your world. And here's my little secret: If you're about to do something scary, see if there's a video about it on the Internet. Before we went ziplining in Costa Rica, I watched a couple of videos that tourists had posted on YouTube, from the very place where we were going. That's why I seemed so cool, calm, and collected when we got there. I already knew what was going to happen. And before I went paragliding off a 1,000-foot cliff in Oman, I watched a video too. It really helped.

I put my favorite quote of all time at the top of this introduction: "A ship in harbor is safe, but that is not what ships are built for." I live by that philosophy, and I highly recommend that you, too, set sail from your safe harbor. Feel the wind, see new sights, and make your world bigger.

And thank you for being one of our readers.

— Amy Newmark —
April 1, 2023

Reinvent Yourself

Fear Is the Doorway

Once we believe in ourselves, we can risk curiosity,
wonder, spontaneous delight, or any experience that
reveals the human spirit.
~E.E. Cummings

've heard it said that middle age is the time when God/the Universe grabs you by the shoulders and yells, "Okay, I've been suggesting so far, but now I'm insisting. It's time to use the gifts I gave you!"

It took many decades for me to figure out what my gift was and how to use it. I had been a cinephile all my life, even before I knew what the term meant. As a child, I would sit through movies I loved over and over (when that was allowed), disappearing completely into the worlds they created, often to escape my own. I dreamed of someday having the ability to create films that would transfix others the same way. But school was difficult for me for many reasons (that's a whole other *Oprah*), so I struggled just to get by and never made any serious effort to learn how to write fiction. Becoming a screenwriter seemed as unlikely as building a spaceship and flying to Mars.

When I was fourteen, I took my first timid step at writing for public consumption by submitting a poem to a "talent showcase" at my junior high school. I was shocked when it made it into a booklet that was passed out to every student. For a week or so, I was treated very differently. Previously invisible, I was now a "published poet" receiving praise and slaps on the back. In the humblest of ways, I had discovered the power of the written word.

I began to read more and dabble with writing, but an already deep-seated lack of confidence prevented me from having any serious hopes for a career in literature. I felt like those things only happened to other people. However, as more years passed, I began to have a strange feeling when I walked into bookstores and libraries. I would look at the thousands of books and ask myself, "Are all these people smarter than me, or did they just try harder?"

So, I kept reading and maintained a journal of quotes that resonated with me. I wrote stories that embarrass me now — my first timid attempts at creativity, like a bird trying to fly for the first time. And I started watching movies not only for entertainment but to break down how great stories are told. As I struggled to develop the necessary skills, find my own writing "voice," and convince myself it was even possible for me, I toiled at more than twenty unrelated occupations. More years passed. The lack of confidence that afflicted me early in life took decades to shake. My writing improved, but it didn't matter how many people told me that something I wrote had touched them; the wall within me was too strong to believe I could make a living at it. I began to fear I would never make my childhood dream come true. Then I had children, and the need to make a living became even more important and constricting.

I had a job that paid well, but I detested it. Suddenly, the company went out of business. Being set adrift was frightening, but it forced me to choose between getting yet another job I didn't like or finally committing to a career as a writer — or at least something that would improve my writing. The solution was copyediting. It wasn't writing, but it was in the ballpark. I spent more years awash in a sea of words and loved it.

But creativity always found a way out. One of these ways was through a CD of songs I wrote and sang for my first child. The composer I worked with became a good friend, and, coincidentally (or not), we shared a desire to write for film. He said he had an idea for a Western TV series and asked if I'd like to script it. It was way outside my comfort zone, but I jumped at the opportunity. We wrote twelve episodes together. Though we had a lot to learn, it felt very purposeful, like taking a gasping, flopping fish out of a bucket and putting it in water. I knew more than ever that this was what I was supposed to do. What I didn't know was that it wouldn't be that show that would launch my career, or that writing it was how I would cut my teeth as a screenwriter. The show got bogged down in legalities due to our inexperience, but we didn't quit. We wrote other scripts and then created a production company — Temple Gate Films — with a third partner. I wrote several feature film scripts that have not been produced yet. Paying dues before one can reach the lofty heights is not just a cliché. Like real taxes, there is no way to avoid paying them.

Well-meaning friends and family members warned me that "it's a very hard business" (which it is), and I should "have something to fall back on" (which I did: copyediting). I also heard another cliché — "It's who you know" — which is also often true. But the people in the entertainment business who are helping me now are people I met along the way, and I wouldn't have met them if I hadn't taken action.

Others accept whatever we say we are without question. When I began to define myself as a writer, producer, and production-company owner, I began to make connections and receive help. It was sometimes mysterious how I would meet the right person at the right time. Like the movie *Field of Dreams*, we built it, and they came.

There were a thousand great reasons to quit along the way, but I didn't. I couldn't. The alternatives were unbearable: Spending my one sacred life in "quiet desperation." Betraying that kid who sat in the movie theater wondering if he could do it. Never knowing what it feels like to fully master my greatest passion. So, I forged ahead. I let myself rest after disappointments, and there were plenty, but I always got back up, which is all success really is. Some call it dogged determination. Working twice as hard as everyone else. Never quitting. Calvin Coolidge said it best: "Nothing in this world can take the place of persistence. Talent will not; nothing is more common than unsuccessful men with talent. Genius will not; unrewarded genius is almost a proverb. Education will not; the world is full of educated derelicts. Persistence and determination alone are omnipotent."

I'm here to testify that constantly stepping outside of one's comfort zone pays off eventually. A few weeks ago, my production company received funding for our first feature film. Principal photography will begin this fall. I will finally sit in a movie theater and see actors performing my dialogue. It took eight years, but I did it. (Well, forty years really, but eight since I fully committed.) It's also worth noting that I didn't do it alone. Success requires a lot of reshuffling. I eliminated people who discouraged me and surrounded myself with people who believed in me. I broke through the walls of my comfort zone by becoming a copyeditor, then a screenwriter, and then a production-company owner. Along the way, I submitted stories to books and magazines, which also required some comfort zone demolition. I'm proud to say that twenty-nine of those stories are in *Chicken Soup for the Soul* books, for which I am eternally grateful.

I achieved my goals not only because I walked through fear repeatedly but because I embraced it as a doorway to knowledge and achievement. I don't regret the decades it took to "make it" because I use every emotion I felt back then in my writing now. We can be crushed by failure or we can make it mean something. When I write a character who's frustrated or heartbroken, I'm not faking it. I'm also not faking it when those characters are happy and victorious at the end of the movie. As the poet Edwin Markham wrote:

Ah, great it is to believe the dream
As we stand in youth by the starry stream;
But a greater thing is to fight life through
And say at the end, the dream is true!

— Mark Rickerby —

A Bright Idea

*I don't focus on what I'm up against. I focus
on my goals and I try to ignore the rest.*
~Venus Williams

At 10:00 A.M. on an ordinary workday, my supervisor called me into his office, shut the door and gave me the bad news. "I'm really sorry, Kathleen, but you're part of the company-wide layoff. You have to clear out your desk and leave immediately. I hope you don't take this personally."

Who was he trying to kid? Not take it personally? I was devastated! After all, I had been doing a good job as a technical writer, according to my last evaluation. Customers had been calling to tell me they could finally understand the instructions on how to use the electronic instrument they had bought from us.

I remember saying to him as I pointed to his office door, "Go out there and pick someone else; I'm supporting a family." I laugh about it now, but I was serious at the time. As a single mom supporting my daughter, Anne, I had lots of responsibilities. I couldn't just go home and tell her we would be cutting back on things and eating spaghetti without meatballs. Or maybe we'd have to move to another city; her life could change radically. Later that day, when Anne came home from school, I told her. A typical teen, she didn't seem too concerned. She just said, "Don't worry, Mom. You'll think of something."

The only trouble was that I was in an emotional tailspin. I couldn't think straight. Unable to come up with a plan, I dragged myself around for the next week. I did the bare minimum in the apartment, but I mostly sat around in a semi-daze, watching soap operas and game shows on TV. Finally, I told myself I had to get off the sofa and look for a job.

I did the usual résumé thing: updated it, adding my last but fateful job to the list, and sent it to all the companies in a thirty-mile radius that I hoped could use a good technical writer. There were only a few. I didn't feel very optimistic.

My next move was to stand in the unemployment line so I could at least pay some of my bills. While I was waiting for a woman to process my paperwork, a man approached me and asked, "Excuse me, but weren't you part of the recent layoff?"

"Yes," I said. "Why?"

"Are you familiar with the Dislocated Workers' Program?"

I wasn't.

He explained that it was a retraining program for people who were laid off in high-tech fields and wanted to change careers. "If you're interested, go see Mr. Hill. He's in charge of the program."

I found Mr. Hill's office. He was a personable man who repeated what the first man had told me. The government would pay the tuition, books and fees for a person who was laid off in a field in which jobs were scarce in the area.

Months ago, a friend of mine had left the company to attend nursing school at the local university. I had briefly considered doing the same, but I didn't have the courage to quit my job and attend college full-time. I told myself to keep an open mind as I talked with Mr. Hill.

"You mean the government will pay all my tuition to go to, say, nursing school?"

"Yes."

"Would they pay for me to attend the university?"

"No, it's too expensive. But they will pay for you to go to the community college."

Just like the little light bulb that goes on over people's heads in the comic strips, I felt something click on in my brain. I thought, *Maybe I should start listening. Maybe the answer to my predicament is here in Mr. Hill's office.* He must have sensed my growing enthusiasm because he suggested I go to the college to see if I could get in.

"Classes started yesterday," he warned, adding that the nursing school usually had a lengthy waiting list, so I might not get in. On my way to the college, I reminded myself again that this could be the answer I was searching for and to keep an open mind.

I arrived on the campus around 11:00 A.M. My first stop was the counseling office. The fellow I spoke to was pleasant but not encouraging as he repeated what Mr. Hill had told me about the nursing school being filled and having a waiting list. My next stop took me to the Continuing Education Office where another pleasant person told me the same thing.

I needed a breath of fresh air, so I stepped outside into the warm August sunshine. Thoughts ran through my head: *Do not give up. Don't let those people discourage you. Who is the right person to talk to? Who has the authority to let me into the nursing school?* My experiences in the business world told me to go to the person at the top.

I found the nursing office and asked the secretary if I could speak with the head of the nursing school. She was on her lunch break, I was told, but would be back shortly. The secretary told me I was welcome to wait.

The dean returned. She had a formidable look about her as she waved her hand toward the chair in her office, indicating that I should sit down. I felt like a little kid in the principal's office, apprehensive and nervous. I introduced myself, told her I wanted to become a nurse, and that the government was paying my tuition.

Fifteen minutes into the interview, she snapped, "Be here tomorrow morning, 9:00 sharp, for a nursing lecture. We'll take care of the necessary paperwork later," meaning my transcripts and official application, and her letter of acceptance. An hour and a half after I had begun my quest, I was an official member of the nursing class! Later, I learned that two people had dropped out the day before. Apparently, I had arrived at exactly the right time. Everything had fallen into place perfectly: Mr. Hill, the director of the nursing school, and the openings in the nursing class.

Attending college full-time for two years, borrowing a large sum of money for our living expenses, and working twenty-four hours a week wasn't easy. I graduated with an associate degree in nursing, was offered jobs in both hospitals in town, and passed my nursing boards. I was a licensed registered nurse! I acquired a flexible career that allowed me to work almost anywhere in the world at a wide variety of jobs. All it took was an open mind, faith in myself, and motivation.

—Kathleen Cox Richardson—

Milk and Meat

*To free us from the expectations of others, to give us
back to ourselves — there lies the great,
singular power of self-respect.*
~Joan Didion

had drinks with a friend a week after my husband and I separated, and she asked me what I was going to do to celebrate my newly claimed life. Dance around the house naked? Have a party for myself and invite all my friends?

"A turkey-and-cheese sandwich. That's what I'm doing," I said, already smiling at the devil I was becoming.

When Eric and I decided to marry, it was assumed we would keep kosher, the ancient, traditional Jewish practice of separating all dairy and meat. And, for the next thirty years, I never mixed the two. There is a biblical reference to this concept — something about not cooking a calf in its mother's milk. But, in modern times, the practice is less about the sacred text and more about the deeply held belief that food is sacred, mealtime is precious, and families should be thoughtful about what and how they eat.

My husband was raised in that tradition. I was not. Still, I agreed to this arrangement without a second thought. That was the first step toward losing myself — to what, over the next three decades, became reflexive — putting aside my wants and needs in service to the marriage and family.

I understand the value of ritual. In a land where we are not the dominant culture, maintaining customs helps us hold onto that part of our identity, to the physical reminders of who we are, especially with kids. I used to cook Shabbat dinner every Friday: homemade challah and matzah-ball soup. It was good for the kids, but ritual and rules were never really my style. When I was a kid, I wore a "Challenge Authority" T-shirt to threads. Why were these ancient rabbis lording over my kitchen?

Learning new routines in the kitchen is like learning a new language, and I'm bad at languages. Keeping kosher means having two sets of everything because nothing that touches dairy can touch meat: two sets of dishes, two sets of silverware, two sponges — not to mention all the extra towels, pots, and pans.

So many of the foods I had grown up eating — tacos with ground beef and cheese, turkey and cheddar toasted on a bagel, steak with blue cheese — I had to abandon. Frantic after-work scrubbing of the morning milk dishes formed the roadblock between me and the shoulder roast I needed to cook for dinner. Clearly, I mumbled as I tossed the dairy sponge into the cabinet, keeping kosher was sanctioned by men before women left the house to work. Over the course of thirty years, this sacred ritual evolved into a symbol of the sacrifices I had made, of the person I had left behind when I became a wife and mother.

Now, here I was in the regular, pedestrian grocery store, standing at the deli counter, where I had not dared to tread for three-plus decades. (Kosher meat only comes from the kosher butcher.) I took a number and surveyed the selection. Several kinds of turkey — but wait! There was bologna. Salami! And it was all hanging out, casually, right next to the cheeses. I almost walked away from the sheer excitement of it all. But then they called my number, so I did it. I ordered a pound of roasted turkey and a half-pound of baby Swiss. I took the packages and placed them together in the cart. I grabbed some bread without checking the label to see if it contained non-kosher ingredients and then sashayed nonchalantly to the checkout line. I'd gone rogue.

I drove home with the contraband. Back in the kitchen, I placed my packages on the counter. I stared at the meat and cheese. There we were, me and my future. I walked away to look in the mirror and make sure it was still me. I was shocked to see the same self as always — curly hair still intact, limbs still attached.

I prepared my sandwich, slapping cheese on top of meat like a seasoned pro, and sat at the table to eat. Slowly, with each bite, I felt the possibilities burst open, the long-lost combination reminding me I could reclaim myself, reclaim what I wanted to taste in my own life.

Maybe tomorrow I would try a patty melt.

— Debbie Chase —

Reaching New Heights in the Navy

Do the thing you fear, and continue to do so. This is the
quickest and surest way of all victory over fear.
~Dale Carnegie

joined the Navy in 1981 because I stumbled across an ad in *The Atlanta Journal-Constitution*: THE NAVY. It's not just a job. It's an adventure.

I wasn't looking for adventure, but in fine print was the clincher. The Navy needed instructors. Bingo! I had seven years of teaching experience so I signed up.

On a crisp October morning, I started training at Officer Candidate School in Newport, Rhode Island.

I didn't grow up in the military, so everything was new, from doing an about-face to learning how to salute. In many ways, that was to my benefit. I had no preconceived notions about Navy life and no bad habits to break.

Every day, my company followed the Plan of the Day. We attended classes from Monday to Friday, played sports at Mandatory Fun on Saturday, and endured daily room inspections. The only time I was in my comfort zone was at Chapel on Sunday morning.

One day, the Plan of the Day told us to report to the swimming pool. The Navy had instructed us to bring a one-piece bathing suit, a terrycloth bathrobe, and a thick towel, so I knew there would be a swimming test.

I didn't expect it to be a challenge because I had recently overcome my fear of water. When I was twenty-four years old, I took swim classes at the YWCA — Guppy classes, in fact. They were for people like me who had to build up the courage to stick their big toes in the water.

To my amazement, I enjoyed the Guppy class. I signed up for the next one (Tadpole), and the next and the next. I learned all the basic strokes, how to drown-proof, how to swim to the deep end without panicking, and how to float on my back. When I saw that the next class involved the diving board, I decided I had learned enough.

As it turned out, that wasn't necessarily the case.

The day came, toward the end of Officer Candidate School, when we had to prove that we could swim.

Piece of cake, I told myself. I felt comfortable in the water.

The first exercise was easy. We had to swim from the shallow end of the pool to the deep end and back using any stroke we wished.

Next, we had to drown-proof for an hour. Again, a piece of cake. While the men struggled to keep afloat, I leaned my head back and counted the ceiling lights. The only odd thing was looking down at one point and seeing a fellow officer candidate walking on the bottom of the pool. I had never seen anyone do that before. I later learned that men are less buoyant than women.

And then the officer in charge of the swim test told us that our next exercise was to swim underwater — under a pretend ring of fire.

Here, my buoyancy kicked me in the rump. I dove underwater but kept popping up to the surface. I made several attempts to swim under the "burning oil" around our pretend ship but never could do it.

The instructor grinned at me and said, "Officer Candidate Wells, you are a French fry!"

Women weren't allowed on ships back in the early 1980s, so I wasn't overly concerned about swimming under burning oil. Neither was he.

Then, we were told that we were going to jump off a twelve-foot platform. We were to fold our hands over our chests, take a deep breath, hold our noses, and jump.

We went up the stairs and lined up for our turn. One after the other, officer candidates jumped in and surfaced.

When it was my turn, I went to the edge, put my toes in the proper place… and froze.

There was no way I was jumping twelve feet into the water. Until that moment, I hadn't realized I had a fear of heights.

I was holding up the line, but I couldn't move.

The guy behind me said, "You need a push?"

"Yes, because that's the only way I'm getting off this platform."

It was the most terrifying thing I had ever done.

Later, when I thanked him for the shove, he gave me a Cheshire smile and said he had fun pushing me off the platform.

I'm glad someone enjoyed my leap of faith.

Seventeen weeks of Officer Candidate School challenged me and made me a better, stronger person. I learned how much I could do that I didn't know I could do.

Did the Navy cure my fear of heights? No. To this day, I can't climb a six-foot ladder without my head swimming. That never interfered with my naval service at all and made me glad I had chosen a career that kept me at sea level.

Getting outside my comfort zone was good for me. Learning what you can't do can be just as important as learning what you can.

— Lila W. Guzman —

Eating My Words

*Coming out of your comfort zone is tough in the
beginning, chaotic in the middle, and awesome
in the end... because in the end,
it shows you a whole new world.*

~Manoj Arora

As I approached mid-life, friends and relatives questioned where I might retire someday. I'd often dreamed of living on an exotic island somewhere, but, in reality, I figured Pat and I would probably stay put in our house on the hill in Jamesville, NY even though it was too big for us now that our children were grown. We had many interesting conversations about places we could consider, but each time I always ended by saying, "I'll never go to Florida! I hate golf."

Pat suggested we step out of our comfort zone and travel around the United States to search for the perfect place, but we never found anywhere we both liked. We continued to pour money into our forty-year-old house, grimacing with each check we wrote for landscaping, driveway resurfacing, fireplace maintenance, and snow removal. We were tired of spending money on things we weren't enjoying, and the cold seemed less kind as each winter passed.

"I'm thinking about watching ocean waves," Pat said dreamily.

"Oh, that sounds nice," I concurred. "A place where we can walk the beach for hours and collect shells?"

"I could do that," Pat said. "I'm thinking about driving to a restaurant in a Jeep with the tropical breezes blowing through our hair."

"Oh, I could do that," I murmured. "And ride bikes?"

Pat nodded. "Swim?"

"Oh, yeah!"

"No more shoveling snow!"

"I agree!"

We were both on the same page, but we didn't know what book. I was dreaming of someplace south, craving warmth, but I didn't know how far south I would go. I heard horror stories about snakes, deadly spiders, frogs, and brain-eating ameba. We decided to sell our home while we figured out where to go. But first we had to tackle the basement.

As basements go, ours wasn't horrible. Half of it was a converted family room. The other half was an accumulation of forty years' worth of stuff.

It took two years to downsize. During the purging phase of our life, my sister invited us to stay in her retirement home in Florida during January. I didn't want to go there, but I didn't want to endure the brutal cold at home. Additionally, I wasn't well, and it gave me an opportunity to recover in sunshine and bask in warmth. My sister was giving me a free vacation in her beautiful home in Florida, away from snow and the stress of cleaning out our home and deciding where to retire. It was in an oddly named place: The Villages.

I thought my sister was too young to have a home in a retirement community surrounded by old people — especially in Florida. She told me to step outside my comfort zone and embrace change. I figured I wouldn't do that in Florida, but I agreed to be open-minded for her sake.

When we arrived, her house was clean and comfortable. We thought it was a perfect home, square footage-wise, and we agreed we could live in something similar. But we didn't want to be surrounded by a lot of old people who sit around in rocking chairs on their porches, snooping in our business.

The second day there, we went for a long walk around the village. It was lovely! Many people were outside early in the morning, walking, biking, and jogging. They were checking their Fitbits. They weren't old; they were my age! No one was rocking in a chair. I peeked in the pool area and saw people swimming laps. As they were toweling dry, they said they swam a mile every day! I saw people scurrying into classes — not biomolecular engineering but dance aerobics. The teacher was eighty-three years young. She didn't look it, nor did she act it. She pointed to several of her students who were also in their eighties and nineties!

That night at dinner, Pat and I discussed this retirement community. It was different. We drove around in golf carts and loved it. Each night, there was a different band playing music in the town squares. We loved being outside in the fresh air, under the swaying palm trees, and basked in the moon glow and starlit sky. We weren't sitting in front of a TV like zombies. We were out dancing.

On the third day, I went to an open house. I definitely could envision myself living there. I signed up to take golf lessons and, much to my surprise, I hit the ball and liked it. I found a golf store near the town square where we both bought a set of clubs. I didn't want to go back home. This Shangri-la made me feel happy, young, lively, and free-spirited. I didn't want any of it to end.

By the end of the month, we had bought a house about a mile from my sister's. Our relationship blossomed, and, unexpectedly, I was excited to grow old together in this paradise. Within two years, we relocated to Florida permanently. I had to eat my words: I was living in the place I said I would never go, and I was golfing three times a week. Thank God I had the courage to step outside my comfort zone because now I'm the happiest person in Florida!

— Barbara Sue Canale —

A Recovering Perfectionist

*Being a mother is learning about the strengths
you didn't know you had... and dealing
with fears you didn't know existed.*
~Linda Wooten

've been called a perfectionist my entire life. The all-A's, well-mannered, tidy child turned into an adult with a successful career, immaculately organized home, and picture-perfect family. But I'll let you in on a little secret: It's easy to appear perfect when you only do things you know you'll succeed at. I have a habit of quitting when I don't think I'll live up to my own unrealistic expectations. When I didn't make the varsity team my junior year, I quit playing softball altogether. After getting a B- in Chemistry, I changed college majors. As a new mother, I quit nursing my first baby after one day of struggling.

The truth is, I enjoy creative things like making music, drawing, and writing, but I stopped doing them. A note slightly off-key or a line of prose that didn't quite flow had me throwing in the towel. Perfection in artistic things is too subjective, and I always deem my attempts as not good enough and therefore not worthy of my time. I tend to stay in my comfort zone of measurable outcomes. One hundred percent on the test. Winner or loser. Success or failure. Perfection or... not.

As I entered motherhood, I was met with a world full of measurable outcomes: milestones, growth percentiles and school grades. My older daughter met and exceeded expectations. She talked at an early age and was reading before kindergarten. I kept up with the other moms: "Sally said 'mama' last night!" "Billy started walking!" "Johnny can already write his name!" Having the perfect child meant I was the perfect mother, right?

When my second daughter was born, everything was perfect again. I got pregnant the first month of trying, had an unmedicated birth, and she took to nursing immediately. Motherhood success. She was the most beautiful, happy baby with a splash of dark hair and piercing blue eyes. She always had a smile on her face with the sweetest dimple on her delicate right cheek. She was drawn to music from an early age and would bob her head to any beat. No matter how quietly it was playing, she would find the music and dance along. She was the picture of perfection.

But things changed. With each passing month, she failed to meet developmental milestones. The older she got, the more behind she fell. I kept hoping she would catch up, knowing some kids just needed a little more time. But at eighteen months she was just starting to crawl and was nowhere near walking. That's when we had her first evaluation. The doctors asked me questions like "Can she pull herself up to stand?" "Does she wave goodbye?" "Does she say 'mama'?" The answer to every question they asked was no. She was below the 5th percentile for height and weight and more than a year behind on all milestones. The doctors ordered more tests and prescribed a variety of therapies.

Tears quietly streamed down my face the entire car ride home from that appointment. My life was suddenly unraveling. There was part of me that feared the worst. A piece that wondered what the future held. Another piece screamed: Why my baby? Another piece felt the pang of guilt: What did I do to cause this? My beautiful baby, whom I loved more than life itself, wasn't perfect.

As I pulled into the driveway, I wiped away the tears with the back of my hand and glanced at her in the rearview mirror. She was buckled in her car seat, head bobbing and body wriggling to some song on the radio that, in my strife, I hadn't realized was playing. She had a huge grin on her face and that little dimple in her right cheek. In that moment, it felt like something hit me square in the chest, taking my breath away. My tears changed from ones of grief to those of a mother feeling her heart explode with love for her child. And I knew it all didn't matter — not the milestones, or the growth charts, or the hope that she would "catch up." It didn't matter if my baby, my family, or my life was perfect. The only thing that mattered was the pure joy I saw on her face, and I knew I wouldn't change anything about her, or this life, even if I could.

My daughter is now three years old and has diagnoses that include global developmental delay and cerebral palsy. We have been to countless specialists, therapies, and evaluations. She can walk now with the help of braces on her feet. She wears sparkly purple glasses and can say a few words. Even though this journey is not what I expected for my child, I still wouldn't change anything. She is tenacious, loving and joyous. And she loves music. She still dances anytime she hears a beat. She hangs onto the couch and sways her hips, bouncing to the rhythm. She waves her tiny arms and claps her hands. Even though she often falls, and her movements are uncoordinated when she dances, the happiness on her face always shines through.

I still often wonder what the future holds for her. She might not ever make it to Broadway and dance on a big stage, but one thing I am certain of is that when she stumbles, she'll get back up and keep dancing, full of joy, with a smile on her face and a dimple in her right cheek.

Out of the many lessons my daughter has taught me so far in her short life, the best one is this: Life is about seeking joy, not perfection. Perfection is like an oversized wool turtleneck that, when first pulled on, feels warm, cozy and safe. Under lumps of loose fabric, it hides the body from judgmental gazes. But soon it begins to feel too hot. It starts to itch, suffocate, and choke. My daughter has helped me begin to unravel this garment of perfection, exposing me.

I feel free. I'm free to spend the rest of my life seeking joy — not worrying or comparing my life to what it "should" be. I'm enjoying what it is. And I'm going to start doing the things I love to do again. I'll choose to play the song even if a note is missed. Paint the picture that gives me peace even though it might not ever hang in a gallery. I'll run the race that makes me feel powerful, even if I come in last. And I'll write my stories. I'll write for my daughters. I'll write for myself. I'll write, not for perfection, but because it brings me joy. And that's what life is all about.

—Amy Stros—

Sailing Forth

As you begin to live according to your own guidance
and your own daring everything changes completely.
~Leonard Willoughby

I walked to the desk wearing my red flats, otherwise known as my confidence shoes. My new manager introduced me to my co-workers in the neighboring cubicles. I gave them a big smile, but inside I was filled with doubt. I had taken the leap, but had I done the right thing?

For the previous ten years, I had called a different desk my work home — my teacher's desk at my local high school. I was an English teacher at my alma mater, and for many of those ten years, it was my dream job. However, in the last few years of my career, I'd found that things had shifted inside me. I wasn't as passionate standing in front of the classroom as I had been before. I'd found myself wondering if the classroom was really my final career destination or if there was something else calling to me. I'd wondered if I was brave enough to do something about it.

Truthfully, I knew it was time for me to leave education long before I hit "Send" on the first application. However, changing your mind about what you thought would be your forever dream is never an easy transition. We tell ourselves all sorts of things to stay in our comfort zone because, let's face it, change is hard.

As a little girl, I lined up stuffed animals on our stairs and pulled my dusty chalkboard to the bottom. I would "teach" my auditorium of pupils as my mother cooked dinner. I thought teaching was my life path. However, there was another passion within me even then.

From the time I could hold a pencil, stories flowed from my brain. I would fill journals with stories of ladybugs and wily cats. I would write poems and detail my day in my first non-fiction drafts. Writing was my way of connecting with the world. Although I was shy and introverted when speaking, the words flowed effortlessly with a pencil in hand.

When I got older, though, writing seemed like a childish whim and not a career. Thus, I did the next best thing for a bookworm who loved writing—I became an English teacher.

My time in the classroom fulfilled me for many years. Surrounded by books and words, I was able to live out my passion to a certain extent. During my career, I even saw another one of my dreams come true. My first novel was published in 2015, and since then I've had over twenty novels published in both the romance and thriller genres. I even became a *USA Today* bestseller.

Seeing my writing efforts come to fruition in a published work made me realize that teaching wasn't my deepest passion. In reality, I was masking my desires with what I thought was a practical choice.

The heart can only be stifled for so long, however. During the past year I'd started to realize that, more than teaching others how to write, I wanted to make a career out of writing myself.

I started to explore my options and step out of the box I had meticulously put myself in. I accepted that the dreams we have at age five don't have to be our forever dreams.

It took a lot of applications and soul-searching to find my new place. I was rejected many times. I talked myself into all sorts of career options only to realize they weren't where my heart was. Some days, I even talked myself out of leaving teaching. But the restless spirit is relentless in the pursuit of happiness, so I pushed on.

In May, a job posted at a corporation for a Communications Specialist. This job was essentially a full-time writing job. It was a chance for me to pursue my passion in a way that was financially stable.

I'd like to tell you that switching jobs after ten years was simple and that I didn't have any doubts. That would be a lie. Anytime you leave a familiar career, with co-workers you've known for years, it's a little uncomfortable. From the moment I put in the application until the moment I walked to my new desk in my red shoes, I had a lot of anxiety and doubts, even though I was chasing my passion.

Still, months later, I appreciate the decision I made and the courage it took to make it. I am now somewhere that lights up my soul and sparks my passion.

Oftentimes, being truly fulfilled in our career means we must take that tenuous step outside our comfort zone. We must ask the really hard questions of ourselves, such as: Am I really happy? Is this my true passion? Does my job still light me up? And when we get the difficult answer, we must respect ourselves enough to be brave and make the change.

Sitting at my new desk now, I no longer see the change as scary. I see it as an exciting opportunity to unleash new potential in myself, to learn and grow. Most of all, I've learned through the experience that it's never too late to change your mind. So, if in the future, my current desk feels too small and I find my heart wandering again, I know I will have the courage and strength to do what feels impossible — take the leap into a new horizon.

I think we all need to find that courage to chase our passions. Life is short, the world is big, and there are so many ways to use our gifts to make a living. I had a quote from Walt Whitman on a poster in my classroom: "Now voyager sail thou forth to seek and find." It worked for me.

— Lindsay Detwiler —

8

Mic Check

We cannot become what we want to be
by remaining what we are.
~Max De Pree

It started with a simple statement: "I think I want to start a podcast." My husband and I were sitting on the back porch sipping our coffee as we watched our chickens chase a grasshopper. It was our Covid lockdown morning routine. When he mentioned the podcast, there was no parting of the sky or doves suddenly appearing. I had no idea that his podcast would unwrap my security blanket of being support staff and jumpstart my own career.

But it did.

As a homeschooling, work-from-home mom living in a farming community, the pandemic hadn't affected me as much as it had most of the world. My husband, however, was a manager at an international company that told all employees to work from home until further notice. He was getting bored.

"Without having the long drive to the office every day, if I was ever going to do it, this is the time," he said.

I assumed my normal role as a supportive wife. Of course, he could do this! Then, he could write a book. Then, he could be a great speaker at international conferences. He could become a leader of leaders.

"How can I help?" I asked.

My journalism background meant that I was a natural at writing questions for him to answer within a given topic. I handled the show notes, press releases, and social-media pages. That evolved into e-mailing people and requesting interviews. The audience steadily grew.

But there were inevitably solo shows, and my husband wanted to try an episode where I was on the mic as well.

"Conversation makes a podcast more natural," he theorized. And it did.

We started with Q&A sessions with me as an interviewer, but then we moved into more banter when there were topics on which I could contribute a unique perspective. Honestly, I think it was just the chemistry between my husband and me that made it work. These episodes were more open-mic conversations with talking points than anything else. But people were drawn to our authenticity and openness.

During the process, I slowly started noticing my much younger self shining through.

In high school, I was pretty fearless. In college, I became even more extroverted. I was the editor of everything, wrote controversial editorials that knocked heads with the powers that be, won some major awards, and went on to be the first student to ever give the commencement address.

We had such difficulty having kids that when we finally did, all my energy went to my family. There was much less Jamie and much more Mom. Between germ infestations and the sheer difficulties of getting three kids under five years old ready to leave the house, I became more and more isolated. That isolation became my security blanket.

I intentionally made the "full-time mom" decision and always thought I'd get back to "me" someday. But I had settled into the support-staff role so much that I forgot what that "me" looked like. It wasn't a bad person to be, but it certainly wasn't the person I envisioned myself becoming.

Slowly, the podcast rekindled the younger me: The woman who asked hard questions and fearlessly answered them when asked. The woman who made a verbal faux pas on tape and laughed at herself. The person who asked for an interview, was declined, and asked again. The fearless Jamie.

And I liked it.

Even as we finished the podcast's final episode, I knew I didn't want to go back into my shell. I had to figure out how to utilize this new version of a younger me — full of gumption and rekindled ambition, but now with the wisdom that accompanies age and experience.

I started by piggybacking on the business podcast and landing writing gigs in the business space. With successes under my belt, I set aside more hours in my day and dove into more writing. Within eight months of daily writing, I had developed a work-from-home, steady-income job that utilized my skills.

Then, I took a stab at my real passion: fiction. I framed my first check and hung it on the wall as a reminder to myself that my husband's dreams aren't the only ones worth pursuing.

It's been a couple of years since we stopped making the podcast. Last week, my husband and I again found ourselves sipping coffee on the back porch when he said, "It's funny, I didn't know it at the time, but the podcast may have been more for you than me."

And he's right. Yes, he benefited because he is recognized as an expert in his field. But, for me, that mic changed my life in a way I never anticipated. It reconnected me with... me.

— Jamie A. Richardson —

9

My Soul Song

We are not our age... We are our energy.
~Author Unknown

always wanted to learn how to fight. Yes, you read that correctly: FIGHT. Fifteen years ago, I watched a mall security video online. In the video, I saw a male snatching a purse from an unsuspecting female shopper. He ran away through the crowd. This caused a commotion. In the thief's path was a male shopper walking the mall with his friend. Due to the yelling behind him, and the fact that a guy was running through the crowd, he quickly realized what was happening. With one fluent backwards kick, he floored the thief. Yes, you read that right: With one kick, he floored an adult male. I was seriously impressed, and my desire was born to become like him.

Years passed, and I never forgot the video or my desire. I still wished I was able to do something cool like that, to protect myself with one kick or punch.

As a woman, I felt vulnerable walking alone in the woods or to my car in a parking garage at night. I disliked feeling powerless but I thought I was too old, or that a female couldn't learn to fight. Maybe I would make a fool of myself if I tried.

I did check out a taekwondo school in my neighborhood. But, looking through the windows, I was intimidated by the sandbags, boxing balls, boxing gloves and other scary-looking fighting equipment. It confirmed my fears that it was not a place for a woman over fifty. Time passed, and every time I drove by the taekwondo school, I glanced over longingly.

I was in an unhappy marriage where I had chosen for too many years to relinquish my power. The smallest incident could set off my husband. In order to protect myself and the children, I had learned to hide my true self. I didn't speak up, contradict, or question, and I definitely didn't fight back because this would unleash verbal rage. I chose to be submissive to keep the peace. I became a shell of who I really was.

I found solace and strength in my spirituality. It gave me hope and I found peace in my daily, hours-long walks with my loyal German Shepherd. Nature was my home, my temple. Journaling became my safe haven, the place where I could connect with my true self and start the process of valuing and loving myself again. The more I distanced myself from the toxic behavior in the home, the stronger I became. I eventually left the marriage and chose my happiness.

Thus came the day when I finally entered the dojang (training hall) of my taekwondo school. I was going to learn to fight even though I was terrified. When I entered the class and realized I was the only female I had to talk firmly to myself. The instructor was welcoming and encouraging, though, and luckily another female showed up.

Putting on those boxing gloves and punching those sandbags liberated my soul! I never even knew what I was missing until I punched and kicked those sandbags with all my might. With every punch or kick, I felt alive and healed. I let go of my anger and pain. An uppercut, a hook, or a punch? Preferably all three back-to-back. Kicking? Yes, please. Forward, side kick, backwards or all three? I come alive and soar high when I unleash and reconnect with my inner and physical strength.

Am I as strong and fit as the young male fighters? Of course not. Can I kick as high and hard? Definitely not. I try not to compare myself to others. I appreciate my "old" body, and I firmly believe in the power of my thoughts.

Today, four years later, I almost have my black belt in taekwondo! I even joined kickboxing. You can find me in the dojang four times a week. I am a woman who is nurturing, caring, and loving but also strong, confident, and powerful. I am a bad-ass fifty-seven-year-old grandma, and I can floor you with one kick!

—Shirlene Raymann—

10

Seizing Bliss

You have the power to choose bliss.
~Amy Leigh Mercree

The repetitive squawking of an overeager bird stirs me out of my slumber. Before I open my eyes, the soundscape of the African bush fills my ears. Each bird, cricket, and creature plays its part in perfect harmony with the rest. I never tire of the ever-changing rhythm of their songs.

This life is a dream, my wild and wonderful utopia. We live in an animal sanctuary deep in the heart of Kruger National Park, hidden in the African bush. We work here on keeping harmony between humans, animals, and the vastly diverse natural landscape. We protect wildlife from poachers and human interference. We are silent partners, standing in solidarity with the natural world and all its species.

This was not how I always lived. I had an office job in a big city. I was part of the rat race. I wouldn't say I was unhappy by any means. Just apathetic. Comfortable. I woke up and went to sleep with this nagging feeling that surely there was something more to life. I just never had the courage to chase it. I thought I had what I had, and that was that. I could always dream or fantasize about shaking things up, but my comfort was something to be valued.

I thank my lucky stars every day for the moment that shook me out of that frame of mind. I ripped off the warm embrace of my comfort zone, shook myself loose from the shackles of obligation, booked a flight and embarked on a journey with an unknown destination. And it led me here.

The mornings are frosty. I welcome the steam rising from my coffee as I look out on the river stretching in front of our living quarters. As far as the eye can see, the unadulterated, natural landscape stretches in front of me. It is a sight I will never tire of, ever-changing and always breathtaking.

We start our days taking a drive through the bush. Each morning is an adventure. We never know which animals we'll encounter. The energy of the bush is incredible. The animals move around with ease, coexisting the way only nature can. The overwhelming smells, a mixture of dry, sandy dust, aromatic flowers, and animal musk, remind me of the distance between us and the artificiality of urban life. As we drive, the sun beats down on my face, and I survey the scenery for signs of life. I do not have to look long. A herd of springboks grazes up ahead, munching peacefully. The younger boks shake what their mama gave them, hopping to and fro animatedly. We watch them for a while, getting entrenched in the hierarchy of pack life. We follow the boks as they move in synchronicity toward the watering hole.

We usually spend a few hours at the watering hole, observing the comings and goings. Endlessly entertaining, it strangely reminds us of a school cafeteria, each animal representing a different clique. Elephants, with their magnitude and gravitas, are the highlight for me. Their strong, silent wisdom and stern beauty make them endlessly fascinating. I am perpetually captivated by the family dynamics within herds of elephants, and the sharp contrast between their extremely playful nature and their fierce protectiveness and loyalty.

Baboons are equally as enthralling. Watching them, I forget that these are not humans because their behaviors and interactions feel extremely familiar — aside from combing each other's hair for bugs. I have yet to witness humans doing this — but never say never.

Each time I think I have decided on my favorite animal, another will come along and change my mind. Zebras, giraffes, rhinos, buffalos, hyenas, wild dogs, the big cats — all are captivating, beautifully stunning, and irreplaceable in their own way. That is why we do this. These are special creatures whose land is being stolen from them.

Unlike humans, they just want to exist. They have no concept of profit or development. They have an amazing unhuman-like ability to appreciate everything—every leaf, every stone—just the way it is. If you ask me, that is true bliss. After a few hours of watching the animals, we make our way back to the sanctuary.

We spend the day nursing the animals we have in our care. Some are victims of poachers. Others were caught in mangled fences. Others were harmed when they strayed too far into human-settled areas. We care only for the animals that have come to harm through human intervention. We allow the natural world to function as it does. Once the animals have been nursed, we release them into the bush as soon as we can, which is a bittersweet feeling. We grow attached to these animals, all with unique, wonderful personalities. It is a joy to witness them reintegrate into their world once we have helped them. The rewards here are endless.

The downtime of our days is filled with creation. We paint and draw. We write stories, poetry, plays or scripts. We dance, sing or act for the joy of it. We try to express ourselves artistically for our own benefit, not to attempt to sell or profit from our art. It is entertainment for the sake of entertainment—the way art was meant to be created. We exercise, do yoga, and relax before cleaning and getting ready for our evening bush drive.

The evening bush drive feels a little more sinister. We follow tips and leads that have been called into us about possible poacher activity. We pray every night for an uneventful trip, with an absence of poachers. Should we find them, we approach them, sharing with them our intentions to protect the animals at all costs. We chase them away and then patrol the area to ensure they do not return. The nights in the bush are a whole different terrain. The nocturnal animals roam the land. On rare occasions, we have been lucky to witness a leopard dragging a dead animal up a tree for his dinner.

Our life is one of routine and simplicity, surrounded by people we love and a world we never get tired of. It is the kind of lifestyle that forces us to live in the moment. We seem to truly function on a higher level. It is a joyful life, where we cannot help but be reminded of our own insignificance when taking in the nature of our surroundings. We want to feel and spread love for the short time that we are here and hope that these animals will still exist to dazzle future generations.

—Vanessa Schaefer—

Face Your Fears

11

The Birds

Nothing diminishes anxiety faster than action.
~Walter Anderson

intentionally walked in front of an oncoming car — to avoid a pigeon. As the car screeched to a halt just a few feet away, I panicked, realizing I almost got killed.

"What's wrong with you?" the driver yelled, adding some choice expletives. "Do you want to die?"

I knew what was wrong with me. I had a lifelong fear of birds. My mother claimed that, when I was an infant, I started to cry if a bird flew past my baby carriage. During my childhood, I darted away from bird cages in pet stores. The sound of chirping outside left me shaking. Well-meaning friends of my parents tried to break my phobia by taking their talkative bird from its cage and letting it fly around me. I'd bolt from the room screaming, convinced their screeching parrot would peck out my eyes.

"Birds are more afraid of you than you are of them," people often explained.

"That's not true," I said, believing they were mistaken.

When I watched Alfred Hitchcock's *The Birds* on television I was vindicated. In the plot, ordinary birds tore open roofs and viciously attacked people. I always knew that birds would rise up against humanity someday.

In my thirties, I took a twilight walk on the beach and unwittingly came close to nesting sandpipers. The next thing I knew, two sandpipers dive-bombed my head. I sprinted away, flailing my arms. This experience only proved I'd been right all along.

At forty, I went to the beach with my twelve-year-old daughter. When some particularly aggressive gulls circled above us and swooped down to grab our sandwiches, she snapped her towel at them. "Get out of here," she yelled. She fought them off, while I sat on our blanket whimpering. I felt ashamed of this unnatural role reversal. It was the worst experience I'd had with birds — until a decade later when I nearly got run over avoiding that pigeon.

I realized my phobia had turned dangerous. If I were to survive, I had to coexist with birds — because they are everywhere. However, I was attached to the fantasy that birds would attack me, gnaw my face, scratch out my eyes, and possibly kill me. I didn't know if I could change.

With much embarrassment, I confided to a friend, a psychiatrist, that I'd lunged in front of a car to avoid a pigeon.

"You know this is a problem," Arnold said.

"What can I do?" I asked.

"You need to de-sensitize," he explained, "by exposing yourself to birds."

I shuddered, remembering my parents' friends opening their bird cage and pulling my arm so their parrot could perch on it. "I can't do it," I croaked.

"Start with one second and build up your tolerance," Arnold said. "Every time you see a bird, do not turn away. Stay still… for one second. See how it goes. Once you feel comfortable with a second, increase it to two seconds. Eventually, you'll be okay for a full minute." He promised that, over time, I would be able to tolerate birds.

Following Arnold's advice meant taking a leap of faith. But I had no choice. The next day, a robin tweeted from the branch of a nearby tree. My body stiffened with fear. But I forced myself to last five full seconds before I fled.

I heard Arnold's voice in my head. "Tell yourself you made it. You're okay." He was correct. Nothing horrifying had happened. From then on, each time I encountered a bird, I increased my exposure. Sometimes, the bird in question flew away while I was still counting seconds. The day I made it to a minute, I rewarded myself with Ghirardelli chocolate.

One morning, I spotted several tiny sparrows pecking at breadcrumbs on the sidewalk. I peered at them from the corner of my eye. Getting up my nerve, I walked into the center of the group. Much to my shock, they scattered. Were they really afraid of me?

Days later, a pigeon boldly pranced toward me. "You don't own the sidewalk," I told him, stamping my foot. He stopped in his tracks until I passed by.

I still didn't like birds, but I no longer panicked in their presence. I called Arnold and thanked him for freeing me from a terrible burden. I couldn't believe I'd come this far.

Several years later, my husband and I went on safari in Kenya. A guide drove us around in a Jeep. Much to my surprise, I was fascinated by the exotic birds we encountered. I found the ostriches gawky and amusing. I photographed them all.

When I got home, I glowed, showing pictures of colorful birds to my daughter.

"I don't understand," she said. "You were always petrified of birds."

"I'm changing," I said.

She looked at me as if a stranger were inhabiting her mother's body.

Recently, my husband and I bought a condo on a lake in Florida. I was amazed by the tropical beauties that landed in our back yard: elegant egrets as white as cotton balls, hardy herons, sandhill cranes that walk like they're on stilts, Egyptian ducks with dark feathers around their eyes that mimic sunglasses, and ibises with their long, curved beaks. Every afternoon, a mother duck assembled her babies in the shade next to our hedge. While they dozed, one on top of the other, she kept her eyes trained on the lake where alligators swim.

"There's always something to see outside our door," I told my husband. "The ducklings are getting bigger. That family of six ibises descend together, pecking the grass for insects. The little terns are so light that they walk on our hedge."

"Look at you," he said. "You sound like a bird lover."

— Linda Morel —

12

Spiders, Scorpions, and Snakes

Life shrinks or expands in proportion to one's courage.
~Anaïs Nin

With my fiftieth birthday approaching, I pondered how to celebrate. Friends were also facing milestone birthdays. One — soon to be sixty — booked a Mediterranean cruise. Another — thirty imminent — had saved up for a week in Hawaii. A third was looking into a posh spa in Arizona.

None of those ideas appealed to me. I felt like Goldilocks, unable to find just the right bowl of porridge. My Mediterranean-cruise friend offered sage advice: "Pay attention. You'll know it when you see it. Just pay attention."

That very evening, as I was purging the day's emails, I saw the announcement of a "vision quest," a week-long wilderness retreat. Ordinarily, I would have hit delete instantly, but I remembered Nancy's words: pay attention. I looked more closely. Something about solitary time in nature rang true. And the spiritual aspects seemed moderate, nothing too woo-woo.

One quest was scheduled a month before my birthday during a week — miraculously — when I had nothing immovable on my busy business calendar. Surely, that was a sign. A few details gave me pause: camping al fresco in the Mojave Desert, fasting alone for three days. My mind pushed those particulars aside.

My husband was incredulous when I described my plan.

"Camping for a week in Death Valley? There's a reason they call it

Death Valley, you know. Have you ever camped? As long as I've known you, we've never even hiked or backpacked."

He was right, of course. I had never camped, slept outdoors, or backpacked. As for fasting, three square meals had been my practice for fifty years. Was I really equipped to go three days with only water?

"And what about scorpions and snakes..." he paused, "and spiders?"

He had me there. I did not like snakes, and I was deathly afraid of spiders. Over the years, Bill had uncomplainingly captured countless arachnids from the walls and corners of our home in peanut-butter jars and put them outside.

I remember exactly when my fear of spiders began. I was about four years old. We were in a neighbor's back yard, enjoying a summer barbecue. I wandered over to a pile of firewood stacked neatly by the fence. My attention was captured by a shiny, fat spider. It had a flash of enticing red on its belly.

"Daddy!" I called. "Come look at this pretty bug." My father and our host had been talking. Cold drinks in hand, they came over to peer at what my pudgy finger pointed to.

"Good God, that's a black widow!" said our host. At the same instant, my father snatched me away from the woodpile. Dr. S. picked up a length of firewood, carefully aimed it toward the spider, and then smashed it with a direct hit.

By then, the other kids and parents had gathered to see what was left of the spider. My mother held me tight and shuddered as Dr. S. told us all to stay away from the woodpile.

"Black widow spiders are dangerous," he warned. "If they bite you, you can get very, very sick."

"Or even die," offered one of the older kids helpfully.

From that day forward, spiders struck terror in my heart. It didn't matter their size or color. If it had eight legs, it was treacherous and must be avoided. I think perhaps other fears were born that afternoon, too, along with the awareness that the world was not always a safe place.

Despite my fear of spiders, this adventure still beckoned. I silenced the warning voices in my head and signed up. I purchased a sleeping bag and borrowed a backpack. I carefully broke in new hiking boots and read books about desert survival and the flora and fauna I was likely to encounter. Thirty days before my departure, I cut sugar, meat, and caffeine from my diet, allegedly to make a transition to fasting easier.

By the time I boarded a plane to take me to Las Vegas, where I would meet up with three other questors and our guides, I felt ready… mostly. I was nervous about fasting and tried not to think about scorpions, snakes — and spiders.

Around the campfire that first evening, we shared our reasons for being there. Each of us was marking a milestone — a landmark birthday, death of a parent, a recently empty nest — and each sought some new understanding. Our guides were experienced outdoors-women. They shared their love and respect for the terrain and the inner work we would be doing, and expressed a confidence in us we didn't yet have in ourselves.

Over the next two days, we spent time preparing for our solo days in the desert. We learned to erect a makeshift shelter with rope and a light tarp. We watched the sky for weather changes and talked about how to ration our water to last three days. We learned how to use a snakebite kit.

By the time we headed out for our solitary days, we were prepared. On departure day, we left at dawn with a sleeping bag and pack on our backs and a gallon of water in each hand.

I made camp in a sheltered canyon. It felt welcoming and safe. High stone walls offered some shade, and a few large rocks became furniture. I felt held here. In the profound silence, I listened to the beating of my heart.

In those magical three days. I connected with a peace and strength I hadn't known. I reveled in the uninterrupted blue of the sky, the star-studded nights, and the hot days that quickly turned to cold at nightfall. There were critters — birds hopping among branches of scrubby bushes, a few small, skittering rodents, and a wide variety of bugs, including spiders. Instead of fear, I felt a kinship with them.

Fasting turned out to be surprisingly easy. As each of the fears I had brought into the canyon evaporated into the dry desert air, I felt a lightness that was far more than just going without food.

My quest ended almost before I was ready. I was getting to know this fearless desert woman. I liked her very much. As I gathered my possessions to leave on that final day, she whispered not to worry; she was coming home with me. We were one.

I still have fears — large ones and small ones. I fear for my country. I fear for our planet. I fear for the safety of my loved ones. Spiders and snakes? They don't really bother me anymore. Looking back on that week in the desert, I still possess the strength I found in that quiet canyon. Whatever challenges and obstacles may be ahead, I know I can face them with courage.

— Donna Cameron —

Flying Through My Fear

The quickest way to acquire self-confidence is
to do exactly what you're afraid to do.
~Author Unknown

n my single days, I loved to travel. My girlfriends and I would pack our bags and head off to fun and fabulous destinations. Jumping on an airplane was adventurous and exciting.

Once I got married and kids came along, those carefree days came to a halt as it was not in our budget to fly the friendly skies with four little boys in tow. I said hello to minivans and road trips. My wings were on hiatus… at least for a while.

My husband and I always talked about traveling once the kids were grown. We'd head off to romantic getaways and exotic locations; we'd jet off into the clouds and live the life of the "not so rich and famous."

Then, horror happened: September 11, 2001. Like the rest of the world, I watched as airplanes were used as weapons, and my anxiety level soared. I vowed I would never fly again. If I could not get there by car, I would not go. Our future dreams of faraway destinations were shattered.

In March 2003, our oldest son was in a tragic car accident while serving in the United States Army, and we were summoned to Kansas where he was in a hospital being treated for a spinal-cord injury. We lived in North Carolina, and the only way to get to Kansas in a hurry was on a plane. It is no exaggeration to say that my husband had to drag me onto that plane as I dug my feet into the carpet at the entrance.

I was sweating, my heart racing, tears running down my face. I was petrified, and the fear was crippling, but I had no choice. My child needed me, and I had to get on that airplane.

I prayed the entire journey — for my son and, selfishly, for myself. I examined the face of every passenger around me. I struggled to breathe as I spotted many potential terrorists in the seats around us. Once we made it safely there and back home, I again swore off flying.

For nineteen years, I sat back as friends and family flew from one fabulous place to another. We were not completely housebound, we just selected trips that were available by car. We discovered a love of cruising. We could drive from our home in North Carolina to Florida where we'd board a huge ship and sail away to beautiful islands with crystal-clear waters. Holding a fruity drink with the sound of calypso music in the background, I convinced myself that we weren't missing out by not flying. Awesome vacations were always just a car ride away... or so I told myself.

Then, out of the blue, my husband said, "I want to go to Alaska. It's been on my bucket list, and we're not getting any younger."

I looked at him and asked one question: "Can we get there by car?"

He laughed it off as if I was joking. (I was not.) He went on to tell me how it was a lifelong dream to head to the Last Frontier. He wanted to see wildlife, visit glaciers, and experience a beauty that can only be found in our forty-ninth state. My reply was simple: "I appreciate the offer, but no... thank you for asking." I felt terrible for crushing his dream, but no way was I getting on an airplane.

Our fortieth wedding anniversary quickly was approaching, and I wanted to do something special for Al. I wanted to let him know how much I loved and appreciated all he had done for our family over the past four decades. I knew the perfect gift. I tossed and turned for many nights, trying to convince myself that I could do it. I could get on that plane, fly to Vancouver, B.C., and board a ship for a once-in-a-lifetime adventure on an Alaskan cruise.

After weeks of reflection, I embraced my fears and booked the trip. Making the deposit was easy — a simple click on the computer — but as the final payment date got closer, I found myself in full-blown panic attacks from morning until night. If I thought about getting on that plane, surviving a layover, and then having to do it again, I would feel the walls closing in around me. I convinced myself that even if I made it to Alaska, knowing that I'd have to get on a plane again to come home would surely ruin the trip. I did not want to spend all this money and then have this heaviness following me through the tundra. I was in a quandary for sure. Vacations are supposed to be fun, not stressful, right?

My husband was beyond excited and immediately began his research. He ordered books, maps and pamphlets. He bought a new jacket, hiking boots and binoculars. I loved seeing his excitement and hearing him talk about excursions like whale watching and dog mushing. He shared his good fortune with anyone who would listen. While he was planning, I was wondering if I would survive the next ten months waiting for our departure. I was suffering behind the smile I showed him each day.

The plan was set. On June 24, 2020, I would reach outside my comfort zone and allow Al to drag me onto a plane again. I watched videos, read books and began planning my Alaskan wardrobe. I was doing my best to be excited, but all the while I was freaking out on the inside.

Of course, our cruise was canceled due to the pandemic, and our vacation became a staycation. I was perfectly okay with that. My feet were planted safely on the ground.

When cruising resumed, so did a certain conversation.

"Are you ready to re-book?"

"Um, not really." But I was out of excuses.

I started a diet to lose the thirty pounds I gained during our life of isolation and quarantine. I booked a doctor's appointment to get a little something to help ease my anxiety. I wanted to have a back-up plan just in case I lost control at the gate. I ended up canceling the appointment and did research online instead. I watched YouTube videos about overcoming a fear of flying.

On June 23, 2022, I took a deep breath and walked through the doors of Charlotte Douglas International Airport. I looked around at the thousands of men, women and children who were filled with excitement about their trips. If they could do it, I could do it.

As the engines roared, I practiced my deep breathing. As the plane lifted higher and higher, I kept breathing. Before long, we were far above the clouds, and I was okay. Hours later, I did it again as we took off from Houston to Vancouver. When I got off the plane and walked toward the cruise ship the next day, I felt a few inches taller. There was a skip in my step.

I enjoyed every moment of our vacation, never once worrying about the flight home. Instead of fear, I switched gears and got excited about the wildlife we were seeing. I trekked through the rainforest and stood at a magnificent waterfall at the base of a glacier. I ate the best salmon, drank a few Bloody Marys, and absorbed the untouched beauty of Alaska. I looked at Al and saw a smile on his face that I had not seen in the years since our son's accident.

The hundreds of photos we took cannot capture what we saw in person, but they allow us to relive our trip. Al looks at the images of mountains, icebergs and fishing boats and remembers the twelve days of awesomeness. I look at the images along with him, and while I too enjoy reminiscing about this memorable adventure, I see it more as a reminder that I climbed a mountain of fear and reached the peak. I pushed through my anxiety and flew through my fear. I did it!

— Trish Bonsall —

14

Humphrey and Me

The brave man is not he who does not feel afraid,
but he who conquers that fear.
~Nelson Mandela

An unfortunate incident in my youth left me with an almost paralyzing fear of snakes. No matter how much I tried to desensitize myself to images of snakes or learn about snake identification, I found myself frozen with fear at so much as a photograph in a magazine or a toy snake. Heaven help me if I encountered a live one.

Then, I became a mother. The world takes on a whole new perspective when viewed through the lens of motherhood. When my son reached Cub Scout age, I enrolled him in the local pack. Within a short time, I found myself in the role of den mother.

A family camping trip to the local Scout campgrounds provided opportunities for the boys to work on merit badges and learn at a variety of nature stations. I accompanied my den from one post to another, intrigued by the wonderful resources provided by the Council. All my positive feelings evaporated, however, when the staff member pointed us up the trail to the next post.

"You guys are going to love the reptile station," he announced. "They've got a live snake you can handle."

Live? Handle? Was he insane? I almost turned and ran away until I remembered I was responsible for these boys. I couldn't abandon them.

The boys ran to the reptile station as though pulled by a magnet. I forced my reluctant feet to follow them.

The young man there went through his presentation on the importance of snakes in the environment with good humor and lots of information. He shared visual aids on identification and tips for avoiding run-ins with the critters. So far, so good.

"Are you ready to meet Humphrey?" he asked.

The boys cheered. I cringed. The young man plucked a snake from a covered aquarium beside the display table.

He identified Humphrey as a hognose snake who had served as a camp mascot for a few years. As he talked about the traits of the species, he held the snake on his arm. The snake rested quietly there as the young man spoke. He explained the snake was not a threat to humans.

"Watch this," he said, and placed the snake on the tabletop beside him. The snake promptly flipped on its back and stayed there. The species has two defense mechanisms, he told us. One is to puff up and pretend to be dangerous. If the threatening critter isn't intimidated by this behavior, a hognose will flip over and "play dead." Humphrey was accustomed to being handled and went straight to playing dead.

The young man reached over and turned Humphrey right side up.

"Nope, I'm really dead, see," responded Humphrey by flipping on his back again.

Once the boys stopped laughing, he offered them a chance to touch the snake, even hold him if they chose. He explained the proper technique to them so they could support the snake without hurting it. Naturally, they all wanted to hold him.

I tried to keep a "safe" distance from the snake but then one of the boys said, "Don't you want to hold him, Ms. Mary Beth?" He held out the snake toward me.

With a silent prayer for strength, I accepted his offering of one hognose snake and prepared to die on the spot.

I expected cold and slimy. What I got was dry and velvety. Humphrey positioned himself along my arm and looked at me with ancient eyes. Could this snake read my mind? Did he understand how scary this was to me?

In those moments, Humphrey brought me out of a world of fear and into a world of wonder. He taught me to look past labels like "snake" and see beyond to individuals like Humphrey. His grace and gentle acceptance of this nervous woman gave me confidence and a chance to appreciate his sinuous beauty.

I don't claim to love all snakes. After all, there are too many dangerous varieties here in the South to allow me to be casual about them. But I will never forget Humphrey and the lesson he taught me.

—Mary Beth Magee—

15

Claustrophobia in a Coal Mine

The cave you fear to enter holds the treasure you seek.
~Joseph Campbell

A tour of a historical coal mine was not my idea of a fun vacation stop. But my husband Tim expressed a desire to visit one during our West Virginia trip. So, I said yes, despite my claustrophobia.

When we drove up to the mine site, everything looked friendly enough, just like the photo from the website. Before I could change my mind, we bought our tickets and joined the others waiting outside at the picnic tables. I focused on the bright sunshine and wide-open spaces while I still had the chance.

From a distance, we heard motorcycles rumbling down the road. As we watched, four of them turned into the parking lot. If you looked up "bikers" in the dictionary, there would be illustrations of the guys right in front of us. As they dismounted, the riders stood staring at the mine, checking out the opening, the tracks and the "man coal cars" that we would be using. The bikers bought their tickets and joined the rest of us at the picnic tables.

For many years, so as not to be labeled a "coward," I just said no to any opportunities that involved dark and confined spaces. Saying yes to a mine tour was all new to me, so I started devising a coping plan in case I had a claustrophobia meltdown. Should we choose our coal car in front, back or in the middle of the bikers? What would they think of my whimpering, crying and (heaven forbid) screaming?

When the three coal cars arrived on the track to start the tour, the guide told Tim and me to sit in the closest car behind him. The bikers were placed in the last car. I was thinking this wasn't so bad. Of course, we were still on the outside of the mine.

As the cars started moving, the guide assured us he was a veteran miner. I didn't pay attention to his entire speech because all I heard were the words "dark mine." As we entered first, I squeezed my eyes shut and Tim's hand at the same time with the same intensity.

"Just breathe. You can do this," Tim said. "Take a look. This place is amazing."

I didn't want to disappoint him, so I opened my eyes and eased up on his hand. My vision adjusted to the dark and the dim wall lights.

By that time, the last "man car" with the bikers entered the mine. For just a moment, I saw the guide glance backward. Then, he braked us to a standstill. Again he looked back at the end of the train of cars. He squinted and cocked his head to the side.

When all of us looked back, the toughest-looking biker leaped out of the last "man car." Without pausing, he hightailed it straight back toward the picnic tables. His three buddies stayed inside.

The guide said, "First time I've ever lost anyone."

One of the other biker buddies said, "He has claustrophobia."

Who would have believed that five-foot me and the tall biker shared something in common? At that moment, my phobia became bearable, at least for this part of the tour.

As we moved on, I took deep breaths and let go of Tim's hand. Instead of focusing on myself, I concentrated on learning about the mine and hearing stories of the guide's experiences.

I wondered what the other three bikers thought about their riding companion's anxiety. Once in a while, I heard the bikers voice their concerns about their buddy, but none of them made any disparaging remarks.

When the tour was over, we noticed the biker at the picnic table with his head down, avoiding eye contact with anyone in our group. His buddies teased him a bit with a punch on his shoulder, but for the most part they sympathized with him. The rest of us took cues from them and did not laugh or make comments.

Tim smiled, gave me a hug and said, "I'm proud of you."

For one brief coal-mine tour, I conquered my fear of dark and confined spaces with the help of my supportive husband and a biker with claustrophobia. That gave me hope because Tim is planning our next vacation to Kentucky. And I said yes to a tour of Mammoth Cave.

— Glenda Ferguson —

16

Crossing the Street

Fight your fears and you'll be in battle forever.
Face your fears and you'll be free forever.
~Lucas Jonkman

've often wondered where my fear of dogs came from. I had very few encounters with dogs as a child, although I do recall my mom telling a story about her hand being bitten by a dog as she was walking down the street. Perhaps she pulled me away from any dogs we encountered, inadvertently instilling a sense of fear in me.

The first encounter with a dog I recall was when I was about twelve years old. I was walking from a friend's house when a Chihuahua, leashed to an aluminum chair, jumped out of a yard, barking and chasing me down the block. That must have been a sight: a six-pound Chihuahua chasing a teenager!

When I was fifteen, I would walk a little over a mile to my boyfriend's house and home again at suppertime. I encountered a few dogs on the way but fearfully crossed the street to avoid them. One day, my boyfriend met me partway. As we walked to his house, a German Shepherd slowly approached me, sniffing my feet. He probably wanted to say hi, but I panicked and screamed. My boyfriend chased him away.

I continued to avoid dogs and crossed the street if one approached all through my teen years and into my late fifties!

In 2008, I purchased my first home, and my teenage grandchildren came to stay with me for a few months. The boys were big into sports and spent every afternoon at the basketball courts. My thirteen-year-old granddaughter, Kayla, however, didn't have any way to spend her time. She had always expressed an interest in dogs, so I thought it'd be a good idea to volunteer at the local animal shelter. Due to her age, it was required that an adult accompany her in working with the animals. So, there we were: my granddaughter, me, and ten dogs — Shepherds, Rottweilers, Pit Bulls and sometimes a Chihuahua (agghh!) or Terrier. They needed to be let out individually into the yard to exercise and get some interaction with people. Part of our job was to play with them and train them so they hopefully get adopted. Understandably, I was fearful of being alone with a dog, but I pushed through for my granddaughter. I didn't want to make her afraid like me.

It didn't take long for me to become comfortable with the dogs, and I actually enjoyed romping in the yard and playing catch with them. Like most people, I was more afraid of the Pit Bulls than the Terriers, but that proved to be wrong. The small dogs were more timid, fearful and subsequently aggressive whereas the large dogs were playful and lovable. When I approached a large dog's pen, it would usually wag its tail and playfully jump up on the gate, panting gleefully. When I approached the pen of a Terrier, he would growl, bark and leap at me, showing his teeth. When a small dog was taken into the kennel, we would have to sit with our backs toward it, heads down, and wait until it approached us before we could be sociable.

Soon, I began to enjoy my time at the shelter and looked forward to it. I continued to volunteer even after my granddaughter moved down south.

I volunteered at the shelter for about two years and made some good human friends as well as animal ones. One day, we had a ten-year-old white female Lab surrendered when her owner was admitted to a nursing home. She cowered at the back of the pen, looking fearful. My heart went out to her, and I adopted her immediately. Her name was Precious, and she was precious to me for the rest of her life. She contributed such a calm presence to the house. Anyone entering would stop when they saw her lying there and bend over to give her a gentle pat. If any of us were distressed, she would come and cuddle to comfort us. I started daily walks with her, making friends with neighbors as we strolled along. Her passing still brings tears to my eyes.

Currently, I have a six-pound, fifteen-year-old Silky Terrier, Shiloh, in addition to three cats I've rescued over the years. I adopted Shiloh from one of my grandsons when he moved. Shiloh is such a joy and greets everyone at the door with a wagging tail. No matter how bad my day is, Shiloh always brings me comfort and a smile.

Ironically, over all the years of having pets and volunteering at the shelter, the only injury I've sustained was from a cat when I unwisely attempted to break up a fight. It was severe enough to send me to the emergency room!

So, now I'm retired, enjoying myself and my time with my three cats and Shiloh. We're all aging, and a few of us are taking supplemental medications. Between us, we have frequent doctors' visits. Shiloh gets me up and out of bed in the morning and out for a walk. I thought I was doing that for him, but now I wonder if he's taking care of me.

Recently, Shiloh was diagnosed with congestive heart failure. It's clear that his time is running out, and I dread the day I'll be without him. In fact, I don't know that I could ever be without a dog again! Now I cross the street to greet any dog I see coming my way. They've given me companionship and forced me to get outside and go for walks, no matter the weather. I ran into the local animal control officer in the store yesterday, and we chatted for a minute. He needs a volunteer for the mornings. I think I'll stop by. I could do a morning or two, but this time I won't adopt. (Yeah, right.)

— Carolyn Roberts —

17

Cold Comfort

The water is your friend... you don't have to fight
with water, just share the same spirit as the water,
and it will help you move.
~Aleksandr Vladimirovich Popov

was already afraid of the water. After experiencing a shark attack when I was eight years old on a family trip to Florida, I barely went in the ocean any deeper than my knees.

By shark, I mean dolphin, and by attack, I mean he was bobbing around in the water about five miles from shore, but people were screaming "SHARK!" and waving their hands around along the coastline. Real shark or not, that moment stuck with me. That memory, coupled with being freezing in any weather less than thirty degrees Celsius, made the idea of plunging into cold water a hard pass.

My husband had been cold plunging for years and would present me with facts to prove that submerging your body in freezing-cold water was a good thing. Using calculated breathing techniques, you prepare your body for the challenge. By doing so, you experience benefits such as heightened energy, reduced inflammation, immune system support, boosted mood, better sleep, and stress reduction. It was an appealing list of benefits — none of which mattered to me. What was presented as a clear "wonder drug" was still not psychedelic enough for me to get out of my warm house, drive to the ocean in the dead of winter, take off my clothes, and go swimming.

Did I mention that I live in Canada? It's minus twenty degrees

Celsius here sometimes. Add windchill to that, and it can measure up to minus forty. Unless you're on fire, chances are you're already cold.

On New Year's Day, my husband invited me to his celebratory cold dip. I had been thinking less about health data and more about my confidence. *How do you want to feel this year?* I asked myself. *Do you want to do something hard? Something brave? Something completely scary, uncomfortable and seemingly ridiculous, or do you want to say no and focus on all of the reasons why you wouldn't dare?* I put on my swimsuit, covered it up with eighteen wool sweaters, and joined Mike for the adventure.

In fairness, it was a beautiful day. This made the scary thing feel a little more reasonable as I negotiated with myself the entire twelve-minute drive. My heart was already pounding. We had packed a bag with towels, blankets, warm water for cleaning (defrosting) our sandy feet, and a hot cup of (spiked) coffee to warm our hands post-dip. The water, however, was still the ominous abyss of ankle-biting creatures that had protruding spikes and multiple sets of teeth.

Nike had it right when they said, "Just do it." It's the only piece of advice I had in that moment on the beach, with the wintry winds at my back and test of will to my front. Normally, I'd dip a toe in the icy waters, clench my arms tight against my chest and complain about it being far too cold to go in. Slowly, I'd inch my legs forward until the waves unexpectedly climbed up to my kneecaps. "Far enough for me!" I'd cry, whether I was in Aruba or Antarctica. But today would be different. Today, I was determined to do the hard thing: to prove to myself that my spirit was tougher than my thoughts. I stripped down to my swimsuit and ran straight for the liquid blue.

My first cold dip lasted one second. I was out of that water faster than a ball from a cannon, running frantically across the sand towards my heap of towels. I screamed, laughed, and tripped. I had done it. The feeling of accomplishment washed away all my fears. I was so proud of that one second; I had virtually rewired my brain. There were no shortcuts or comforts. It was simply a matter of deciding and doing. The slightest moment, about the length of a sneeze, changed my life forever.

Having overcome the "just do it" part, I was ready to attempt plunge number two the following week. I would try to go a little longer this time. I already knew I had the courage to go under, but now I had to work on staying there.

The second time would prove just as challenging as the first. My mind ran through all the reasons why I should stop. How ending the experience would bring comfort and ease. How I could be warm instead of cold. Watching instead of wading. Taking the easy way out...

But I stayed.

I taught myself again that I could trust myself to show up and do it. I was more powerful than that taunting voice in my head. I was exhilarated.

I have now been cold dipping for over a year. In the fall, I have stayed in the water for up to thirty minutes. In the depths of winter, I have broken through ice and breathed through the tingling cold.

I am more present in those moments than any other part of my day. I am thinking only about survival, not my car payment, the plants that need watering, my grey hair, or if I need to buy cat food. The first thirty seconds are still challenging, and I always get a little nervous before I step into the lake or ocean. But I have learned to relax in this state of immersion, teaching my body and brain that I am capable of resilience and being in control. What began as a place of fear has become a place of finding.

— Kristen Herrington —

18

Risk-Taking at 65

Curiosity will conquer fear even more
than bravery will.
~James Stephens

I told the woman who answered the phone at the local stable that I only wanted to sit on a horse. I didn't want to go anywhere. No need to sightsee. I just wanted the experience of sitting on a horse.

My idea of exercise is turning a page in the latest Louise Penny mystery. So, for me to want to sit on a horse was a very big deal.

She said I'd have to take a lesson.

Okay, I was game. It was to be a celebration of my sixty-fifth birthday. I wanted to mark this special day by trying something new, something outside my frame of experience.

On the following Saturday morning, with a good friend in tow — one who would not laugh but would record this moment of triumph — we arrived at the stable and went inside. I was nervous. Scared. And beginning to doubt if this was really such a good idea.

I looked around the large indoor ring. It appeared to be populated by seven-year-olds with perfect posture, dressed in complete riding habits, nonchalantly moving around in the circle. I was wearing jeans, a sweatshirt proclaiming a love of books, running shoes and the helmet they loaned me for the hour. I felt old and was anything but nonchalant.

Nancy, my instructor, teacher, and all-around-first-lesson caretaker, walked over to greet me. Could she even be eighteen? My adventure-for-the-hour cheerleader stood about five feet tall and nodded to me with a smile that wouldn't quit. The horse, whose reins she held, was introduced as Lightning. He was sidewalk gray and looked quite bored.

I thought I could stand on a box or stepstool and get on the horse. Wrong. Nancy felt it was important to use the left stirrup and haul myself up and over, hopefully landing in the saddle at some point.

So, my foot was in the stirrup, and I was doing this hop, hop, jump step and holding onto the saddle. (Nancy said I could pull Lightning's mane, but this seemed too cruel.) Once, twice, no luck. I was still on the ground. I was now soaking wet from exertion and anxiety. Once again, I was thinking of using a box or even leaving. I got myself there, didn't I? That should count for something.

Nancy was urging me on. I quickly bargained with myself for a total of four tries, and that was going to be it. I would be done. Later, I could only guess that I must have blacked out because, lo and behold, in a magic moment, I was sitting on the saddle on the third try.

And, OMG, I didn't realize I'd be up so high! I was sure I was going to fall off. Sweat poured down my face. But I was content. Just sitting. I got my wish. Now, let me be. But, no, Nancy told me to take the reins and move. She called out encouragement. "You can do it! You're looking good!" Lightning and I did indeed move, twice, around the large ring. It was a miracle.

Finally, I was allowed/told I could stop. It took two tries to get down to terra firma. I patted Nancy on the shoulder and thanked her and Lightning. She told me she knew I was scared but thought I was very courageous. I walked outside the stable on wobbly legs, hugged my friend who was standing there smiling, and burst into tears.

I'm not going to run away and join a rodeo. I have no desire to ride another horse. What I took into my heart and soul was an intensely powerful experience of having a wish and making it come true. I'm so glad I did!

— Jane Seskin —

The View from Above

Make a bucket list and fill it with dreams
that have no boundaries.
~Annette White

I hate heights. I flinch when a hotel clerk places me higher than the third floor. On sightseeing trips, I've been coaxed onto the observation decks of the Empire State Building, the John Hancock Center, and the CN Tower, but I counted the minutes, queasy and trembling, until their elevators returned me safely to the ground. Even on the second floor of a mall, I'd just as soon keep my distance from the railing.

But I love the water. I could spend weeks at the shore and still not get enough. Growing up, my sister and I were blessed to spend beach vacations with our parents, grandparents, and extended family. I loved being bumped and jostled by the waves. I loved digging into the sand. I loved the midday bustle — the patchwork of towels and umbrellas, the murmur of radios, the scent of sunscreen. I loved the quiet mornings and evenings when we gathered shells and watched sandpipers scuttle along the water's edge. I was hungry for everything the beach had to offer.

At least a few times during each trip, we'd hear the rumble of a speedboat. We'd glance up to see someone waving from beneath a brightly colored parachute, and we'd wave back. What would it be like to see the beach from high above, surrounded by wind and warmth and all that blue?

I knew I wanted to try parasailing someday.

Years went by, and I made a bucket list. Parasailing made the cut. It was fun to imagine a bolder me tackling the gutsy dreams on my list — but not just yet. *Someday,* I thought. *I'll do it someday.*

More years went by, and our family planned a trip to Lake Erie's islands. The three of us agreed that we would each choose one thing we most wanted to do. Ride a ferry? Visit a museum? Hear live music? We poked around online, researching the options.

And then I remembered those parasailers. Maybe now was the time.

Or maybe not, I told myself. It was a little pricey, after all. We had to book in advance. What if the weather didn't cooperate?

What if I waited until next year, or the year after that? Or another decade?

There are always plenty of reasons to say no, and the more reasons that popped into my head, the angrier I became. I needed to know that I could do this. We booked our reservation.

The night before we flew, I lay awake, listing each thing that would keep us safe. We would be tethered securely to a boat being driven by an experienced crew. We would be held aloft by a giant parachute. We would wear lifejackets. We all knew how to swim. We would be just fine.

Even if we were 400 feet in the air.

Yikes.

On the morning of our flight, we ate a light breakfast and arrived early at the beach. I signed our waivers and tried not to think too hard about all that fine print. Part of me wanted to scrap the whole thing, hand back my life vest, and shake my head. "Keep the money," I'd say. "I just can't."

But another part knew that if I didn't fly today, I never would. Those trepidations would never magically vanish; those discouraging voices would never pipe down if I didn't tell them to. Someday was now.

As we rose higher and higher, I kept waiting to panic. I'd imagined it would be like those skyscraper visits, gritting my teeth and powering through those ten minutes of air, proving something to myself.

It was the very opposite. High above the boat's rumble and the shouts of thrill-seekers at Cedar Point, it was gentle, quiet, and peaceful. We pointed out the rides and laughed, tickled by how tiny they looked from above. We floated on the warm breeze, surrounded by blue: a sunny, wiped-clean sky and softly rippled water that sparkled in the morning light. The lake looked as joyful as we felt.

Viewing that summer day from above, I knew it was a moment I'd remember for the rest of my life.

The folks on the shore waved up at us, and we waved back.

— Kelly Close —

Chapter 3

Believe in Yourself

Just Take the Compliment

Low self-confidence isn't a life sentence. Self-confidence
can be learned, practiced, and mastered — just like
any other skill. Once you master it, everything in your
life will change for the better.
~Barrie Davenport

I was the undisputed world champion of deflecting compliments. Receiving a compliment was uncomfortable for me, and I would brush it aside with a joke. Let's say you told me that I looked nice. I would respond, "Thanks! Oh, I guess I clean up well... once or twice a year!" Maybe you really enjoyed those cookies that I baked for you. I would say, "You're welcome! But, well, they are really easy to make, even for an idiot like me!"

On and on it went...

My deflection of compliments could best be described as a thirty-year tennis match complete with serves and volleys. Every compliment (the serve) that was given to me always had to be returned with some kind of self-deprecating response (the volley). But why? Why did I feel I was undeserving of any praise? Why did I have to tear myself down?

It turns out the answer was surprisingly simple: my very low self-esteem. I believe my self-esteem issue was two-fold: a family trait inherited from my mother's side of the family, exacerbated by growing up very poor, surrounded by children from affluent families. In my mind, I was not as good as the other kids.

Instead of accepting compliments, I made a big effort to compliment *other* people. In the short term, the strategy worked; I was very much accepted by my classmates. However, over the course of time, my strategy completely destroyed my own self-worth.

Looking back, it's funny how some seemingly miniscule event from your youth can stand out. One such happening best illustrates my compliment deflection. In fact, it is the first time that I recall using the strategy.

It was during seventh-grade physical education. We were playing a game of football. I can still remember the teacher barking out, "This is the last play!"

The game was tied, and our team had the ball. Upon breaking the huddle, our quarterback gave us one command: "Get to the end zone." It was Hail Mary time.

Years later, I remember running a route toward the back right corner of the end zone. I managed to elude my defender, and I was open, maybe three yards in front of him. I can still see that poorly thrown football wobbling through the air. It was not only wobbling but sinking at a rapid pace. In the fleeting seconds before the ball struck the ground for an incomplete pass, I dove, fully extended, and managed to cradle the ball in my hands.

It was a touchdown. We had won the game! As expected, there were lots of high-fives, smiles, and compliments like "Great catch!" In fairness, it *was* a great catch! But, even in that brief moment of childhood jubilance, a moment when I should have basked in the adulation of my teammates and friends, I immediately began deflecting the compliments. When the quarterback congratulated me on the catch, I responded, "Well, it was a great throw, too. And, if I wasn't so slow, I would have caught it in stride!"

So, even at age eleven, I just couldn't accept the compliment. Worse yet, I took what should have been a happy moment and completely squashed it. Why? I didn't want to be perceived as arrogant, and I wanted the quarterback to like me.

This became my M.O. The deflecting became so habitual that I barely recognized it as an adult. But as my unwillingness to accept a compliment grew, something else was growing inside my heart, mind and soul, something much more sinister: my own self-loathing. By my early thirties, I had come to completely loathe the person I was. I felt unworthy of not just compliments but of friendships, happiness and love. I was in a dark place — one I had crafted for myself.

Around the age of thirty-three, my darkness and self-loathing reached its absolute crescendo. I will spare the details, but saying that I am extremely fortunate to be telling this story some seventeen years later would be a huge understatement.

Around this time, I finally decided that if I wanted to live a long, productive life, I couldn't keep dealing with my issues the same way. So, for the very first time in my life, I stepped outside my comfort zone and began to talk about my perceived shortcomings.

There was much work to be done. Luckily, I had coaches like Jeffrey, Joe, Nancy, Les, Gary, Jessica, Amanda and Muhammad, who were more than up for the task. I was in very capable hands. Making these life-altering changes was not going to be easy. My coaches told me as much. I believed that I was up to the challenge; I just had no idea how difficult unlearning thirty years of behavior would be.

There were tears, anger, sadness, and days I just wanted to quit.

But I never stopped putting in the time and effort, and I changed the way I looked at not only myself but others and the world as a whole.

I had my share of slipups, but, generally speaking, I made steady progress. I discovered that, as I began to like myself, receiving compliments became easier. I finally felt worthy of them.

Years later, I'm much happier. Now, upon receiving a compliment, it's almost second nature to just respond, "Thank you!"

And to the quarterback from my seventh-grade physical education class who told me "Great catch!" I say, "Thank you! And, next time, maybe get the ball up a little bit!"

— Brian Michael —

The Mountains Are Calling

Fresh air is as good for the mind as for the body.
Nature always seems trying to talk to us as if
she had some great secret to tell. And so she has.
~John Lubbock

By my mid-fifties, I was at a crossroads. After decades of married life, I realized that I was afraid to venture out on my own. My life was limited, and even having friends frightened me. "Either I change, or I die" kept going through my mind.

To relieve my anxiety and depression, my husband and I ventured to the Blue Ridge Mountains about an hour's ride from home. We drove on the Blue Ridge Highway until we came to a trailhead. We looked at the map there and chose a trail that was only a couple of miles long. I put one foot in front of the other and, in no time, was getting into the rhythm of something positive in my life. I hadn't felt anything spiritually in years, and the simple process started to soothe my aching soul. Being one with nature slowed down my racing mind. Up and down the trail we went. The trees gently swayed in the breeze as we glimpsed views of valleys below us.

I knew this was my way to heal.

How would I do it, though? My husband was not a big fan of hiking. He was a golfer. Riding in a cart around eighteen holes was his idea of outdoor activity. I had to leave my comfort zone and branch out on my own.

I found this Internet site called Meetup. I told the Meetup people that I was interested in hiking, and their hiking guru spit out a couple of groups I might find interesting. I picked the most unintimidating group and signed up for a five-mile hike in Shenandoah National Park.

All my insecurities came into play when meeting the hiking group. The hikers were at least ten years younger than me and sported well-worn hiking shoes, moisture-wicking clothing, and graphite hiking poles. I didn't let on that I was a newbie, but my attire of a cotton shirt, jeans, and sneakers made it obvious.

The fifteen hikers started slowly, crossing many little streams on rocks that were slippery in spots. My husband had converted a mop pole into a hiking pole for me. It did the job of keeping me out of the water. I placed myself toward the back of the group, not wanting to slow anybody down. We hiked to the Hoover retreat complex, Rapidan Camp, where the President and Mrs. Hoover went to escape life in Washington. We toured the complex with a park ranger. I enjoyed the tour but worried about keeping up with the hikers when the journey continued.

Upon leaving the retreat, we started going over a mountain. With labored breathing and my heart pounding, I struggled to keep up. After a half-mile of this torture, it slowly became more comfortable; my steps got into the rhythm. I was doing what I desired and felt a part of all that surrounded me. After two miles, we started to descend the mountain. I had made it over the crest and into a new way of life.

I have been actively hiking since that day. I've walked thousands of miles, with several worn pairs of hiking boots to prove it. I retired the mop pole for actual hiking poles, though I don't have or need the latest and greatest ones. I keep thanking God for giving me legs to hike with — merely putting one foot in front of the other — and taking me to places I never dreamed I would see.

I hiked in the Great Smoky Mountains seven years ago for my sixty-seventh birthday. With ten of my gal-pal hikers, I summitted Mount Le Conte at 6,593 feet. It was a challenging hike, sometimes walking on rocky cliffs with only a safety cord to hold onto. The girl who feared going up the bleachers in high school was killing it.

I have hiked the Dingle Peninsula in Ireland with five other women, trekking more than a hundred miles of green hills and valleys filled with baby sheep and their mothers. My husband, sister, and I did part of the Camino de Santiago in Spain, walking along stone paths into little villages that led us to Santiago's cathedral on our seventh day.

I am fortunate to have the Blue Ridge Mountains nearby. Before Covid, I backpacked on the Appalachian Trail, falling short of my 100-mile goal but enjoying it immensely. I met through-hikers along the way, camping next to them and listening to their determination to hike the entire 2,200 miles.

Being one with nature outdoors is my key to serenity, and I don't intend to give it up anytime soon. We all are responsible for our peace and happiness. I have found mine one step at a time.

— Carole Olsen —

A Vote of Confidence

What you do makes a difference, and you have to decide what kind of difference you want to make.
~Jane Goodall

I live in a village. It's not big enough to be a city or a town. Some time ago, I noticed that in each election cycle the same candidates would run and get elected, sometimes unopposed. The village had become stagnant, with nothing changing and no new businesses or growth.

Having daughters in high school, I felt I had my finger on the "pulse" of a younger generation. I listened to their ideas about what could be better in our village, or why they had to go one town over to use the new skateboard park or have a burger at a new diner.

And that was the moment when I, a divorced mother of three, thought about running in the upcoming election to become a Village Trustee. I felt that our stagnant economic development needed to be addressed to relieve the burden of rising property taxes on the residents.

So, I gathered up my courage and picked up a packet from Village Hall on running for election. I did some serious research and enlisted friends who had run in various town elections before to make sure I chose the correct petition, filled it out accurately, and got the right number of signatures to get them turned back into Village Hall on time. Little did I know, this would be a life-changing experience for me.

I truly believed that the Lord helps those who help themselves, so I did my due diligence in learning how to run a campaign. I checked other campaign websites for ideas. I chose campaign colors that were appealing on my sign but not being used by anyone else. I made sure my campaign signs could be read within a matter of seconds by people who were driving by.

Once I filed my paperwork and word got out that I was running, I began to receive phone calls from friends offering to put my sign on their lawn. Another friend offered to create and maintain a website for me. There, I was able to post a short bio, highlighting my education, work experience, and mission statement. I listed events I would be speaking at and shared pictures of myself and family. The website also listed information about free health-care events and elderly services.

My brother and his son drove around putting up my signs at the designated addresses and kept a list of where they were placed so we could easily find them to pick them up after the election. It was wonderful to not feel alone in my journey and know I had support where it mattered.

As I walked in our Good Neighbor Parade as a newly elected official, the mayor smiled at me and said, "It's very humbling, isn't it?"

I paused and nodded. "It absolutely is," I replied. To know that so many people believed in me and wanted me to help them achieve good things for their hometown was an incredible feeling. During my four years as a trustee, I worked hard with our mayor and state representatives to help our village obtain the resources we needed. I learned to write grants for funding and went to see our representatives at the state capital.

Finding the courage to run in a small-town election changed my outlook on life. It gave me hope that dreams can come true and small ideas can grow into something big.

— Nancy J. Lucas —

23

Conquering My Fear of Fifty

Running allows me to set my mind free. Nothing
seems impossible. Nothing unattainable.
~Kara Goucher

I clicked the blue link: Sign up here. This wouldn't be my first half-marathon; I had run a flat half when I was thirty-eight. But that was eleven years ago. Now, it was November 2021, and I had spent the better part of eighteen months locked away in our house. I'd had Covid twice, and shoulder surgery, and I was turning fifty. So, as daunting as running 13.1 miles seemed, I was going to do it.

I signed up for a women's training group, a group of strangers with whom I would spend a few months virtually preparing for the race, and then I was directed to sign up for the actual race. I imagined a course somewhere in Florida near a spa. Or perhaps sunny California, again near a spa. My jaw dropped in horror when the race website opened, and I was greeted with the words, "Zion at night, half-marathon in the darkness." In Zion? Oh, no.

I looked at the website. Was it too late to quit? Granted, I had just signed up for a coaching group that was meant to "motivate me through running." Giving up before I even started seemed like a terribly wimpy thing to do. I scrolled through photos of the race.

My stomach sank. Runners kitted out with headlamps and trail shoes filled the computer screen. *I cannot do this,* I thought. *I don't run on trails in Delaware. I don't run on trails or up hills.* I clicked onto the next photo and looked at the happy runners cruising alongside a terrifying-looking cliff. I am also afraid of heights.

A text came through my phone. It was Nicole, our training group's fearless leader, a woman who has run hundred-mile ultramarathons. This is what happens when you run a race with someone who has the mental toughness of a Navy SEAL. "Sign up for the 4 am start time," she wrote.

As I filled in my name and address, I tried to figure out how likely I was to get injured during training. Realistically, that was my best way to get out of this race. I filled out the form and started worrying. About everything.

At our first "meeting," seven other women's faces popped up in the Zoom tiles. I looked at the group and realized that I was likely the oldest member. Our dauntless leader Nicole told us how beautiful the course was and raved about running toward the cliffs as the sun rose. And I nodded along, smiling, wondering how I could possibly conquer my fear of flying to get to Nevada; conquer my fear of strangers to spend three days with these women; overcome my intense dislike of waking up early; and then overcome my fear of trails, animals and the dark to run this insane race.

At the beginning of the school year, I had set a goal for myself: to run five miles by my fiftieth birthday in December 2021. And I was getting there. Running post-Covid was no joke, though. Every three-mile run felt like I was going to have a minor heart attack. Bouts of vomiting, something I had never experienced in all my years of running, plagued me during almost all my training efforts. But as January neared and my fiftieth birthday came and went, I noted an internal shift. Maybe, I began to think, just maybe I could do this.

Typically, I spend January under my duvet, keeping my toes warm and occasionally riding my Peloton. But this January was different. Come rain, snow, or ice, I had a training plan to follow. During one of our one-on-one sessions, Nicole, whom I was discovering was one of the kindest, most understanding women I had ever met, told me that she was with me in spirit on every run.

I told her how difficult it felt just to get out of bed some days. The double whammy of losing both my parents followed by a worldwide pandemic left me so tired, both physically and emotionally, that the idea of running six or seven miles in the snow was overwhelming.

Nicole told me to process some of my pain while I ran. "My hand will always be on your back," she said. I could tell she meant it. I made a playlist for my long runs. I decided that perhaps getting out from under my duvet was the best way to avoid my typical mid-winter depression.

By March, I could run seven miles. I tried not to think about the fact that I was running on a road and not a trail, or that I was running in the daylight. I just needed to put one foot in front of the other.

As our race date, May 20th, approached, the women in my group and I started hammering out logistics: which flights we would take, who would share hotel rooms, who would drive. Try as I might, my anxiety would occasionally get the better of me. "I can't share a hotel room," I blurted out. "I occasionally scream in my sleep, and none of you need to hear that." Then I worried that I had overshared. But no one judged me via Zoom. I saw no eye-rolling. This group was beginning to feel like a fellowship, a safe place.

The week before my adventure on the mountain, I found myself wishing I would catch a cold or twist my ankle — anything to keep me from having to meet strangers and run in the dark. But the week came and went. I was tapering, so I didn't have a long run. And on Thursday morning at 6:00, my husband drove me to the airport. He and my children had all the faith in the world in me. "We know you can do this," they said. I did not know I could do it but decided to believe the people who knew me best.

When I landed in Las Vegas and met the other women with whom I was running the race, I felt at ease. Nicole's genuine excitement for all of us was contagious. But I couldn't stop myself from asking, "What about these large rocks we have to run across at the top of the mountain... the lava rocks?"

"It will be okay," said Nicole. "They are just rocks. One foot in front of the other, and you will be fine."

The morning of the race, the alarm I had set for 3:00 A.M. didn't

go off. Somehow, I woke up on my own at 3:23 and realized I had seven minutes to get dressed, put on my headlamp, find some food, and get into the car. This may have been for the best as I didn't have any time to process what I was about to do.

We drove to Zion and milled around until 4:00 A.M. I had my phone in my fanny pack along with a bottle of Gatorade. I secured my headlamp and walked to the staggered start line with my friends. We started together, but I fell back quickly. I couldn't see anything and didn't want to risk falling on the gravel road before the sun came up. I ran alone along the five-mile stretch to the mountain trail. My nerves were quieted by the silence and dark.

As I neared the end of the stretch, the sun began to rise, and runners gathered at the scenic drop-off to take photos. I looked from afar, balancing my fear of heights and my desire to see. I was almost at six miles when the gravel turned to rocks—large flat, jagged, uneven rocks that had been there for eons. As I traversed the first of many of these "slip rocks," I was overcome by an emotion I hadn't felt in years: joy.

I began to sing Sting's song about walking on the surface of the moon. I was alone. No kids, no husband, no one else. Just me. I was conquering the mountain, but I was also conquering so much more: my fear of heights and rocks but, more importantly, my fear of being alone when my kids left for college.

When I got back to the trail that took us away from the mountain to finish the course, I came across an older gentleman who was having some trouble with his footing. I helped him and then kept running when another man joined us and told me he would run the gentleman across the finish line. As I continued down the path, I heard the older man say it was his seventy-sixth birthday.

It hit me hard in the chest. So what if I was fifty? So what if I had endured Covid twice? I was here now, doing something that had seemed impossible just a few months before. Who was I to say that fifty wouldn't be amazing or that this was the end of my journey and not the beginning of a new one? And as I ran the last few minutes of the race, I recorded myself finishing. I sent the video to my family with the note, "You were right. I did it!" And with that one race, I redefined my idea of what I am capable of. The possibilities are endless.

— Helen Boulos —

24

The Candy Counter

Believe in your flyness... conquer your shyness.
~Author Unknown

The museum had not yet opened, and my fellow gallery associates and I were perched around the break room, sipping coffees and bottled water while others scarfed down a quick breakfast burrito. We must have looked like a flock of cardinals in our red blazers. The museum was closed on Mondays, so Tuesdays felt like Mondays for people in our department. We were hoping for a day that did not involve telling people to not touch the art, or get near the art, or use flash photography that just might damage the art. Our hopes were dashed when some school buses pulled into the museum's lot.

"Maybe it'll be a guided field trip," a co-worker said hopefully.

"Don't count on it," someone else replied. "Looks like high-school kids."

"Ugh. Remember last week when that little punk stepped over the ropes and touched the Warhol?"

For a moment, no one spoke. We all remembered that unruly group of high-schoolers who had swarmed about the galleries like insects. They terrorized the art museum for well over an hour, making silly faces as they took selfies, laughing too loud, daring one another to get close to the artwork, and smirking whenever their behavior was corrected.

"You know, I used to teach kids like that," said one of the older gallery associates. He shook his head like a war hero recounting a long-ago battle. "Thirty-five years of teaching sophomore biology. Makes me glad to be retired."

It was my turn to speak up. "I hated high school." I adjusted my bracelet with the single charm. "I was so shy."

"You? Shy?" another co-worker said in disbelief, and I nodded. "But you talk to EVERYONE!"

I laughed. It was true. Yet, during my teenage years, I had walked silently through the halls, unnoticed and overwhelmed by the noise. I talked to no one, and no one talked to me. Occasionally, a class-mate — and sometimes a teacher — would make a hurtful remark about my quietness. "She spoke!" they'd say in mock surprise whenever I opened my mouth. They did not realize that comments like that made it much worse for me.

It got a bit better in college, although I remained shy and with-drawn. I didn't really overcome my timidity until I got a job in retail. It was at a gift shop that sold everything from candles to greeting cards. The managers had me stationed at the service center, which suited me fine for there was very little interaction with customers. But one manager, exasperated by my inability to wrap gifts, eventually had me moved to the candy counter. There, I was forced to talk to people. I wanted to cry. The idea of even saying, "Hello! How are you?" was terrifying. So I busied myself wiping down shelves and straightening up jars of jellybeans, even offering to decorate the display windows, doing everything I could to avoid the customers.

Christmas was approaching. Every day, more and more customers filed in for their holiday shopping. They'd approach me, flipping through the winter catalogue and pointing to whatever they wanted. I would nod nervously and escort them about the gift shop like a professional tour guide. I was also forced to use the cash register, an out-of-date and temperamental piece of machinery that seemed to hate me. I'd walk out in tears when my shift was over, dreading the next day.

One evening, a customer asked for a pound of gummy worms. "It's a gift for someone," he added.

Hearing that, I switched the plain paper bag with a cellophane one, tying it with green ribbon that I then attempted to curl with scissors. But the ribbon refused to cooperate. I tried again, slowly running the blade against the ribbon. Nothing.

"This is why they don't want me in gift-wrapping," I said in annoyance. And, to my surprise, the customer laughed.

My job miraculously got easier after that. The number of customers dwindled after Christmas and then increased for Valentine's Day, only to dwindle back down during the spring. Hardly anyone stepped into the store that summer. The candy department was cleaned, polished and organized, for there was nothing else for me to do. In order to pass time, I began to seek out customers, as few as there were, and ask, "Is there anything I can help you with?" I learned to smile and greet people.

Slowly, I established friendships with my co-workers. Most of them were considerably older than I was, and they'd hug me whenever I felt flustered. When the owner was not around, we laughed and recounted tales of unpleasant customers. My favorite story involved a man who walked into the store one September and asked, "Do you have any Mother's Day cards?"

"Well," I answered back with a grin as I stacked the shelves with pumpkin-flavored truffles, "you're either several months too late or way too early because we don't have any!"

The man glared darkly at me, clearly not appreciating my attempt to be humorous. He proceeded to call me a smart aleck and left.

I was sad when I made the decision to leave the gift shop several years later. My co-workers, who by then were like overprotective aunts, pitched in to buy me a going-away gift: a silver bracelet with just one charm — a heart-shaped box of chocolates.

"So you'll never forget your time behind the candy counter," they said.

When I got the job with the art museum it was even more necessary for me to interact with strangers. But it was okay. I had long ago realized that I could usually make people — both co-workers and visitors — laugh. I was friendly. I was bubbly. I'd entertain the other gallery associates by reciting video installations or wearing headbands with plastic eyeballs around Halloween. ("So I can keep an 'eye' on the artwork!")

"Yeah," I now said. "I used to be painfully shy. Working in retail did wonders for me."

It was nearly ten o'clock, and the high-schoolers were filing out of the bus. They stood around with their arms crossed, and from the break room we could see the looks of boredom. Suddenly, one of the students leapt up to snatch hold of a tree branch. He began to swing back and forth like a trapeze artist. The chaperones did nothing.

"Look at that," the retired schoolteacher lamented. He disgustedly pointed at the window. "They're not even in the museum yet, and they're already acting like little jokers."

"Well, if the chaperones can't control them, then I'll say something." I grinned. My fingers again brushed against the candy charm that had become slightly tarnished over the years. "I'm not afraid. If I can handle speaking to cranky customers, I can certainly handle unruly teenagers."

— Cristin Wenninger —

25

The Sacrifice of the Class Ring

*It is hope that gives life meaning. And hope is based on
the prospect of being able one day to turn the actual
world into a possible one that looks better.*
~François Jacob

"It's beautiful," I said, admiring the teen's high-school class ring. Since I was a regular at the coffee shop where she worked, the excited girl extended her hand closer to allow me to inspect the glittering gem.

The red center stone glistened in the café's track lighting. In that instant, my mind traveled back in time to when I had experienced the same feeling of pride in my own high-school ring. I bought it with the hard-earned money I saved while working at a fast-food restaurant in Lima, Ohio.

I don't have the ring anymore. I had to sell it when circumstances got challenging a decade later. I suppose my story is every single mother's story in a way, except I was a married single mom.

When I was seven months pregnant, my son's father and I separated at the advice of a counselor. When my young husband went out west for employment in Nevada, our apartment rent was due. I was unemployed with a mere ten dollars to my name.

After nearly suffering a miscarriage early in the pregnancy, I'd had to resign my demanding position as a local newspaper reporter. Thankfully, our kind landlady took pity on me, returning our deposit even though we hadn't given notice.

My mom and stepfather let me stay with them for as long as they could, but they were in the process of relocating out of state for my stepdad's job. Eventually, I moved to my grandmother's house temporarily, but Gram was extremely upset with me.

To say I felt alone and abandoned is an understatement. Gram had been supportive in the past, but she was angry with me for getting pregnant and then getting married, in that order. Having a wedding and then my husband leaving only heightened her humiliation.

That's why I couldn't stay at Gram's without contributing. Plus, I didn't have a reliable vehicle, and bills were piling up.

It seemed like a minor miracle when I was able to trade an antique chest of drawers for an old Ford station wagon. Steve, the owner of the wagon, was a family friend who, out of the kindness of his heart, gave me the amazing deal. It would be a safe vehicle for a baby, but I wondered how I could possibly afford auto insurance.

Then, I remembered my class ring. I didn't wear it often, but I was incredibly proud of owning it. Yet the gold market was high, and selling it would bring in a few more desperately needed dollars.

While walking through the square in downtown Lima, I noticed a small storefront with the sign in the window, "We buy anything gold." After contemplating what to do, I made my decision.

A young woman about my age was behind the counter. She weighed the ring and told me what it was worth. It wasn't a lot, but it would help. She wrote out a sales receipt and handed me the cash. All of a sudden, she stared at my protruding belly, and asked, "You're alone?"

How could she tell? That day, I felt forsaken and frightened at the prospect of raising a child by myself. Did I also have the word "Rejected" stamped on my forehead?

The sensitive clerk must have noticed how startled I was because she quickly added, "I'm alone, too."

She shared her story of having a seven-month-old girl. She had to work all the time to support her little one, who had been sick quite frequently since she was born. There had been hospital stays and lots of doctors, although the petite mom was grateful her daughter was finally doing better.

"Sometimes, I'm so tired," the clerk admitted. "I look at the stack of medical bills piling up on the counter. Then I look into my little girl's face and say to myself, 'It's all worth it.'"

It seemed like divine intervention meeting a kindred spirit who knew what it was like to be alone and terrified because another human being was dependent on you. In that instant, I realized things were never going to be easy, but our brief conversation gave me hope that my baby and I were going to be all right.

Selling my ring happened forty-two years ago. I know because that's how old my son is now. Somehow, the years flew by, and my little boy grew to be a dependable and protective man. He never forgets my birthday, Mother's Day or special occasions, even after I remarried when he was twenty-one. Being Zach's mom truly is one of the greatest gifts God has given me.

"What was your most important accomplishment?" I was asked this question at a job interview near the end of my career. The interviewers eagerly awaited my answer, expecting me to cite the books I've written or my former work as a TV reporter/producer. They seemed surprised when I replied, "My most important accomplishment was being a mother." There was a brief pause, but instead of being taken aback, several of them reached for their cell phones and showed off photos of their own children and grandchildren.

I wasn't a perfect parent, far from it. I didn't know how to parent, and finances were awfully tight for much of my son's upbringing. We relied on secondhand shops, Hamburger Helper, and the assistance of quite a few folks along the way.

My grandmother became our steadfast advocate the minute she saw my newborn's precious face. Despite being divorced, Zach's father always helped, along with my brother, "Uncle Don," who stepped up to support us in countless ways. There were also compassionate teachers, doctors, good neighbors, and caring pastors who empowered me to bring up my boy. Like the famous saying goes, "It takes a village to raise a child."

Still, I don't believe I could have done it without a divine appointment in a long-gone retail shop while selling my class ring. That afternoon, another single mother's encouraging words gave me hope that my baby and I were going to make it. And we did!

— Christina Ryan Claypool —

26

On Your Bike!

*Inaction breeds doubt and fear. Action breeds
confidence and courage. If you want to conquer fear,
do not sit home and think about it.
Go out and get busy.*
~Dale Carnegie

Being an adult who didn't know how to ride a bike became a bit
of a joke about me. "Oh, that's just Hannah," friends and family
would laugh. "Of course, she can't. She's so uncoordinated. I'm
surprised she can even tie her shoelaces." I would usually laugh
along with them, acting as if I was in on the joke. After all, it's better
to be laughed with than laughed at. But no matter how thick I tried
to make my skin, I found myself slowly using those words to fuel the
already burning fire of self-loathing that was crackling inside me.

It might sound silly to some people that not being able to ride a
bike would affect my self-esteem so much, but it was only one of the
many things for which I berated myself regularly. It is often not one
big thing but lots of smaller things that can weigh us down.

When I was first dating my now partner of ten years, Matt, he
casually mentioned over dinner that he enjoyed a bike ride along the
lake now and then. My stomach sank, and I could hear that ever-
nagging voice in my head pipe up. "Just wait until he finds out you
can't ride. He'll assume you're not fun, and there goes your chance of
being with this great guy." I took a big gulp and decided to tell him. I
figured it was best to get the conversation over and done with before

I got too invested in the relationship.

"Um, well, I don't actually know how to ride a bike." I smiled weakly. "I never learnt."

I waited for his laugh or scoff, but instead he gave me a look of total kindness.

"Well, how about I teach you someday?" He smiled, reaching for my hand across the table.

"Oh, maybe," I said back, still processing his response.

As our relationship went on, from time to time Matt would ask me if I was ready to start learning, and I would quickly make one excuse or another. It wasn't like I hadn't tried to learn before. Well-meaning friends and the occasional date would offer to teach me, and I would agree, only for the process to end up with me in tears and them frustrated. One not-so-nice partner reminded me, "There's no hope for you. You can't do anything right."

So, naturally, I was hesitant. Anyone who has learnt anything difficult as an adult would probably agree that it can be challenging and requires a great deal of vulnerability and resilience. Matt is a kind and patient partner, but I didn't want to do anything to jeopardise our relationship.

Inevitably, though, my arm was twisted. We decided to plan a trip to Europe, and one leg was going to be a visit to Sweden to see a friend's hometown. We were having coffee with her one morning to discuss the trip when she exclaimed, "We can borrow bikes and do a tour through the village. It will be so fun!" Suddenly, she realised I was there and turned toward me with a look of pity. "Of course, walking it will be just as nice."

"No, no, I'll ride," I replied. "I have plenty of time to learn," I continued, hopefully sounding more confident than I felt.

That afternoon when I got home, I sat down on my sofa next to Matt, taking a deep breath as I faced him. "Can you please teach me how to ride a bike?"

"Of course." He grinned, kissing my forehead before opening up his laptop to begin his research into his new role as biking instructor. The next few weeks, Matt fully embraced this role. He watched videos online, visited local biking shops to speak to the staff, and purchased a helmet for me that he knew I would love.

Finally, the day came, and early that morning we walked a bike to the local park. I won't lie: The negative self-talk was coming in hot that day. *You'll never be able to do this. What's the point? You've gotten this far in life not knowing how to do this, so why bother now?* I knew that to learn, I was going to have to step far out of my comfort zone, and I didn't think I was ready. When we got to the park, the lesson began exactly as I suspected it would. Nothing was working. I was resisting everything he said to me. And, to make matters worse, the pedal had scratched the back of my ankle, leaving me grazed and close to tears.

"This is not working," I wailed. "I was stupid for trying, and I shouldn't have bothered!"

I waited for Matt's response, for him to agree and for us to head home, both quiet and dejected. But I didn't expect what he did next.

"Wait here," he said abruptly before jumping on the bike and riding off.

I flung myself onto the grass with my head in my hands. I shouldn't have been surprised that he had just ridden off. Who would want to be around someone as hopeless and unworthy as me? Someone who couldn't even muster up the resilience for half an hour would hardly make an ideal life partner.

But, as I sat there on the grass, I felt another train of thought pop into my head. *Who says you're not resilient?* I was surprised by this thought, but I decided to follow it. I thought consciously about what I was thinking. I began exploring all the times I had been resilient, when I had overcome things that were hard or different, and how proud of myself I had been. The longer I sat there, the stronger my resolve grew. By the time I saw Matt heading back towards me on the bike, I was determined to embrace the lesson and try my best.

Matt pulled up with two things that made everything even better: a cup of my favourite coffee and a screwdriver to remove the pedals. He had totally forgotten that when an adult is learning to ride a bike for the first time, it is best to remove the pedals so they can practice rolling on the bike to learn balance. By mid-morning I was rolling down the hill with ease. By that afternoon, to my surprise but also with great pride, I was riding a bike. I was in shock that I was now doing something that had terrified me for much of my life. It was a great big "shut up" to that negative self-talk.

A few months later, I had the opportunity to fully embrace this change of thinking as I rode around Sweden with my friends and Matt, through gorgeous seaside villages, fields and parks. Yes, I had shaky moments, and I may have fallen once or twice, but instead of using that as an opportunity to question my abilities and drag myself down, I reminded myself, "You've done this before, and you can do it again." I now use this mentality in many aspects of my life, and I can honestly say I am a different person. I am more open and willing to try new things, and, most importantly, I am kinder and more patient with myself every day. With kindness from a loving partner who encouraged me to step outside my comfort zone that day, I have turned into someone who loves myself — and knows how to ride a bike.

— Hannah Castelli —

27

The Beauty of a Challenge

*There's nothing more addictive or incredible in life
than reinventing yourself and allowing yourself
to be different every day.*
~Thalia

Looking at my bucket list and all the items that had been crossed off, I realized something. When I was young, I had experienced the excitement of new adventures. But then, during the pandemic, I had lost my job and I had started to live a safe, comfortable life, one without new challenges. At seventy-four, I was content to take things as they came. Or was I?

One day, I was corresponding with a dear friend on the computer. During the conversation, my friend started talking about the Ms. Colorado Senior America Pageant. Years ago, she had participated in it and won. I had never even heard of it; the only pageant I was familiar with was the Miss America pageant. I grew up near Atlantic City where the Miss America pageants were held and attended parades of the contestants on the boardwalk. My friend stressed that this was not a beauty pageant. Rather, it honored women over sixty. The best part, she added, was there was no swimsuit competition. I told her I would think about it.

When I was younger, I entered talent contests, but that was years ago. I didn't even own a gown anymore. I agreed to meet with the pageant administrator just to talk. We met at a coffee shop, and when she entered the shop, I was thinking of a way to say I just wasn't interested. I felt bad, though, because she had made a one-hour trip to come and talk to me about it.

At the end of our talk, I realized I was starting to feel like a child on a new adventure. Participating in a pageant would be a new challenge. I knew if I made the commitment, I would not back out. I started thinking about what it would be like to tell people about it. Rene Green, the pageant administrator, gave me a packet of forms to fill out, and I left the coffee shop feeling good about myself. I remember thinking that even if I didn't place, I would be proud of the fact that I tried.

I spent hours on the computer typing up a bio, composing my "Philosophy of Life," and answering the many questions on the form. Then, I thought about my talent. I was a singer and quite a good one. But, fifteen years ago, as a result of neck surgery, my right vocal cord was paralyzed, and my singing voice was gone. After the surgery, I was very depressed. For a while, I thought I would never get over it. I talked to my pastor about it, and he told me that I might have lost my singing voice, but I could still speak. I auditioned for a play and got the role in a community-theatre production.

I've always loved telling jokes and decided I'd give standup comedy a try. When I was in my twenties, I enjoyed performing in small clubs. Unfortunately, the pay was not enough to live on, so I became a legal assistant. Recently, I was working for a home health-care service as a CNA. One day, I was assigned to a woman in her nineties who lived in senior housing close to my home. I only worked a few hours a day, but Gladys and I formed a special relationship. One day, when I arrived at her apartment, there was a note on her door. It was an announcement for all residents to attend a special music performance by a trumpet player in the activities room at 3:00 P.M. Gladys got very excited and asked if I would take her.

The trumpet player was delayed in traffic, and the room was full of about fifty residents wanting to be entertained. I got up and asked if they would like to hear some funny stories. I performed a routine for them that lasted twenty minutes and got rousing applause. That was the beginning of "Why Nott Laugh?" It was comedy designed just for seniors, and I started entertaining at assisted-living homes on weekends.

My talent for the pageant would be "Stand Up for Seniors," and I started putting together a routine. In the guidelines, it stated that I would have two minutes and forty-five seconds to perform. However, if I went over the time limit, points would be deducted. It was a challenge but one I could definitely handle.

Because of Covid, the pageant was rescheduled to take place a year later. At first, I was disappointed, but then I realized I would have more time to prepare. I worked on completing the form and doing some research on the pageant. The more I read, the more excited I became. I needed an evening gown, a little black dress, and an interview outfit. Evidently, "bling" is something the women in the pageant loved. I never wore much jewelry, but I started looking at "pageant jewelry" online.

When it was safe to go out, I donned my mask and hit Macy's. When I told the saleswoman I was going to be in the Ms. Colorado Senior America Pageant, she offered her services and took me around to various stations in the store to introduce me. I was now on a first-name basis with women in the make-up, jewelry and evening-gown departments.

Planning for the pageant was invigorating, and I was proud of myself for taking this step. At the first rehearsal, all the contestants met, and it felt like the first day of school. All the women were beautiful and had led exciting lives. We all told our stories, and soon it became a convivial gathering of like-minded women.

As the only contestant who had no pageant experience, I had to learn how to walk, smile, interview and present myself. We learned basic movements and, toward the end of rehearsals, we wore our pageant outfits and shoes to get used to them. Close to the date of the pageant, we practiced at the theater and saw our dressing rooms. We had singers, dancers, musicians, motivational speakers and a comic.

The pageant itself was surreal, and I smiled through the entire performance. When my name was called as the winner, I stood still until a bouquet of flowers and trophy were placed in my arms. I will never forget the crowning ceremony.

I now make appearances and share my comedy with other seniors. When I hear someone say they could never do it, I tell them, "Challenge yourself. The experience will change your life."

—Jeanne Nott—

28

Stepping Out of the Bashful Box

Once we accept our limits, we go beyond them.
~Albert Einstein

"Hello, Mrs. Briggs. It's so nice of you to speak to the juniors in my business class. I try to prepare them for the world outside of high school, which they'll soon be entering," Ms. Johnson said, eagerly shaking my hand.

"Besides," she added, "doesn't it make it more fun with your daughter, Holly, being in my class?"

"Oh, I'm sure Holly will get quite a kick out of me being front and center. I'm happy to help, but I confess that my line of work doesn't require me to speak in front of groups. In fact, these days I'm operating Grime Fighters mostly from home," I said, not meeting her gaze.

A few weeks earlier, Ms. Johnson had reached out to me about speaking to her class. She'd read an article in the local paper where I was featured in a piece about women in business. She was particularly interested in my story because I'm a female who started a business from the ground up.

Because of the article, Ms. Johnson assumed I met and interacted with the public every day. She couldn't have been more wrong, as meeting new clients was always one-on-one. I'd suffered from bashfulness since early childhood. Speaking to groups was way out of my realm of experience.

She was clearly passionate about prepping her high-school students for the world that lay ahead. She knew they'd go in many different directions after graduation. Some would go to college, while others would opt for blue-collar work, the military or entrepreneurship.

Ms. Johnson's enthusiasm was somewhat contagious and her self-confidence seemed to help bolster my own. I felt a little better about doing this presentation although my knees felt wobbly as I looked into the faces of the thirty students. Most appeared reasonably eager to hear what I had to say about my house-cleaning business; others, not so much, which I understood about teenagers.

I shifted from one foot to the other while giving myself a silent pep talk. After Ms. Johnson introduced me, I took a deep breath and began to speak.

"I'm here to speak to you today because I'm an entrepreneur. My company, Grime Fighters, was born three years ago out of a desire to work outside the home yet be home for my kids when they came home from school.

"It all began with a bag of cleaning rags, a pair of household gloves, and a long-time friend who asked me to start by cleaning her house. I didn't know it at the time, but she gave me the break I needed. She was pleased with my work, dependability and trustworthiness. She then passed on the name of my company to her friends. Since then, Grime Fighters has grown steadily, relying strictly on word-of-mouth, which gives me a consistent and quality clientele. I guess the rest is history," I said, smiling at the sea of teens.

"I started alone with just myself cleaning houses. I began hiring employees as the business grew. I now have seven women who work part-time five days a week with hours that perfectly align for them to meet their kids when the school bus drops them off in the afternoon. These hours work smoothly for my employees as well as my clients," I explained.

I took another deep breath, and it appeared the kids wanted to hear more. "Owning and running a business, whether it's five, fifty or five hundred employees, is basically the same process, and it prepares one for all aspects of business. A small business like mine prepared me and gives me the confidence to operate any size of business should I be given the task or forced to do so because of unforeseen circumstances.

"I confess to being a born neat freak. So, in essence, I work at what I love to do and what I'm good at. It sounds crazy to most people, but for me cleaning is cathartic. The old saying, 'Do what you love, and the rest will follow,' is very true for me. Grime Fighters, I'm proud to say, made money the first year, which is not the norm for a newly formed company," I explained.

Beginning with purchasing a business license, I went on to describe some of the responsibilities of starting, owning and operating your own business. "Keeping financial records is crucial. Not keeping proper records is the number one reason that small businesses fail." They all peered at me from their seats with a classic "deer in the headlights" expression.

"Okay," I said, laughing. "I can see I'm making it sound overwhelming. It's not. The beauty of starting your own business is that it's taking baby steps at first. And, before you know it, you're in the swing of things, and you've learned all the ins and outs of your business.

"Other than raising my children, starting Grime Fighters is the most valuable thing I've ever done in my life. It's my belief that being an entrepreneur, no matter how small the business, prepares us for functioning and thriving in the business world. Running your own business fundamentally puts you in place for understanding most businesses."

I decided I'd talked long enough. Without meeting anyone's gaze, I chanced it and asked, "Are there any questions?"

A young man raised his hand. Holly giggled and flushed pink, which told me this fellow was her latest crush.

"My name is Todd (oh, yes, he was the crush), and I'd like to know if it's a hard job."

"Do you mean starting the business or the actual work of cleaning the houses?" I asked, smiling.

"Oh, I mean setting up a business," he replied.

"It's not really difficult. I suggest taking one step at a time and asking a lot of questions. Other business owners are always ready with helpful advice, and there is plenty of government how-to assistance readily available.

"Oh, my gosh, I hope I haven't scared you all." I chuckled. "Remember that starting, owning and running your own business is fulfilling. It's hard work and a big responsibility that can be tedious at times. But, at the end of the day, it's gratifying. The best thing is being your own boss, and, trust me, the day will come when you'll contemplate becoming the boss." I smiled with more confidence than when I'd started.

"Thank you, Ms. Johnson, for inviting me to speak. I've enjoyed meeting you all, and I sincerely hope I've helped shed positive light on some of the decisions you make in the years ahead."

Whew! My knees didn't buckle. I stayed on track without my tongue getting tied around itself! It occurred to me that this presentation was a new step in overcoming my bashfulness. It was somewhat of an acid test, speaking for the first time to a room full of people, especially when it included my teenage daughter.

I'd accomplished one shyness hurdle with this presentation. Did I feel like jumping in the air and clicking my heels as I left the building that day? You bet I did!

— Cynthia Briggs —

Challenge Yourself

- ✓ Try avocados
- ✓ Go ziplining
- ☐ Sign up for art class
- ☐ Make a new friend
- ☐ Run a 5K
- ☐ Buy a bathing suit

29

Lynne's Life, Part II

The vision must be followed by the venture.
It is not enough to stare up the steps —
we must step up the stairs.
~Vance Havner

really, really disliked my husband's favorite sport. I never wanted to hike to remote mountain and desert areas, attach myself to a rope, and climb up a rock face. But I followed Dan on his adventures, even though I would rarely initiate one on my own. My role was to take climbing pictures and pack food and water.

Once in a great while, Dan managed to coerce me into trying what he loved. Absolutely terrified of heights, I whined, kicked, and even shed a few tears until I got to the top of the rock. And then the feeling of accomplishment was euphoric. That is, until the next time.

Without warning, when Dan was sixty and I was fifty-nine, my adventure man died. Alone now, I had to decide whether to become a couch potato or figure out how to create adventures of my own. Without Dan, there would be no more van trips down Highway 1 in Mexico to Bahía de los Ángeles or exploring remote areas of Alaska. I never wanted to go on any of his adventures, but once into them… Well, words really can't describe how supremely wonderful they were.

Something curious happened at Dan's Celebration of Life service. A number of his old climbing friends surprised us by showing up. A severe storm raged that day, yet the climbers, all from out of town, came to our home afterward to continue their visit with our family.

I had a great reunion with them. I have absolutely no idea where it came from, but a small spark lit something inside me.

One day, soon after Dan's memorial, I thought about returning to rock climbing and its community—a group of great diversity but like-minded in their love for rock climbing. The group takes in all kinds of people with all levels of ability. Dan had climbed in his twenties and thirties, but I did only a handful of climbs with him. Now that I was sixty, how would this work? Or even could it?

Okay, I thought, *it's terrifying, but I'll try, just a step at a time. But first I need gear to climb. And, more importantly, I need to know how to climb.* I'd picked up quite a bit of information watching Dan and his friends over the years, but now I needed to know how to climb without Dan.

A few days later, I went to the local climbing store, Nomad Ventures, where Dan bought all his adventure gear. I asked the twenty-something manager to help me with climbing shoes, pack, belay device, harness, chalk bag and a few all-purpose carabiners. That much I still remembered.

I settled on a cool pair of soft, pale green leather Mythos shoes because I liked the color and feel. I learned later that I lucked into a great pair of shoes. Next, the pack. I saw a lovely one, ruby red with black overtones. It said Mammut on it and had an elephant logo. Cool. I bought it. Again, I lucked out. Packs are made for function not looks, I found out later. The harness was my next purchase and a pale blue chalk bag to match, of course. The carabiners were a no-brainer. Dan's friends owned Black Diamond, a climbing equipment corporation, so I bought their brand.

I owned the basics. Now what? The manager at Nomad's had given me a free pass to the local climbing gym. "It's a good way to start," he encouraged. I'd never climbed indoors on plastic holds before. In the 1970s, there were no climbing gyms. You climbed on real rock.

I agonized for days. A sixty-year-old woman going to a climbing gym? But I knew I would die without adventure. I would cease living, resigned forever to the couch, watching people on TV live my life.

I called the climbing gym and asked if they gave lessons. "Of course," the young person on the phone replied in a tone that said to me, "Lady, what kind of question is that?" So, I signed up for lessons with Marcel, the manager.

Lesson day arrived. I told my staff I had to leave work early. I was going to a rock-climbing lesson. I saw their shocked expressions. I drove to the gym, a cavernous place that looked like an airplane hangar. *God, help me,* I told myself. *Why do this to myself? Why not just do nothing — go to work, live normally and forget adventure?*

Walking through that door into the unknown was one of the gutsiest things I've ever done. Inside, it was like the Twilight Zone, dim with huge gray plastic rock walls. Attached to them were multicolored, varied shapes of plastic looking a bit like leeches clinging to the walls. And, after a glance around, I confirmed that I was the oldest person there and the only female.

But at least I was in the door. I walked up to a busy eighteen-year-old attached to a cell phone. "I have a lesson with Marcel," I said. His expression was priceless.

Climbing that day, I realized that the familiar terror that had gripped me in the past was gone. I also realized that Dan had already taught me the basics of rock climbing. At the top of the last, most challenging route, I heard a holler. "Aunt Lynne, is that really you?" I looked down, and there was my teenage nephew.

What is Luke doing here? He doesn't even live around here, I asked myself. He and his friend had watched the entire climb. I had done well, but I was embarrassed, mortified even. *What do they think of me... an old lady climbing?*

When I got back to the ground, the first words out of Luke's mouth were, "Aunt Lynne, that was awesome! I'm so proud of you."

You know, I thought, *I'm proud of me, too.*

That one door I walked through was the beginning of a new life for me. It opened up other opportunities. I learned to ice climb. I got a job working summers at Tioga Pass Resort, elevation 10,000 feet, close to the entrance to Yosemite. I made many new friends.

Walking through new doors is still hard, but not walking through them is not an option.

— Lynne Leichtfuss —

30

My Own Happily Ever After

*The best piece of advice someone has
ever given me was "do it scared."*
~Sherri Shepherd

Once upon a time, there was a young girl who watched so many fairy tale movies that she believed the only ending involved a prince at your side. That young girl was me. Most of the books read to me as a child ended with the princess marrying the prince and the words "happily ever after." Even my dolls had significant others. Barbie had Ken to take her out on dates, and my Jasmine doll had Aladdin to sweep her off her feet on a magic-carpet ride for the night.

As I grew older, my goal became to find myself a prince so that I could have my own happily ever after. When I went out with friends, my mission for the night was to meet a guy. When that did not pan out, I turned to online dating sites in search of him.

Finally, after meeting many frogs, my "prince" came along. We had that magical connection and bonded over shared interests like rock music and travel. He even brought me a beautiful bouquet of pink roses before our first date night. We started seeing each other frequently and were soon caught up in a whirlwind romance. He cooked me surprise dinners by candlelight, even printing out a menu. We were going on road trips for weekends away, which turned into airplane trips to tropical islands. Before I knew it, we were engaged.

Unfortunately, this story did not end well. Arguments ensued and grew progressively worse as other issues arose. We ultimately ended up getting a divorce.

While all my friends were married, some even with children, I was back to checking the "single" box. Weekends were a challenge. After all, I couldn't possibly go to dinner without a date. The movie theater was also out of the question as I could not bring myself to sit alone anywhere besides my living room couch.

As I was driving home from work one Friday afternoon, I contemplated what I would do that weekend. My friends were otherwise busy with their families, and I had no plans. Just by chance, I tuned into my favorite radio station right when the two hosts were discussing their weekend plans. The male host asked the female about her plans for the weekend. "Got any big dates lined up?" he probed.

"Actually, yes!" she said excitedly. "I'm taking myself out on a date, going to a restaurant I love!" I was intrigued and admired her confidence and courage to go out alone. If she could do it, why couldn't I?

When I got home, I hurried straight to my closet on a mission. I searched through the sea of colors for an outfit before settling upon a V-neck magenta dress with dazzling rhinestones along the collar. I lined my blue eyes, on which I often received compliments, to help draw attention to them. Then I headed off to my favorite waterfront steakhouse. For the first time in many months, it was date night again.

When the waiter approached my table, he greeted me with the question that had prevented me from going out solo in the past. "Are you waiting for someone?" I smiled, shaking my head. *Actually, yes, but that could take years!* I thought to myself. *But life is way too short and precious to allow my single status to inhibit me from doing the same things that people in relationships do.* I still deserved to enjoy that delicious steak dinner with the incredible view of the water, even if it meant the only conversation would be with my waiter.

I went on several dates with myself after that night. I stood in the front row at a concert and danced and sang along with one of my favorite bands. One afternoon, I took the ferry over to New York City for a day of exploring and even caught a Broadway show. I took myself on several breakfast, lunch and dinner dates. As time went on, I became more confident as I told the host staff, "Party of one, please!" I went to places I had never been before and did things that my exes in the past never wanted to. I went to different wineries and took a painting class, just to name a few. I even bought myself a colorful display of pastel roses just because, and I cooked myself gourmet dinners that I ate by candlelight.

Over the years, I have found love and I have lost love. Finally, I was falling deeply in love again, only this time it was with myself and the life I was living. Who knows, one day I may even meet a man who will love me the way I love myself. But regardless of whether that happens or not, I will continue to go out and enjoy my life, even if that means doing things on my own sometimes. And I will be living happily ever after.

— Michele Vagge —

31

Lessons from the 5K

Life begins at the end of your comfort zone.
~Neale Donald Walsch

nstead of merely driving my son to a 5K race, which had become our Saturday tradition, I made the leap from spectator to partici-pant. Attempting a 5K was worth a shot, despite being a recover-ing couch potato who, up until six weeks ago, hadn't run more than eighteen feet at once — the distance from the couch to the refrigerator and back.

The quest to be a positive role model for my kids prompted the decision. "Take healthy risks," I told them. "Try things beyond your reach. Put yourself in situations to gain skills and confidence." While my mouth was saying the right things, my actions were not. The boundary of my comfort zone hadn't moved in so long that I wasn't sure it could budge. I'd always mocked parents who told their children not to smoke as a cigarette dangled from their lips, yet the hypocrisy of my advice was equally laughable.

Determined to take a healthy risk, with the endorsement of my teenage son, and knowing the race was far from home where I would know no one, I accompanied him to register.

As soon as we registered, waves of doubt overcame me. *What if my six weeks of exercising hasn't been enough preparation? What if I can't finish?*

Other runners started to arrive — young, fit runners. Women with perky bodies clad in form-fitting running gear in stark contrast to the industrial-strength sports bra I required and the oversized T-shirt and shorts strategically chosen to cover myself.

I stretched while avoiding eye contact with anyone as I imagined them wondering how an out-of-shape, middle-aged woman like me could think she belonged here.

Temporarily brushing aside those thoughts, I approached the starting line, knowing I would have a story to tell after the next 3.1 miles. At the "on your mark, get set, go" command, I joined the swarm of runners headed toward the finish line.

Mile One

I reflected on a recent conversation with my doctor, which had served as a nudge to start exercising again. "You're rather young to be having these symptoms," he said, "and there's a lot you can do to take control of your own health." Prior to that conversation, I hadn't broken a sweat in months. I'd long neglected the exercises my chiropractor recommended to keep back pain at bay, and I'd abandoned taking brisk walks to reduce stress. It was time to start treating my body with more respect.

I'd long neglected the exercises my chiropractor recommended to keep back pain at bay, and I'd abandoned taking brisk walks to reduce stress. It was time to start treating my body with more respect.

No more, I thought. *When so many people struggle with health problems, I will no longer say, "I'll get in shape someday," when others don't have the luxury of that option. No more will I forget I'm blessed with an able body that I bear responsibility to care for.*

"10:37," the timekeeper yelled as I completed mile one.

Mile Two

I joined the track team for one year in high school, purely for social reasons. I wasn't much of a runner but was assigned to the mile and two-mile races. The two-mile races were especially humiliating. Inevitably, during the eight laps around the track, I would be lapped. Sometimes twice.

I always garnered applause at the end of each race, though. Some applause was the "Oh, bless her heart for finishing" applause, and some was applause of gratitude that finally we could move on to the next event.

Even as a teenager, I wasn't able to run more than two miles without stopping. In track practices, I frequently had to stop and rest. And when I crossed the finish line of the two-mile races, exhausting every ounce of energy, I wasn't about to continue with a "cool-down run."

"21:47," the timekeeper yelled as I completed mile two. Surprisingly, I had come this far without walking. Despite the steep incline marking the start of mile three, I decided to try something I'd never accomplished: finishing a 5K without stopping.

Mile Three

What a stupid idea, taunted my mind as everything from my thighs down burned as I ascended the hill. Though my speed had diminished to an ever-so-slow trot, I refused to walk. I would give it my best even if it meant collapsing in the arms of the volunteer EMT stationed at the top of the hill.

If my grade-school friends could see this, I thought. I was always one of the last kids picked in gym class, regardless of the sport. I could sense collective groans as I'd walk up to bat. My teammates knew a strike-out was imminent. I could stand on the basketball court without a defensive player in my vicinity, yet my teammates would not pass me the ball.

The closest I came to athletic glory was in fifth grade. While playing kickball, I smacked the ball with my foot and proceeded to round first base. The kids were yelling in excitement as I rounded second, then third, and then jubilantly crossed home plate. I quickly learned the screams of excitement were actually my classmates telling me that I'd kicked a foul ball.

I smiled at the EMT as I passed him by. Still running.

I'm sure had my gym teachers known that being chosen last haunts the last-chosen for years, they would have done things differently. Yet, they unknowingly taught me that being an athlete equals being good at organized sports. They unknowingly taught me that some people are accepted as athletes, and others aren't. I was clearly in the latter camp.

I wonder how many adults spend time in therapists' chairs re-hashing memories of being chosen last, feeling inadequate and wishing gym class didn't exist.

I approached the church where its congregants gathered, holding handmade signs bearing words of support. They cheered and clapped as I passed by, and I hoped my smile would convey what I didn't have the energy to say, "Thank you for being here, for caring." Spurred by a fresh dose of encouragement, I knew finishing without stopping was attainable. Then, the small, still voice within said something I'd never heard it say: *You are an athlete.*

"Hi, Mom," my son yelled as I completed mile three. "Didn't think I'd see you so soon."

The Final Stretch

He ran alongside me. "You're doing great. It looks like you're going to break thirty-five minutes."

He had finished his run far ahead of me, giving him time to walk back a hundred meters to meet me. Later, I would learn he had won the race. He was well-familiar with being in the lead pack, but this was the first race he'd won. Yet, as he greeted me, he contained the excitement of his accomplishment as he encouraged me through the final seconds of my own.

"You're almost there," he yelled, stepping to the sideline, allowing me to continue toward the cheering assembly of strangers yelling, "Good job!" and "Way to go!"

I sprinted those final strides because I could. When I crossed the line, I was sure of two things: I was capable of running a 5K without stopping. And I would do it again.

— Dawn L. Hauter —

32

Euphoria

Two roads diverged in a wood, and I —
I took the one less traveled by,
And that has made all the difference.
~Robert Frost

There are few things that put sheer terror in my heart like the thought of public speaking. All eyes on me. All ears waiting for some great wisdom. To somehow walk to the podium gracefully without falling on my face. The level of panic that goes through my body is similar to how it must feel jumping out of an airplane.

As a new business owner, I was asked to speak on a small-business panel for the Kirkland Chamber of Commerce. Not one ounce of me wanted to do it. I was absolutely terrified. But I thought it could be great exposure for my growing business.

I was told it would be a panel of four speakers. I'd be third to speak. I would do a two- or three-minute speech. I'd be up there with all the other speakers. And it would be "no big deal."

From the moment I agreed to do the panel, I started writing my speech. I would read my speech to my son. He must have heard me repeat that speech a hundred times. I would write and rewrite. I'd wake up in the middle of the night with a great line to add.

"Ken, let me read this to you again."

He'd listen each time as if it were the first time.

It was all-consuming. I wanted to get it right. I wanted to be informative. I wanted to be helpful. I felt like my business depended on this three-minute speech.

The day of the panel, I walked into the event hall. I had gone to Kirkland Chamber luncheons many times before. I never noticed how large that room truly was. It felt like a football field.

I asked Bill Vadino, the Executive Director, "How many people are coming today?"

Without skipping a beat, he said, "Over one hundred people are coming today. They are all so excited for the small-business panel."

He said it as if that would ease my mind. It did not. I regretted I had asked.

Just then, I got a text. It was from my son. He said, "Good luck today, Mom."

A little smile came over my face. Then, I heard, "Can everyone please take their seats?"

As I sat there looking out over the crowd, I heard Bill proceed to introduce key audience members.

He said, "I'd like to thank the mayor of Kirkland for joining us today. Our local state representatives are here. I'd like to welcome the president of the Seattle Seahawks and the president of Puget Sound Energy."

What now? Who? The mayor? The president of the Seattle Seahawks? What is happening here? These very important people are going to listen to me? Me? A thirty-six-year-old, single mom with a new small business? What could I possibly have to say that they want to hear?

Sheer panic.

Next thing I knew, it was my time to speak. As Bill introduced me, I grabbed my notes and headed for the podium.

At this point, I was blinded by nerves. I couldn't even see my notes. I read the first line. My mind went totally blank. I read the first line again. Only then did I notice I was shaking so badly that the mic was picking up the sound of my paper rustling.

I put the notes on the podium. I forgot about my speech and just began to talk. I talked about being a business owner and the accounting needs of small businesses. It felt as if I was up there for about three hours. I was not. It was maybe three minutes.

I didn't even hear what the next speaker had to say. I was so wrapped up in all the things I did wrong.

I blew it! Why did I agree to do this? I was shaking. I looked like a fool.

As the event ended, a woman walked up to me. She said, "Diana, I want to show you something."

She handed me a flyer from the event. On it was a handwritten note. It said, "Diana is the best speaker."

She continued to say, "The lady next to me wrote this on the flyer and handed it to her friend. When I saw what she wrote, I asked if I could have it. I wanted to share it with you. That was so effortless. That was so good. I could never get up and do what you did. You didn't even read from your notes."

I let out a nervous laugh.

I don't think I've ever been as scared as I was in that moment. But, in that moment, I realized that to grow, really grow, you must step out of your comfort zone. I've heard we all go through pivotal moments in life. We can choose one road or another. That afternoon was one of the biggest moments for my business. It propelled me to the next level. I gained a level of respect that day that has stuck with me for over seventeen years in business.

Who knows what would have happened if I had decided to play it safe? Take the easy road. Take the safe road. Who knows? But what I do know is that there is a feeling you get when you do something you are scared to do. A feeling when you come out the other side victorious. It's a feeling like nothing I've ever felt. I will forever take the less traveled road. I will forever take the scary road, for now I know the less traveled road always leads to euphoria that you can never receive taking the easy one.

— Diana Lynn —

33

Flying High

Leap and the net will appear.
~John Burroughs

spent my childhood wishing I were a bird. I envied birds' graceful flights as they took advantage of the wind currents that made
their flying seem so effortless. If wishing would make my body
sprout wings, I could have flown around the world. However, as
an adult, I realized the irony of my earlier desires to be a bird. I am
afraid of heights. Even climbing a ladder is a challenge.

On an April day several years ago, my daughter wanted to do
something special to celebrate my seventieth birthday. I was entering
a new decade, and I knew my daughter well enough to anticipate her
wanting to do something unique that year. In casual conversation one
day, she asked, "Mom, what would you like for your birthday this year?"

"I want to skydive!"

Her facial expression told me she thought I was kidding. In total
astonishment, she asked, "You want to do *what*? Are you serious? Mom,
you are afraid of heights."

"So? I am serious. You asked me what I wanted, and I told you."

As my daughter's shock wore off, and she accepted the reality
of my request, we began making plans for my adventure. But two
scheduled dates for jumping were canceled due to bad weather. I realized after the second cancelation that I had mentally built up courage
by "flying high" in my mind, only to "come down to earth" when the
jump was canceled.

As I mentioned my upcoming birthday present to friends, their reactions ran the gamut. One laughed at the funny joke I had just shared. Some gave a blank look and merely shook their heads, while others expressed sheer terror and commented, "Carol, you can't be serious. You could break every bone in your body."

One close friend said in astonishment, "I thought you were afraid of heights."

"I am."

"Then why are you going to do this?"

"I am tired of being afraid and wonder if I can really do it."

They say the third time is the charm, and so it was with the third scheduled jump date. It was a go! As excited as I was, my stomach did flip-flops as we neared the location where my special birthday present would soon become a reality.

During the instructional lecture, I learned I would have not only one parachute, but three, in the event that one or two failed. That thought was both comforting and terrifying and brought back my fear of heights in full force. Suddenly, everything became real.

While reaching the 10,000-foot altitude for jumping from that small Cessna, my anxious mind kept asking, *Whatever made me think I could do this? And why am I jumping out of a perfectly good plane?*

As I sat in the plane's doorway, waiting for the command to jump, I realized this was going to be the most exciting — and terrifying — thing I had ever done! How could something be both exciting and terrifying at the same time? Well, I was about to find out. There was no turning back.

I heard the reassuring hum of the plane's engine one second, and then I heard only the roar caused by my body falling at one hundred miles per hour in tandem with my instructor. That sound was almost deafening. I felt my skin sliding backward as Mother Nature gave me a natural facelift.

At 5,000 feet, my body jerked violently upward as my parachute opened. And then it became quiet as I descended. I then knew how the birds feel as they circle in the sky. I could see for miles as the Earth became a checkerboard of farmland, subdivisions, and concrete roads.

I was finally flying—not as freely as birds, but as freely as any human could experience. My determination to overcome my fear of heights was, at last, a reality.

I knew I was falling, but I didn't have that sensation. I felt total peace as I quietly surveyed the ground from my amazing vantage point. Although I have flown commercially many times, domestic and international, my view was not through a plane's thick window. I was actually out there in that open space. I felt a complete release of daily cares and responsibilities. I felt engulfed in absolute peace. I wanted these new sentiments to last forever.

As I touched down, my heels dug into the sod and I landed on my behind. My body was still seventy years old, but my mind and spirit felt an excited youthfulness. My determination to step outside my comfort zone permitted me to achieve one of the scariest endeavors of my life. The thrill had outweighed the fear!

But now, I was again bound to Earth by the law of gravity until I could "fly high" during my next dive. Oh, yes, I was going to do it again! I had fallen 10,000 feet, and the only mishap was grass stains on my jeans.

However, my next jump was not meant to be. Two weeks later, as I was anticipating another skydiving experience, I stepped sideways off a friend's three-inch porch step. That small miscalculation resulted in two torn ligaments in my leg, a complete spiral break of my foot, and an ankle so badly damaged that my orthopedic surgeon cautioned against ever skydiving again.

I had fallen 10,000 feet without mishap, yet I was unable to step from a three-inch porch step without being in a cast for eight weeks. One of the ironies of life!

By my willingness to "fly high," I learned that stepping out of one's comfort zone can bring tremendous, satisfying rewards. And that realization gave me courage to consider trying other new adventures.

—Carol Goodman Heizer—

34

My Language Journey, Beyond Words

A different language is a different vision of life.
~Federico Fellini

I had no idea it was possible to sweat so profusely without exerting any physical activity, yet there I was with droplets of moisture excessively dripping down my back.

I wasn't peeking out from behind a heavy curtain, gazing out at a huge crowd who waited to hear me impart profound words of wisdom. Nor was I standing at the open door of a plane thousands of feet in the air, ready to jump out into the wild, blue yonder.

Rather, I was simply sitting on my bed, wearing my comfiest clothes, and waiting to hit the "Enter classroom" button on my computer.

As I clicked the button and was transported into the living room of a stranger across the world, my heart rate quickened.

A friendly face popped up on the screen in front of me. At that moment, my mind froze. An appropriate greeting would have been a simple, "Hello" or "Good morning," but I wasn't able to utter either of those salutations.

I had signed up for my first immersive language session with a Portuguese language tutor with the intent that the entire lesson be conducted in Portuguese.

For the past few months, I had been studying the language and knew the next step required me to practice speaking and have conversations with native speakers. Since I was not in Portugal, video chat was the next best option.

Following my tutor's introduction of herself, she paused, waiting for my response.

It's funny how the mind works. I've heard of people pulling up high-school French from the recesses of their memory to barter with a street vendor at a Parisian market, surprising themselves with how well they performed when the moment called for it.

Yet there I sat, my mind completely blanking on even the most basic of words despite the fact I had been studying hours a day for months.

I broke down and replied, "Sorry, I'm so nervous that I can't seem to form a sentence."

Her response was something I will never forget. "Learning a new language is like showing your butt to the world. You're showing a part of yourself that you don't normally show, and it can be uncomfortable. Trust me, I've seen a lot of butts."

The ice was officially broken.

Laughter burst forth as her words both caught me off-guard and resonated with me.

As I've progressed along on my language journey, I often think back to her insight.

Learning a new language is uncomfortable. We take for granted the ability to express ourselves robustly, and when that power is taken away, we are brought to a place of vulnerability.

While it can feel overwhelming and intimidating taking on such a feat, I have come to realize the numerous benefits that accompany stretching beyond my comfort zone.

Learning a new language has made me a better parent.

As the parent of a preschooler, communication can be tricky. My three-year-old son has big feelings but isn't equipped with the vocabulary to properly express himself. This has led to numerous outbursts and meltdowns, with both of us becoming frustrated.

When I started learning Portuguese, it clicked. Although I had a lot to say, I didn't know the words to accurately reflect what I felt, and it was both deflating and frustrating. I finally realized how difficult it must be for him to be understood in the adult world around him.

The tenacity of preschoolers is something to be admired. Each day, he tries out new words and phrases. Sometimes, he gets them wrong, and sometimes he gets them right, but his toolbox of words, along with his confidence, grows every day. As adult learners, we sometimes feel embarrassment over what we don't know and hold back in fear of what others may think. With children, there is no shame or embarrassment; they unabashedly try.

Not only has our relationship improved, but he has become my example of what learning should look like.

Learning a new language humbled me.

I have always loved words. From voraciously reading Nancy Drew books to obtaining my graduate degree in English, my passion has grown along with me. The power of words is profound, and I had taken for granted the ease of which I was able to communicate.

Once that was stripped away, my confidence was replaced with anxiousness.

I was not blind to the luxury I was afforded. I was learning a new language as a hobby, at my own pace and without any true pressure.

Many others do not have that same luxury. Every day, there are people who must leave their country of origin and move to a new country where the language is as foreign as the land. To them, it's a matter of true survival.

I'm humbled by the strength and bravery that it takes.

Learning a new language taught me respect.

When my husband and I finally had the opportunity to visit Portugal, we spoke the language to the best of our ability whenever we had the chance.

There were moments when I used the wrong verb conjugation or the wrong word, and I simply had to apologize and admit I didn't understand what was being said. But there were also moments when connections were made.

As we were ordering gelato in Portuguese at a small shop in Porto, the server asked where we were from as she had heard us speaking English to each other in line. We told her, and she complimented us on our Portuguese skills.

She then said something that struck a chord.

"Thank you for taking the time to learn our language. So many people don't even try to learn, and it means so much that you did."

Attempting to learn someone else's language, especially when visiting their country, shows respect not only for their homeland but for the people themselves. It's not about doing it perfectly; it's about respecting them enough to try.

Learning a new language has emboldened me.

Taking on the challenge of learning a new language has ignited a spark within me. I had previously put a label on myself. I would often say I wasn't good at learning new languages. It was a false narrative that slowly overtook my thinking until I believed it to be true.

I took a hard look at other areas in my life where I had placed self-imposed limits. With honest self-reflection, I realized there were several.

As a result of stretching myself through language learning, I have also stepped outside my comfort zone in other ways. If you had told me a year ago that I would be taking a writing course, competing in competitions at my gym, or learning about car maintenance, I truly wouldn't have believed it.

There's no way around it, venturing outside one's comfort zone can be uncomfortable. It can also be beautiful, fulfilling and rewarding in ways you will never know unless you attempt it.

— Laura Niebauer Palmer —

The Important Stuff

*Since there is nothing so well worth having as friends,
never lose a chance to make them.*
~Francesco Guicciardini

After years of semi-retirement, I decided to join the ranks of the employed once more. Although I enjoyed my daily volunteer gigs and gardening chores, I longed for a weekly paycheck and that tired, satisfied feeling after a good day's work. My former career included performing in theme-park shows in Florida, but my husband and I now resided in Tennessee, so it was time for a fresh start.

That's when our fitness center announced an opening for a part-time front-desk position, checking in members and answering phones. I knew there would be a plethora of technical computer work, which was daunting, but I wanted to step out of my comfort zone and give it a try. I applied immediately.

To call our fitness center a "gym" would be a ridiculous understatement because it's so much more. For starters, it's massive. There are three levels, providing weight machines, cardio equipment, three lap pools, two basketball courts, a café, and a spa. Services include childcare, personal trainers, yoga, cycle, strength, and kickboxing classes, pickleball, and swimming lessons. Basically, there's something for everyone, and it's always brimming with activity!

As a current member, I was familiar with the building and its programs, so I thought I'd be a perfect fit. And at the conclusion of my first interview with Jane, the assistant manager, she agreed. I was set to begin the following week. Yay, me!

My first day was a whirlwind of paperwork and an introduction to the front-desk computers. My co-workers, all efficient, skilled twenty-somethings, negotiated the software with ease. They moved quickly from screen to screen, instructing how to check in members, record guests, complete childcare forms, and take member photos. Although I wrote copious notes and asked them to repeat each action several times, I quickly realized I wasn't absorbing anything. It was all so foreign and completely overwhelming. I failed constantly, each time apologizing and asking for information to be repeated. Frankly, it was embarrassing.

My manager and co-workers were abundantly patient, always kind and encouraging, but my ineptness was glaring. It seemed my constant plea to members was, "Please bear with me. I'm still trying to figure this out!" Most of them smiled, but I sensed their understanding was waning. I had to get this.

One day, Jane announced there was an opening shift available three days a week. Would anyone be willing to take it on a permanent basis? "Opening shift" at our gym meant 3:45 A.M. to accommodate the members who preferred a good sweat before work. I genuinely wanted to help, and no one else offered, so I volunteered.

I woke at 2:30 A.M. my first day, drank lots of coffee and mentally prepared for my new shift. I needed to get this right. I quickly learned one very important quality about our morning workout members: They are consistent and disciplined, showing up daily without fail, and following a strict routine. Opening those doors on time was a valuable part of that routine, and I learned to take it seriously. I was never late.

Unfortunately, I also learned that, except for one other custodial employee, I was completely alone. There was no one to ask for help if my computer froze or a difficult question was posed. It was all me. And it was terrifying.

I was failing again. When Jane would arrive around 8:00, I frequently presented a list of "guesses" I'd made when faced with the morning's issues. She'd explain what to do going forward, but there was always a slew of new problems the following day. Clearly, I was out of my league.

I considered quitting, but I deeply loved this job. I loved greeting my morning crowd, learning their names, and hearing their plans for the day ahead. I took great pride in my ability to get people to smile, even at that hour.

One day, we were informed the corporate office had begun sending surveys to random members each month, asking for suggestions and comments. There was also a section for members to praise an employee who made a difference. I gasped as I read the first lines:

"Joan is fantastic. She remembers everyone's name and is so positive."

"Joan is a ray of sunshine. I look forward to seeing her smiling face in the morning!"

"I love Joan's bright sweaters and positive attitude."

Even those who couldn't remember my name wanted to make sure I got credit:

"That lady in the morning is a delight."

The next day, Jane approached with a smile. "See?" she chirped. "You've been so hard on yourself but look at the difference you've made! I can teach people how to use the technical equipment here, but you've got something more valuable. You've made a true connection with our members; I can't teach that. Great job!"

From that day forward, I focused on "connecting." I learned every name of my morning members, hundreds of them, and greeted them as they walked through the front door. Despite the early hour, we had a wonderful time! I oohed and aahed over pics of grandkids and family vacations. They actively participated when I counted down the hours before my Caribbean cruise. ("How many more days, Joan?") If I was a little slow pulling up their guest pass on the iPad, who cared? There was so much to discuss while it was rebooting!

One day, Jane approached with a grim face and bad news. The corporate office was making a change. There would no longer be part-time workers employed at the front desk. Only full-timers would be permitted. All others were given notice. That included me.

Word of my termination reached the members, and suddenly

there were letters and e-mails flooding the office.

"We want Joan!"

"You're getting rid of Joan? Are you INSANE?"

Jane shared many of the comments with me, even though her hands were tied. She fought hard for me, but it was over.

I was very sad while opening the doors on my last day, but that soon dissipated when people began arriving with flowers, cards, and other gifts. The front counter was covered with beautiful trinkets that my members had brought. Each one stopped to thank me before leaving that day. I couldn't have asked for a finer send-off.

I still work out at that gym as a "civilian," and I frequently run into those dear members. I'll walk across the room to a machine and hear, "JOAN! I miss you!" It never gets old. In the end, nobody cared that I was clumsy at the technical stuff. They wanted to see what colorful sweater I was wearing and to tell me about their weekend. You know, the important stuff.

In a few months, I'll begin my job search again. But it'll be different this time, thanks to all those people who reminded me of what matters. They helped me remember that even if the territory is scary outside of my comfort zone, if I take a risk and focus on my strengths, surprising and wonderful things can happen. I can't wait to see what's next!

— Joan Donnelly-Emery —

36

Try Every Sport Once in a Lifetime

*You never know if you can actually do something
against all odds until you actually do it.*
~Abby Wambach

The wobbly orange ladder led to a small platform twenty-five feet above the concrete floor. When I reached the tiny steel stand, I was instructed to tuck my toes over it and extend my arms straight in front of me. I would need to be ready to grab the bar that was coming my way. I did it! I jumped and then flew through the air, pumping my legs back and forth until I was told to dismount. I wasn't the most graceful flying trapeze artist to ever go airborne on their first attempt, but I victoriously displayed my fingers in the shape of a "W" after dropping to the net as the other women applauded.

One by one, seven women followed my lead, some less brave than me but all eventually accomplishing the same feat — even one woman wearing a dress. The only difference between those women and me was that they could feel the air through their tresses, and I could not. My head was bald from a three-year bout with the autoimmune disease alopecia.

They say grief occurs in five stages: denial, anger, bargaining, depression, and acceptance. After three years of losing my thick dark brown hair, eyelashes, and eyebrows to a disease that affects over 147 million people globally, I was done with the first four stages of grief and onto the last one: acceptance. Part of accepting the new me was acknowledging my lifetime love for sports. I set a new personal goal of trying every sport once in my lifetime.

You see, when people are exercising, biking, running, or skydiving, they don't care what anyone else looks like because they are too busy doing their own thing. No one does a double take when they see me biking bald, parasailing with no hair, or wearing a pink baseball hat when I'm fishing, like they do when I'm banking, grocery shopping, or public speaking. Sports have allowed me to accept myself in this new light better than any counseling session could. So why not get out of my own sports comfort zone and set a massive life goal?

After Googling lists of sports, I created a comprehensive list of 163 sports: 125 regular sports such as tennis, waterskiing, basketball, etc., and thirty-eight adventure sports such as parasailing, rock climbing, and bull riding. I've already participated in sixty-six regular sports and five adventure sports, meaning I'm halfway to my goal with a solid twenty years to go.

Sharing my list of sports has flooded my inbox with invitations from friends, clients, and family members willing to experience some of them with me. My sons are booking us a spear-fishing trip since we have done all the other types of fishing together. A couple of women are interested in boxing, while a big group of women wants to try curling. My husband registered me for a big-game-hunting course because I will accompany him deer hunting this fall.

It turns out that everyone I talk to is interested in getting out of their comfort zone. As I stood side by side with another volunteer, making sandwiches to feed the hungry on the south side of our community and sharing my new endeavor, she told me she wants to learn to fence. Together, we are looking into the opportunity to do it since it is a sport I haven't tried. One thing I know for sure is that excitement begets excitement, and sharing big, bold goals has a way of spurring on, or should I say *sparring* on, others.

The inspiration for my first big sports goal came while sitting around a table eight years ago with thirteen women in New York City. They were talking about running experiences for a new non-profit organization. Each one of them was a marathoner; I was not. In fact, the woman sitting across the table from me had just returned from completing a marathon in Antarctica, and the woman to the left of me ran marathons in Iceland with a gun to protect her from bears. These women were the Wikipedia definition of living outside their comfort zones.

Never imagining I could run 26.2 miles, I gave up on the marathon idea until an opportunity arose to run in the Boston Marathon for a charity. I spent six months training for that marathon as I envisioned the finish line and having the medal placed around my neck. When I finished the race on a sunny April day, I wondered what could ever live up to that jubilant feeling. That's when I decided to do it again... with every sport there was.

My favorite motto is, "If I don't try, I can't fail; and if I fail, I get up and try again." Who would have ever known that by losing all my hair, announcing my intentions, and stretching far beyond my comfort zone, I am inspiring others to do more sports in their lifetime and getting mentally and physically stronger in the meantime?

— Tracy Chamberlain Higginbotham —

37

Soaking Away Body Shame at a Korean Jjimjilbang

The paradox of relaxation is the renewal of the mind,
rekindling of spirit, and revitalizing of strength.
~Lailah Gifty Akita

was twenty years old when I went to a public bathhouse for the first time. I was studying abroad with several other students in Japan and had experienced several cultural excursions, such as preparing matcha in a tea ceremony, wearing a kimono, and playing a koto. I knew about public bathhouses, or sentō, but it wasn't top of mind for experiences I wanted to try in Japan.

But then I found myself in the women's changing room with our teacher and the female participants, getting ready to undress for the bath. The other female students were equally awkward and shifty, and we avoided eye contact with each other. Even our teacher, who was Japanese and very familiar with sentō etiquette, felt awkward standing naked in front of us and went off to the bath area.

A small towel was provided for drying off after leaving the bath, but I found myself trying to decide which half of my body I could try to (futilely) cover up with it. In the bath area, we had to soap up and shower before entering the bath. I knew I had cleaned myself sufficiently in the shower but delayed the inevitable moment when I would have to turn around and bare it all in what felt like a long walk to join the other ladies (including other patrons) in the bath. I finally turned myself around and quickly got in. A few girls engaged in conversation, but I found that hard to do. I was too focused on making my body as invisible as possible in the water.

The bathwater was hot and soothing, but the enjoyment was not enough to make me want to experience a public bath again. I avoided it for a long time, turning down polite inquiries at the gym about joining the bath or booking a private bath when staying in an area famous for its hot springs.

At age thirty, and this time in Korea, I was faced with the option to experience the Korean version of the public bathhouse: a jjimjilbang. Thinking back to the first awkward experience ten years earlier and finding the idea of getting naked in front of my future sister-in-law, who proposed the idea, awkward, I said no. Everyone accepted my response, and we moved on. Of course, I would have had a great time in Korea whether or not I had gone to the jjimjilbang. I now look back fondly on the home-cooked, multi-dish meals, traditional hanbok photoshoots, and the illuminated, snowy sights of Seoul. But I felt this was my opportunity to stop running away and missing out on this particular cultural experience. How long would I continue to live in Asia and avoid this?

Several days later, I announced to everyone that I would like to go to the jjimjilbang after all. I had put it out there, and I was not going to pull away from my verbal commitment. I doubled down on this when, one afternoon, it was suggested we go there while driving back from lunch. I settled the anxious feeling bubbling up within me as we pulled into the parking lot. My fiancé and his brother-in-law went through the curtain leading to the male bathing area, and I followed his sister into the female bathing area.

I saw women and girls of all shapes and sizes strolling around the changing area, chatting away with no coverings at all. I mostly avoided eye contact with my fiancé's sister as we stuffed our clothes into our lockers. I knew better than to try to shield myself with the towel, so I attempted to form some kind of cocoon with my arms and legs while I was being led to the bathing area.

I'm the only Black woman here. My body is clearly bigger and curvier than a lot of the other women. What if they stare? What if they point out something? I really should be in better shape.

These thoughts had kept me away for all these years, and they came to mind again that day.

As I gently eased myself into the 100-degree bathwater, it hit me that no one cared about that. I took in the sight of the freedom with which the other patrons moved and even played in the bathwater. Bodies, and nothing more, surrounded me. I looked my fiancé's sister in the eye as we chatted away.

We got out of the bath to join the guys upstairs for the sauna. After the sauna, we relaxed with some food and drink and took some pictures. I got to try the Korean sauna egg I had heard about on YouTube.

We separated again to return to the bathing area. This time, I had my towel hanging around my neck and walked upright. The anxiety from earlier gave way to calm. My insecurities had given way to the trivial concern of not getting my hair wet as I moved with certainty through the different baths. Nothing distracted me from the mental and physical release of the tension I had felt. Back in the changing area, I looked at myself in the mirror as I toweled off, owning and treasuring my body as it was in that moment. I moved slowly as I dressed, no longer in a rush to hide anything.

The four of us settled into our seats in the car, feeling relaxed and sleepy. We would not have had this experience if I had stayed in fear. Or, to put it another way, my ability to have this experience hinged on my willingness to go. Staying in fear doesn't deprive only me but the people around me as well. I shudder to think of what else I (and others) have missed out on because I allowed fear to call the shots.

— Monique Bloomfield —

Chapter 5

Try Something New

An Introvert Builds a Little Free Library

*The real voyage of discovery consists not in seeking
new landscapes, but in having new eyes.*
~Marcel Proust

"Package!" the UPS man called to me through the window, placing a box on the porch. I jumped and nearly slid out of my chair and under the dining room table, but it was too late. He'd already seen me. I smiled and thanked him as he turned away.

Until my husband and I bought our house, I'd never lived in a place where I felt compelled to hide from delivery people.

Growing up, I lived in the last house on a dead-end street. Our driveway was too narrow for the mail truck to turn around, so our mailbox was a block away.

In college, I had a campus mailbox. In subsequent apartments, there was a centralized location for mail. At none of those places was I ever actually confronted with the people who brought me correspondence and packages. I could work around my anxiety about crowds and people by waiting them out. If I saw someone at the mailboxes, I'd hang back at a distance until they were done. At the apartment, I'd hang my head over the balcony railing to see if anyone was at the mail hub below.

Here, the mailbox is at the corner of the porch. I can see it from the dining room window where I work. I don't know what comes over me in these moments when I'm happily typing on my laptop, and then I see someone approaching the house and have the sudden urge to hide or flee. My husband doesn't know what to make of it when I tiptoe to his office in the back of the house, crouching below the windows, and whisper-yell, "Someone's about to come to the door," especially when it's someone bringing us food—which I would've ordered and therefore knew to expect.

To make matters stranger, all our delivery people are impeccably kind. The logical side of my brain knows that hiding from these sweet, helpful people doesn't make sense.

Then again, there's so much about anxiety and being introverted that doesn't make sense, and yet that's the side of my brain that holds the most sway over my legs. That's why I find myself on my feet and fleeing or on my knees and hiding before I even realize what I'm doing.

Like many introverts, I love books. Once we had a house, I couldn't wait to build a Little Free Library.

"You do realize that means people will be coming to the yard, right?" my husband said.

I tried not to think about that part. I envisioned people being so enthralled with the books that they wouldn't notice me at all, and we could each pretend the other wasn't there. Later, when I checked the Library, I'd see what book they'd taken and be thrilled with their choice. It was a way of connecting with fellow book lovers from a distance.

But that distance grew shorter with time. A letter carrier took a Winnie the Pooh book and told me that she couldn't wait to read it to her son at bedtime. An insurance adjuster took a book about fishing and told us how excited he was because he so rarely finds books he likes. An elementary-school teacher cleaned out her classroom library and dropped off a huge stack of picture books and chapter books and talked to me about the new books she was stocking in her classroom. Dog walkers have taken everything from *Conversations with God* to *Erotic Stories for Couples*. We don't discriminate. We try to keep a little bit of everything.

Since installing the Little Free Library, I've had more conversations with neighbors and delivery people than ever before. And for the most part I've stopped hiding because I enjoy these discussions. I've learned how many people in the neighborhood love books as much as I do, and I can't wait to hear what they're reading. Throughout the pandemic, when social distancing was the way of things, seeing people at our Little Free Library and talking to them through the window was a comforting human connection—necessary, sometimes, even for introverts.

Nowadays, rather than hiding, I have to remind myself not to stare and smile giddily when people approach the Library so I don't frighten them off with my enthusiasm. And I don't slide under the table in panic at the sight of another person in my yard anymore — unless they're carrying a clipboard and wanting me to switch utility companies. I still dash to the back of the house to escape those people.

— Mandy Shunnarah —

39

I Feared for My Life

What would life be if we had no
courage to attempt anything?
~Vincent van Gogh

was beginning to question my sanity. Why did I book an activity
that would take me so far out of my comfort zone?

As a birthday gift for my fun-loving, nineteen-year-old granddaughter, Faith, I had suggested the two of us go whitewater rafting.
She was thrilled.

The excitement of our upcoming adventure carried me through
until we arrived at the launch site.

We were too early to check in and sat in the car watching rain
spatter on our windshield. The unseasonably cool weather dampened
my enthusiasm. I started getting nervous. I attempted to put on a brave
face for Faith, but the cracks in my façade were starting to show.

Check-in time arrived, and we joined a group of about ninety
people who were issued protective gear to put on before going to
orientation.

The safety lesson was far from reassuring. I didn't want to think
about tumbling off the raft into the cold river. I am not a swimmer,
and even wearing a lifejacket didn't give me the sense of security I'd
hoped for.

If we ended up in the water, we would need to float on our backs,
go with the current, and grab the side of the raft. In order to help
someone back into the raft, we were told to push their head down to

submerge them. When we let go, they would pop up, and we'd use that momentum to lift them back on board. Seriously! It would be bad enough to be in the water without someone pushing me under. I was terrified and tried to find a way to stay safely on shore.

Families with young children excitedly made their way to the rafts. My rational mind told me that if it was safe for children, it would be safe for me as well. My rapid heart rate told a different story.

We half-slid down the slippery, muddy slope of the riverbank. My granddaughter had to come back and lead me by the hand when I stood frozen in fear, unable to take another step toward my certain demise.

I felt like I was in mortal danger as she patiently reassured me and helped me board the raft. Did I want to sit near the front? No way! The middle seemed like the safest place to position myself. Faith sat opposite me.

What kind of stupid idea was this? It was hard to believe it had been my suggestion. Everyone else was laughing and full of excitement. I was wondering when I'd see my life flash before my eyes.

Our guide led us through some practice paddle strokes and the commands we were to follow. We learned when our paddles should be in the water and when we should hold them in the air. When he felt we were ready, our raft moved slowly from the shore.

The river was calm, and I started to relax. Soon, we approached our first rapids and navigated through them. Cold water suddenly sprayed in my face, but just as quickly as it appeared, we were back in calm water again.

My fear turned to exhilaration when I realized I'd survived the tumultuous water and stayed in the raft. I'd done it! I actually helped navigate a river raft through rapids. What an incredible feeling of accomplishment.

A short while later, Faith and I were given the opportunity to move to the front of the raft. We'd be the first ones to enter the rapids and face the onslaught of rushing water. I knew she wanted to experience this but wouldn't leave my side. Shocking both of us, I said, "Let's do it!"

We carefully traded places with those at the front and prepared to take a lead role. Entering the next rapids, all I could see was a wall of water about to crash over me. The thrill of adventure took over, and I enjoyed every minute of my time up front. I had no idea I could laugh in the middle of something like that. In fact, I was disappointed to move back to a less turbulent area of the raft when our turn was over.

That night, I reflected on the rafting trip and my drastic change of attitude. I wondered how many experiences I have missed out on because I gave in to my fears and stayed in my safe, little comfort zone. I vowed to break this cycle.

Since that day, I have resisted my initial hesitation and experienced activities I wouldn't have been brave enough to try before. Snorkeling may not sound adventurous to you, but to a woman in her mid-sixties, who had previously been afraid to put her face in the water, it was incredible. So was ziplining!

Faith and I have talked about going whitewater rafting again, with bigger rapids next time. Until we do, I look back at the pictures taken from along our route on the river, see the pure joy on my face, and am reminded of the day I learned to fully embrace the adventure of life.

— Tandy Balson —

40

Out of the Stands and Into the Game

*We have to be in the center of action in order
not to end up on the sidelines.*
~Sunday Adelaja

I was raised in a music-centered home, and I excelled as a classically trained vocalist and saved my competitive nature for the stage, not the athletic field. Everyone knew "Emily doesn't do sports." I opted for the safety of the cheering section, far removed from fast balls and certain death. Staying on the sidelines meant I was in control and would never injure myself or look like a fool.

My husband's career has led to our family relocating a number of times. With each move, in order to make friends I explored new hobbies and joined various clubs and groups. I was good at letting myself be vulnerable and trying new things, such as quilting, playing Bunco, attending *The Bachelor* viewing parties, and joining the choir. All these activities were safe, slow-paced and comfortable, with not a ball or sneaker in sight.

That changed when our family moved to the capital city of Turkey, Ankara. As I found myself exploring a new terrain, a new climate, new culture and new cuisine, I knew I needed to build my tribe, and fast. Without a *Bachelor* fan to be found, it looked like I'd have to reach beyond my norms and get uncomfortable. Very uncomfortable. It turned out that the activity of choice in my new community was tennis. If I wanted a social life, I would have to play, and it was a sport I had never tried before. I cheered myself on with reminders that I enjoy trying new things, tennis skirts are adorable, and, well, how bad could it be?

My first step was to look the part. Tennis skirt purchased. Second step, borrow my kid's cheap, hand-me-down racket. Third step, find a coach. Fourth step, follow the coach's instructions and buy a better racket. Fifth step, lace up, gear up and show up to my first lesson.

I couldn't remember the last time I really challenged myself to learn something new — and not just a craft or concept, but learning to move my body in new and completely foreign ways. With arms, legs, hands and feet all accelerating in different directions, I celebrated at the end of each lesson when I hadn't thrown out my back or pulled a hamstring. My movements were awkward and childish, like a toddler just learning to walk, struggling to put one foot in front of the other.

Klutzy or not, it didn't take long for me to see why this sport was so popular. I was hooked. I simply couldn't get enough of it. With an encouraging instructor, I continued to show up, with a racket in hand and a smile on my face. I accepted criticism and learned to laugh at my mistakes. Despite my new can-do attitude, my swings were often met with nothing but air. Laughing and learning, I kept swinging. I kept trying. I chose to dismiss the embarrassment I felt at my uncoordinated, unpracticed movements and focused instead on the progress I was making.

After a few months of lessons and many hours spent hitting balls with my kids (who inherited their father's natural athleticism), the practice provided me with the confidence to take the next step. Cardio Tennis happened on Saturdays and was well-attended by the tennis-loving members of our community. This was a tight-knit group of skilled enthusiasts and, may I say, fiercely intimidating. Put me in the spotlight to perform to a sold-out audience any day, but hand me a racket and tell me to return that lightning-speed serve? No, thank you. I must have been crazy to think I could hold my own against them, but with their loving encouragement and promises that Cardio Tennis was just for fun, I apprehensively committed to playing.

Adorned in my cutest tennis skirt, neon orange visor and preppy polo, I made my way to the court, confidently grasping my newly strung racket. As they explained the rules of the game to me, I apprehensively declared, "I'm an amateur! Just happy to be here! I apologize in advance!"

The hours we spent together were full of laughter, encouragement and camaraderie. They complimented my forehand and sympathized when I missed a return. I laughed along with them as I dodged a fast ball and forgave myself when my racket caught nothing but air. I showed up. I put myself out there, unashamedly showcasing my rookie status.

My seat in the cheering section had been my shield against appearing weak, flawed, and inexperienced. But by putting myself in the game, I developed a sense of empowerment and accomplishment, learned a new skill, and, best of all, made new friends who are always willing to meet up to rally with me. I might never get past amateur level, but I'm willing to try and fail, learn and practice, swing and miss. I will continue to buy the tennis skirts, practice, jump, reach and swing. Some balls, I'll hit; some balls, I'll miss. But I'll keep showing up to play the game. It turns out Emily does play sports—and still finds room in her life for nachos.

—Emily Ruth Rusch—

A League of My Own

*We should not let our fears hold us back
from pursuing our hopes.*
~John F. Kennedy

When I was four, my seven-year-old brother received a baseball mitt for his birthday. Every night, as we went to sleep, I'd listen to him throwing a ball into the mitt over and over to soften the leather. When he was finally sleepy, he'd put the ball in the mitt, wrap a rubber band around it, and put it under his pillow to shape the leather even more. I wanted a mitt so much that I almost cried. But, back then, girls didn't play sports; they played with dolls.

Fast-forward twenty-six years. Now a thirty-year-old mother of three, I happened to see a notice in my local paper: "Women's Slow-Pitch Softball League opens soon. Anyone interested, sign up at the rec center." I cut it out and set it on the kitchen counter. Could I? After all these years? Was it even possible to think about playing baseball, a game I'd never actually played but had dreamed of playing my entire life? I had been a swimmer in college and, as women became more active in sports, became a competitive racquetball player. But I'd certainly watched enough Chicago Cubs games to know how the game was played.

I looked at that notice on my counter every day. I thought of a thousand reasons I couldn't play. I was too old. I had three little ones to watch. I would/could never be good enough. But the idea of playing baseball stuck in my head and wouldn't go away. Finally, I screwed up my courage and signed up at the rec center. Since I wasn't affiliated with a team, they told me I'd be assigned to one. One week went by. Two. Had they forgotten about me? Maybe there was no opening on a team. Finally, the notice came to report to James Park on Monday night to begin practice. They gave me the name of the team to look for. Since my husband worked Monday nights, I arranged for a sitter. It was a luxury but, at that moment in my life, a necessity.

On Monday, heart pounding, I walked through the park filled with women of all ages practicing at different diamonds. It took me a while to find my team. They were all high-school girls, seventeen and eighteen years old! I waited a couple of minutes before approaching the coach. He was one of the girls' fathers and not at all happy to see me. He had put together top athletes for his team, and he didn't want some old lady messing things up. He looked me over. His girls had fine mitts and metal cleats. They looked like players. I had no mitt and wore an old T-shirt and gym shoes. I didn't care. I wanted to play, and the rec department rules said he had to put me on his team.

That first day, he had me run bases. What that meant was I'd stand near home plate while one of the girls batted, and then I'd run as hard as I could to first base, trying to get there before they threw me out. I did this over and over and over. I never got a chance to bat or play the field. I just ran bases all night. The next morning, I could barely stand. Excruciating pain ran down my front thigh muscles.

I was still feeling sore when I showed up to play the next week. The coach was clearly surprised to see me. He had no idea how determined I was. I could take whatever abuse he dished out... as long as I could be part of this game I'd loved and longed to play for so many years. This time, I brought my kids. The boys were old enough to play in the park. I put my daughter in a portable playpen behind the batting cage.

Every week, I showed up for practice. Every game, I spent the night sitting on the bench. My husband asked why I didn't just forget about it, and I told him this was the only way I was ever going to get to play. If I stayed home, I'd never get a chance. At least, by showing up every Monday, I was around women playing ball, and I felt sure I'd somehow find the right team. During the last inning of the last game of the season, the coach finally told me to go to center field. I had to borrow a mitt from a member of the opposing team and I used it to catch an impossibly high ball, winning the game for us. Again, the coach looked surprised. It never occurred to him that I might be able to play.

After the game, as I was gathering up my kids to go home, a young man approached me and asked if I'd like to play for his team. They were a group from Belize, and he'd been scouting the other teams looking for players. He'd seen the catch I'd made and the way I "moved like an athlete" on the field and thought I might make a good pitcher. I couldn't believe it! A coach who wanted me on his team? The next day, knowing I was actually going to play, I went to the sporting goods store to buy a mitt. "How old is your boy?" asked the salesman. That took me back all those years to when people assumed baseball was for boys. "It's for me," I said. Excited as a kid, I took my new mitt home, remembering how to break it in.

Playing for my new team began a nine-year odyssey. My teammates were women who had all played in Belize, where women's fast-pitch ball was a major sport. They'd traveled around all of Belize's islands to play and told me that big money was bet on the games. Now living in the States, they were clearly the most powerful and gifted players in the league. Best of all, they loved the game the way I did, loved practice, and constantly worked hard at getting better. I knew I would never play as well as they did. After all, they grew up playing in a culture that encouraged girls in sports.

But it turned out their coach was right: I could pitch. I played with them until I retired at age forty. We went undefeated six of those years, and I was named MVP five times. Playing the game with these women enriched my life and the lives of my family in countless ways. My children, nine years older by the time I stopped pitching, grew up assuming women played sports just like men. To this day, memories of those years gladden all our hearts.

And none of it would have happened if I hadn't cut out that little article, nervously signed up to play ball, and dared to take a chance on fulfilling my childhood dream.

—Sue Sussman—

42

Trapeze School of Life

You gain strength, courage and confidence
by every experience in which you
really stop to look fear in the face.
~Eleanor Roosevelt

could hear one of my classmates expressing her impatience with my slow crawl up the ladder. "If she's afraid of heights, why would she sign up for a trapeze class?" *Personal growth is a marathon, not a sprint,* I said to myself as I continued my climb.

My friend was at the top of the ladder, trying to coax me up. "Think of Leonardo DiCaprio! Nathan from *One Tree Hill!*"

How did I wind up on a ladder teetering above the Hudson River? My friend invited me to a trapeze class. I was skeptical, but her enthusiasm and assurances of strict safety procedures won me over.

I had been fearful of heights since elementary school. My gym teacher would make us climb to the top of the ropes to get an invitation to a pizza party. If the pizza party wasn't enough motivation, a group of classmates tracking my ascent surely was. There's nothing like the promise of lukewarm pizza and the fear of teasing to motivate a kid.

Avoiding my fear of heights became second nature. I tried not to look down on balconies or staircases. When necessary, I traveled by plane with my friends and family. I declined invitations from friends to join them on roller coasters. I claimed I would rather eat a funnel cake than wait on a roller-coaster line, which was only partially true.

But here I was, at age twenty-six, facing my fear of heights in a rather extreme way. I had come around to the idea of trying trapeze. I figured it wasn't much different from swinging on the monkey bars as a kid. The one obstacle I didn't expect was the ladder. In order to reach the trapeze, I had to climb up a twenty-two-foot ladder.

My friend's distraction techniques helped to take my mind off my precarious task. I found a rhythm and kept going. With a slow, steady pace that Aesop's tortoise would have been proud of, I made it to the top.

The humid August air was heavy as I stepped forward. I took a moment to take in the view. New York City was on display. The bright, late summer sunshine illuminated Hudson River Park and the Manhattan skyline. It felt different to see New York City on a platform twenty-two feet above the Hudson River instead of safely ensconced behind a glass window. Everything looked bigger, crisper, and clearer, like wearing glasses for the first time. Feeling like I was eye-to-eye with the city gave me the push I needed to get into position for the flight.

An instructor strapped me into a harness and told me to step to the edge of the platform. I grabbed the trapeze bar with sweaty hands, surprised that it was too thick to wrap my hand around. Instead of a firm grip, my hands were in a weak, bear-claw position.

The cheers from my classmates echoed below. An instructor reminded me of the safety protocols, including the net below that would catch me at the bottom. He reminded me to listen to the directions while in the air, so I could perform a trick.

"Maybe I could just swing the first time to feel more comfortable?" I bartered.

"We like everyone to try to perform the trick," the instructor firmly told me.

No wiggle room there.

I stood face-to-face with my fear of heights. The realization that this was something I would have to do alone gave me some discomfort, but also a bit of pride. If I made it through the class, I would have accomplished something in the face of my fear. My stomach dropped as my hands clenched the trapeze bar as tightly as I could. As the instructor counted down, I took a deep breath and pushed off the platform.

The air rushed into my lungs as adrenaline surged through me. The exhilaration of hurtling through space was dizzying. I lost awareness of time and space and let the momentum of the trapeze swing me back and forth.

An instructor's voice came over the loudspeaker, giving me step-by-step instructions for performing a trick. Instead of doubting my inability to perform the trick, I took his directions one step at a time.

Hang straight. Legs up. Go under the bars. Good job! Look at your kneecaps. Point your toes. Hands off! Lean back. Arch back. Keep your hands out like Superman. Tuck your tailbone under. Push yourself forward more. The other direction. Hands off. Lean back. Kick forward. Back. Forward. Hands off!

I plopped onto the net ungracefully and bounced several times before an instructor released me from my harness. I rolled off the net, bursting with adrenaline, and began walking on shaky legs. I couldn't believe I had actually done it!

My second round on the trapeze went a bit more smoothly. I gritted my teeth and slowly ascended the ladder, one rung at a time. This time, the instructor led me through a more detailed trick. I was instructed to let go of the bar and fly into the waiting arms of an instructor on a parallel trapeze. While I couldn't quite get the hang of this trick, I was pleased with my attempt. Instead of seeing it as a failure, I reframed it as a decent try.

During my flights on the trapeze, my fear didn't completely leave me. My palms were clammy, my heart was racing, and my mouth was dry. But I turned down the dial of my fear so I could be present in the experience. I focused my thoughts on the instructor's voice instead of my internal dialogue about what could go wrong.

While my fear of heights is still with me, this experience opened up a new way of seeing myself and approaching challenges. I became more open to trying new things. In the years since my trapeze flight, I've taken an archery class, gone on my first kayaking trip, and hiked along a 200-foot cliff in Nova Scotia.

While these experiences made my heart pound, I completed them, one step at a time. By breaking down the trapeze ascent and flight,

I learned to listen to myself, trust my instincts, and have faith in the people around me. I'm more capable than my fears let me believe I am.

Life is a series of steps. Even in midair, when I slowed down, focused on the present and took one step at a time, I went further than if I hadn't tried at all. My experience helped me realize that I don't want to cave into my fears and spend my life standing still. Whether my steps are small or big, on the ground or in midair, I want to keep moving toward new experiences.

As I walked out of trapeze school, I noticed how different things looked on the ground. There's nothing like twenty-two feet of perspective to help you step out of your comfort zone. Right then, my perspective was telling me I had earned some pizza for dinner.

—Danielle Cappolla—

43

Celebrating Lillördag Every Wednesday

Marriage is a mosaic you build with your spouse.
Millions of tiny moments that create your love story.
~Author Unknown

et me start off by saying that I am a creature of habit. I thrive on routines. I am wary of "surprises," and truth be told, I often enjoy my familiar routines — particularly on long winter evenings, when my comfy couch, television remote, and Netflix subscription beckon.

But even an individual like me sometimes experiences a "wake-up call." And after one-too-many nights of binge-watching the British series, *Midsomer Murders,* I knew something would have to change. My husband and I were becoming way too comfortable in our after-dinner routine, and it was getting a bit boring.

But what were the options on wintry nights for a couple of aging baby boomers? An avid reader, I began my explorations through books, namely those about Scandinavian winters and how those hearty souls passed the time when nightfall occurred in the early afternoon. That exercise led me to the discovery of hygge, pronounced hoo-ga, defined as the Danish philosophy of comfort, togetherness, wellbeing, and warmth.

The Danes practice hygge by incorporating simple, soothing things, such as comfort food, easy conversations, and candlelight, into their daily routines. Most important, they spend this time with loved ones in a cozy atmosphere of contentment and warmth.

That sounded wonderful, and given the geography of where Denmark is located, I wasn't surprised that a country near the Arctic Circle would embrace such a philosophy. But how could I actually practice this? I needed more concrete examples of how hygge could be incorporated into winter evenings in northern New Jersey.

So, my research continued.

Not surprisingly, comfort food and heartfelt conversations were the cornerstones of hygge. But so were activities that had nothing to do with technology, batteries, or chargers. Television, video games, and electronics were replaced by board games, puzzles, and charades, in an atmosphere that relied upon candlelight and crackling fireplaces, not electricity, for light.

My quest to learn more about hygge led me to another discovery in Scandinavian tradition known as lillördag, or "little Saturday." Unlike the American view of Wednesdays as "hump days" to be endured, lillördag is a Nordic cultural tradition whereby Wednesdays are viewed as opportunities for little weekend celebrations. Instead of trudging through a five-day workweek, why not break it up with a little indulgence, a bit of fun, every Wednesday?

That sounded ingenious to me, and I was ready to launch my plan. Not blessed in the culinary department, I located a wonderful bakery, gourmet specialty store, and high-end arts-and-craft store. I was ready.

The following Wednesday, while my husband started his ritual of settling in on the couch, remote in hand, I asked him to indulge me that evening. He joined me in the dining room, where I had placed a centerpiece of lighted ivory candles, two steaming mugs of hot chocolate, and slices of iced almond cake on the table. In the center was a high-end jigsaw puzzle that featured a collage of vintage television programs, including scenes from *I Love Lucy, The Love Boat,* and *M*A*S*H.*

I'll never forget the bewilderment on my husband's face as he surrendered the remote and picked up his mug of hot chocolate. But as he settled into one of the dining room chairs, he declared, "Okay, I'm game." I took a deep breath and began to empty the puzzle box of all its jigsaw pieces.

What happened next was a minor miracle. With a mild gleam in his eyes, which I hadn't seen in months, my husband started separating the various pieces. Straight-edged frame pieces were placed in one pile, with different colors in another. And when he found one of the four corner pieces, he yelled "Bingo!" I hadn't heard that much excitement since the World Series playoffs, which had occurred months before.

But as we settled into the evening, while he worked on the frame of the puzzle and I pieced together parts of the middle, our conversation deepened. Perhaps it was the ambiance of the candlelight, hot chocolate, and almond cake, or even the nostalgic illustrations on the puzzle itself that lent themselves to sharing stories about our grandparents, childhood homes, and first jobs. We reminisced about grade-school teachers, favorite classes, art projects, music lessons, and long-lost friends. We had been together for nearly forty years, but this was the first time that I had heard some of these stories. It was a magical evening.

Somehow, working together on a joint project by candlelight, surrounded with good food, comfort, and warmth during a winter evening, produced a minor miracle. Not surprisingly, we made a commitment to "celebrate" lillördag every Wednesday evening. Of course, we tweaked the specifics depending upon the season. During the warmer months, white-wine spritzers replaced the hot chocolate, and watermelon salad was a refreshing change from iced almond cake. Sometimes, our jigsaw puzzle was replaced by a board game like *Monopoly*, *Clue*, or *Risk*. On other Wednesday evenings, we played hearts, crazy eights, or gin rummy.

But one constant remained: All electronic devices were banned from our sacrosanct Wednesday evenings. And, in doing so, our heartfelt conversations continued while we engaged in a project together.

Looking back a year later, it seems almost unbelievable that taking such a simple step out of our Wednesday evening comfort zone could enrich our lives so much.

— Barbara Davey —

44

The Challenge

*You cannot believe what it does to the human spirit
to maximize your human potential
and stretch yourself to the limit.*
~Jim Rohn

The sun sparkled on the water as I stepped up to the bow of the Commodore cruise ship to take my turn at skeet shooting. This was only the beginning of a week-long Mexican Riviera cruise that started in San Diego. My employer had suggested that since this was my first cruise and the meals were included I should be brave and try new foods. I promised him that I would accept his challenge even though I'm a fussy eater. I then decided to take his suggestion even further and experience more than just new cuisine.

On my first day at sea, I signed up for skeet shooting, something I'd never even considered doing in the past. I gathered with the shooters at the appointed hour and watched as one man after another took a turn. Some hit the clay discs and some didn't. Then my name was called, and as luck would have it, I was the first woman on the list. I walked to the shooting area as people chanted my name in encouragement, "Linda, Linda, Linda."

After a few quick instructions I heard "Pull." I aimed at the sky and missed the target. I needed to determine where the target was going to be by the time the bullet got there, all on a moving ship. I tried again and again. After several tries of hitting nothing, I walked red-faced back through the now silent crowd. Inwardly, though, I was cheering for myself because I'd actually done something new.

On the day we arrived at Puerto Vallarta, I signed up for horseback riding. I'd never been on a horse in my life, and when we got to the ranch and I spied Chili Bean, I knew why I hadn't. He was the biggest animal I'd ever seen. Somehow, I was supposed to get on him. Thankfully, a stool appeared, and I climbed up and arranged myself in the saddle. Then Chili Bean moved forward, and I had second thoughts but didn't want to go through whatever it would take to get back down.

I discovered I didn't need to know how to lead him because he and the other horses knew the route by memory. I just had to go along for the ride. That is, until we got to a river. I held my breath as Chili Bean stepped gingerly down the slippery bank and into the water. As we crossed the river, I had the feeling we were in a Western movie and only needed a herd of cattle to complete the picture. When we finally got back to the ranch and off our horses, and then eventually back to the luxuriousness of the ship, I was tired and sore but smiling as I checked off another accomplishment.

The next day, we docked at Mazatlán, and I was excited to go parasailing. A few of us with the same desire gathered at the beach. After receiving minimal instructions, Carlos, the young entrepreneur, pointed to me and said, "You go first." That wasn't in my script. I'd planned on watching the others to see how it was done. But Carlos seemed to know about weight and wind velocity and decided I should go first. So, I got into the harness with a rope behind me that was attached to a huge parachute and a rope in front of me attached to a boat out in the water.

Before I could get mentally prepared, the boat started to move forward, and so did I. I had no choice. I ran about three steps on the beach and was soon airborne, sitting in a seat of sorts and going higher and higher. When I was way up in the air, I looked down and saw the entire coastline. The people and buildings looked like little dots. I remembered Carlos saying that when it was time to come back down, I should listen for his whistle and watch for the flag he was waving. Sure. From way up high, it was impossible to pick out any one person, so I just enjoyed the ride, feeling free as a bird and unable to wipe the silly grin off my face.

After about seven minutes, I noticed that the people and buildings were getting larger. Lo and behold, there was Carlos waving a flag and blowing a whistle. He knew what he was doing after all. As the ground came closer, I pulled on the ropes to keep me free of buildings and trees. Soon, I stuck a victorious ten-point landing on the beach. I was extremely thankful for my willingness to test myself in new ways.

The next day, we anchored at Cabo San Lucas where I had signed up for snorkeling. I stepped into a catamaran with the others and received a few instructions from the boat owner, Pancho. When we got out past the arch at Land's End and smack in the middle of nowhere, Pancho said, "Here we are."

I said, "Where are we?" I had pictured walking into the sea from the beach, sticking my head in the water and looking at all the pretty fish. But, no, we had to enter the water from the back of the boat — water that was way over our heads. I'll go as high in the sky as possible, but don't put me underwater. I put on the fins and flip-flopped down the steps and into the Sea of Cortez. So far, so good. But then I had to find the courage to put my head in the water. I wasn't at all sure that the little snorkel tube would keep me from drowning.

After stalling a long time, I admonished myself, saying, "Look, girl, you came out here to snorkel and see something new, so stop thinking and just stick your face in the water!" I listened to myself, and when I realized I wasn't going to die, the colorful fish and coral I saw were simply beautiful. All too soon, a whistle blew telling us it was time to get back on the boat, and I could have kicked myself for all the time I'd wasted being scared.

When we docked in San Diego at the end of the cruise, my head swirled with all my adventures and a passion to continue to try new things. I fueled that passion by skydiving.

As for new foods? I kept a list on a napkin and proudly showed my boss that I had indeed tried new tastes — lobster tail, quail, black bean soup, a Tequila slammer, and even frog legs, among other things. The trip was an experience from start to finish. And the best part is that I survived.

— Linda Loegel Hemby —

45

Skater Girl

Don't let fear make your decisions for you.
~Annette White

I didn't choose the skateboard. It arrived on the fireplace, fully wrapped, just in time for Mother's Day.

"Wow," I said.

"Wow" was an understatement. I'd never ridden a skateboard in my life. I was barely able to ride a bike. Walking and chewing gum at the same time was a challenge. How was I ever going to ride a skateboard?

"Do you love it?" my son asked.

I looked down at the long black board. The top, covered in a fine grain of sand, scraped the tips of my fingers.

"Look at the other side!" my husband said.

I flipped it over. Pink, blue and purple. I held it out.

"Santa Cruz?" I asked.

"Oh," my husband said, a look of confusion crossing his face.

"We thought it said Santa Claus," my son added.

I took in their expectant faces and nodded my head, slipping into a smile. "It feels like Santa Claus, doesn't it? It feels like something wonderful."

"You're going to need pads," my son said.

My husband nudged him. "Shh." He passed me a red and green package. "Open this."

I pointed to the evergreens and stockings all over the wrapping paper. "See? Just like Christmas!"

"Just open it already!" they both shouted.

I tore into the paper, pulling out pink and black pads of every shape and size. My kid explained what they were for: "Wrists. Elbows. Knees. And one more thing!"

It was 2020. The first year of Covid. We were trying to live an exciting life to drown out the sadness.

I shook the box. "Helmet?" I asked.

"Just open it!" they yelled again.

They didn't have to yell twice.

I pulled back the paper, revealing a turquoise helmet.

My son smiled. "It's the same as your hair."

"It is!" I was already turning into a blue-haired lady, embracing my books, tea, and slow Covid life. But they were already pushing me out the door, pulling off tags and upending boxes.

I stepped out into the May morning feeling like I was covered in plastic wrap and sunshine.

I set the board on the sidewalk and stepped on. "Let's roll," I said.

Did I fall? Of course I did! Did I get back on? You know it!

Two years later, I'm still rolling down to the stop sign and working my way back toward the house again. Am I the next Tony Hawk? Not even. Am I getting better? Maybe a little.

But really, I've learned two things from my skateboard: One, sometimes you just gotta get on the board. And two: It takes your palms a lot longer to heal when you're in your forties, so wear your wrist guards.

— Kate Ristau —

46

Benefits of Being an Extreme Book Nerd

When we share our stories, what it does is, it opens up
our hearts for other people to share their stories. And it
gives us the sense that we are not alone on this journey.
~Janine Shepherd

When I learned that our community library was hosting a Book Nerd Challenge, I got excited. My granddaughter devoured books and I needed a little inspiration to increase the quality of the books I read, so I suggested we sign up.

How hard could it be? The goal was to read fifty books in a year. I am an English teacher. This didn't seem like much of a challenge.

Then, I read the small print. There were fifty different categories ranging from historical nonfiction to a book with a red cover. Not so easy after all.

The experience created a bond with my granddaughter. We read a couple of the same novels, but mostly read different titles. However, we had interesting conversations based on the similar themes in our books and we discussed the authors' styles, different genres, and our favorites.

I read some nonfiction material I would not have read if not for the challenge. They provided insight and enjoyment. Three books provided new information and a unique lens. Answering the challenge to read a book with a different political position than my own, I picked up a personal memoir written by John McCain since I am a Democrat and he was a Republican. *The Restless Wave: Good Times, Just Causes, Great Fights, and Other Appreciations* appropriately fit the category. It proved to be a stimulating read, reinforcing my long-held belief that John McCain was a compassionate, honest individual who dedicated himself to the fight for democracy. The events of his life reminded me that politics and humanity are two different things entirely.

The second text that I would not have checked out of the library but found rewarding was *Born a Crime* by Trevor Noah. The story shared his growth from poverty in South Africa to fame in America and communicated his belief that we are in control of our lives and empowered to create the world we desire.

The third book I added to my list of must-reads had personal value: *My Stroke of Insight: A Brain Scientist's Personal Journey* by Jill Bolte Taylor. My daughter had a stroke in September. We had to read a book from the 300 category of the Dewey Decimal System, so this was the obvious choice. Taylor shared her personal journey of recovery after a stroke.

The book challenge also introduced me to some obscure pleasure reads: *Love Handles* by Gretchen Galway, a humorous romance, and *Autumn* by Ali Smith, a story of spiritual love set post-Brexit. I also took a break from heavy literature to consume the new release in a series by Kate Collins, *Yews with Caution*, a mystery romance, as well as Janet Evanovich's newest novel. Her Stephanie Plum series is one of my favorites.

With fifty categories to choose from, I reread my all-time favorite, *Atlas Shrugged* by Ayn Rand, and devoured several classics. It also became a habit when walking my dog to listen to an audiobook, increasing the pleasure of my daily chore. Life doesn't get any better than a walk on a beautiful day with my dog and a book.

Initially, inspired by a stubborn need to meet the goal, I forced myself to make time to visit the worlds and characters of the novels. In the past, excuses created reasons to procrastinate, but now I found books provided a better alternative. When a new TV series premiered, I discovered books brought greater joy and engagement. When the house needed cleaning, I remembered it would be dirty again tomorrow. When the dog wanted attention, I held her bone in one hand and a book in the other. And when a task could not be postponed, I turned on an audiobook.

After a year, reading became a habit I craved. My life became more fulfilling as I grew intellectually. The realistic stories of life replaced the unrealistic dramas on the screen.

Perhaps the greatest benefit I realized through my increased reading was the impact it had on my writing. I witnessed firsthand what I had so often preached to my writing students. Reading improved my vocabulary, modeled unique styles, provided new insights, inspired new ideas, and prompted a desire to imitate other authors' successes.

When I began, fifty reading categories looked intimidating, but my granddaughter and I both won the prestigious title of Extreme Book Nerd.

I have listed the categories in case anyone is interested and wants to join the fun.

1. A book about or set during WWII
2. The first book in a series
3. Nonfiction & Fiction about the same topic book 1
4. Nonfiction & Fiction about the same topic book 2
5. A bildungsroman book (coming-of-age story)
6. A book set during a holiday
7. A book with multiple narrators
8. A book recommended to me
9. A book with a green cover
10. A classic novel
11. A book with a weather element in the title
12. A book with a heist in it
13. A book with a Dewey Decimal number in the 300s
14. A book written in the first person
15. A Young Adult (YA) novel
16. A book set in two time periods
17. A book with a baby in it

18. A book set in India
19. A biography
20. A book set in a favorite location of yours
21. A book from a celebrity book club
22. A book set in outer space
23. A true crime book
24. A book by two authors
25. A book that was made into a movie
26. A book of poetry or written in verse
27. A book by a famous non-author
28. A book with a pirate in it
29. A book set during the summer
30. A novel based on a true story
31. A book about the military
32. A book that was translated into English
33. *A Christmas Carol* by Charles Dickens
34. A book with a number in the title
35. A book that scares you
36. A book with a long title (at least five words)
37. A book with a person's name in the title
38. A National Book Award winner or nominee
39. A book based on a fairy tale or mythology
40. A book published the year you were born
41. A book with a cover that is your favorite color
42. A book by a person of color
43. A book found using NoveList
44. A book about a sport
45. A book with a time of day in the title (dawn, midnight, etc.)
46. A title with an action verb in it (running, talking, etc.)
47. A book with a cat
48. A loved one's favorite book
49. A book with a child or teen protagonist
50. A book with "Extreme," "Book," or "Nerd" in the title

— Brenda Mahler —

Be Daring

A Call to Action

Always have a willing hand to help someone,
you might be the only one that does.
~Roy T. Bennett

Ll I knew was that, when I heard a young girl's voice in distress, I had to do something. It was on a flight to Iceland with a dear friend with cancer. He asked me to accompany him as he traveled to get some medical scans in Europe. We were all settled in for a long flight, off on an adventure to a hospital in Holland where I would support him.

It wasn't long before I heard a man belittling a sobbing girl directly behind me. I couldn't ignore what was happening. This was obviously a girl in a very dangerous situation.

My friend didn't hear any of it, so he had no idea what I was thinking. I was witnessing, with my ears only, a guy verbally abusing a girl who was crying uncontrollably. He continued to upset her with no regard for her tears. He didn't let up. He didn't care. He was controlling her, and this was his intent.

I noticed the napkin used for my water cup and recognized it was something I could write on. If I could get a note to her without him seeing, maybe this would help her understand she needed to run away from him FAST.

This was happening behind me, so I thought, *Wait until he goes to the bathroom and pass her the note.* I glanced behind me periodically, and he finally left. I don't know what she looked like. I don't know if our eyes ever met. All I knew then was she now had a note from someone who cared with my e-mail address if she wanted to contact me. I was a total stranger who had observed her desperate situation. It was so dangerous that I couldn't even risk sharing my phone number and taking a chance it would land in his hands.

Sometimes, there are situations we cannot ignore. My dad taught me to never leave a place wishing I had done or said something. That was going through my mind. Did anyone else hear this desperate situation?

Never did I expect a response from this young girl, but almost one year later, her mom e-mailed me. It turned out that my note had started the girl on the path to saving herself. It brings tears to my eyes to share that this innocent sweetheart's life was being threatened in ways I never could have imagined. Her mom revealed there was not only verbal abuse but physical abuse as well, and her life was being threatened over and over. Her mom shared that even while being in therapy, the draw to go back to the abuser was so strong that she stayed with him for quite a while longer. With a lot of hard work in therapy, this smart, articulate, and beautiful young woman is now doing amazing things with her life.

God knew she needed help that day in December. I don't want to think about what could have been if I had not listened to that soft voice of the Lord guiding me to write a note on a napkin on a plane that changed a beautiful life.

— Karen Ambro Bernatis —

48

Open What?

*By leaving your comfort zone behind and taking
a leap of faith into something new, you find out
who you are truly capable of becoming.*
~Author Unknown

Two years had passed since I'd lost my husband, Frank. We'd met in the middle of our lives, with our kids married or getting married. He was a country boy. I was a city girl, a dreamer who loved stories and poems. When we married, I moved into his house in the country. By the time I retired, Frank's kidneys had failed. Dialysis three times a week became our reality. Two years later, the Lord called him home. I was left with a forever ache in my heart.

I'd had a few stories published when I was very young. I'd even had one published locally while married to Frank. He had been so proud. Now that he was gone, I busied myself with estate sales and remodeling. But that didn't mean the sadness and loneliness disappeared. I felt compelled to express my feelings in a poem. Through tears, I poured out words onto a page.

I come from a Latino family, but not the loud, boisterous kind. My people were more the strong, silent types. My own mother was often described by relatives as *muy seria* — very serious. They say we learn by example. I would describe myself as more on the shy, quiet and serious end of the spectrum. That's not to say that I can't be friendly and flirtatious, but I prefer not to be on stage. I keep my feelings tight in my heart.

One day, while Googling poetry, I discovered the Sun Poet's Society. They were a local writing group that hosted "open mic" events. I learned that I could read my poem in front of strangers who would listen to every word. They would watch my face as I read about my feelings. Ordinarily, I would have run away from this type of situation, but the idea tantalized me. When was the last time I had felt this excited about something? It terrified me, but I needed to share my poem.

The Sun Poet's Society met Wednesday evenings at a bookstore on my side of town. The meeting was starting soon, so I needed to grab my poem and get right over there.

When I arrived, I found about twenty people scattered among the folding chairs. A guy walked up to the microphone, introduced himself as Rod, and welcomed everybody. He called for newcomers to introduce themselves. Three of us bravely raised our hands and were welcomed with a smattering of applause. Rod asked if we had signed up to read a poem. I was the only newcomer who confessed to bringing a poem. Yikes! I went up and signed at number 14, thinking, *I can't believe I'm doing this.* At least, Rod hadn't asked if I wanted to share my poem right then and there. Anyway, what could go wrong? At least, I hadn't had to memorize anything because there's no way I would remember a single word.

I returned to my seat next to a girl who had also raised her hand with the newcomers. "You didn't bring a poem?" I asked.

She answered with a fierce shake of her head and said, "Next time."

I enjoyed every single poem I heard that night before I shared mine. I heard lovely love poems, some rants, some fierce political opinions, funny poems, literary twists of phrases and words, beautiful nature poems, and some that sounded like songs without music — rhyming, melodic, orderly. At last, Rod called my name. My name!

"And here is a virgin poet who will read for the first time at the mic of the Sun Poet's Society. Let's give her a hand."

By the time the gentle applause silenced, my knees felt like they were knocking against each other. I prayed my voice wasn't shaky. *Nothing to fear but fear itself,* I thought. Luckily, there was a podium where I could set down my poem because a couple of the previous poets had read from sheets of paper that shook like leaves in the wind. I mean, if I had noticed, everybody else must have, too. And they weren't even virgins.

I set my single sheet of paper on the podium. I had to adjust my bifocals because the podium was too low. I announced the title of my poem.

"Move closer to the mic, Susana," Rod said in a gentle voice.

I inched up. I could almost feel the mic's cold steel against my mouth. I didn't want to touch it with my lips. That would be gross and unsanitary.

I reintroduced myself and explained that my poem was in Spanish but that I would read a full translation afterward. As I began, my lips kept bumping up against the mic just like I'd feared they would. I tried to inch back, but I felt so nervous that my entire body shook, which pushed me up against the mic over and over again. Soon, I thought, everybody would start laughing. I tried to look up at each face as I articulated the words. When I looked back down at my poem again, I'd lost my place, so… awkward pause.

I finally got to the end. Now, I had to read the translation. Great. Now everyone would fully understand every single word of my silly babble. It didn't help that, as I read, I spotted some areas that needed serious rewriting. And why was I suddenly unsure of how to pronounce certain words?

When I finished, I heard another smattering of applause. Rod thanked me and said, "Wonderful, Susana. Please, please promise me that you'll come again."

Really?

But I was hooked. I returned every Wednesday with a new poem. Maybe they weren't all that great, but they were my heartfelt thoughts and feelings. And people applauded every time. I even participated in a city-wide contest, reading my poem in front of an auditorium of people. I didn't win, but I got out there and did it. I was a nervous wreck, but it was exhilarating.

I've continued participating in open mics and poetry performances with yet another group of wonderful poets. They call themselves Voces

Cósmicas (Cosmic Voices) led by a very cool guy named Fernando, a retired schoolteacher. I've had my poems displayed on city buses and art galleries. I've had some published in literary journals and anthologies. Maybe someday I'll have a collection published. Frank would be so proud.

—Susana Nevarez-Marquez—

49

To Thine Own Self Be True

*The caged bird sings with a fearful trill, of things
unknown, but longed for still, and his tune is heard on
the distant hill, for the caged bird sings of freedom.*
~Maya Angelou, I Know Why the Caged Bird Sings

The sound of the scissors making their way along the nape of my neck cut the silence in the room. Then I heard the snip. There was no going back. My decision was now final, and although I'd long thought about it, I couldn't believe that I was actually doing it. I was locing my hair at age forty.

After spending twenty years in the professional world, I'd learned to play the game quite well. It's the game that most professionals know because the rules are pretty simple. Actually, there's only one rule: blend in from nine to five. It required me to straighten my hair, take off the hoop earrings that my grandma, may God rest her soul, would often call gold bicycle tires because they were so big, and replace them with pearls before sliding into an uncomfortable pair of crisp slacks and toe-curling, corn-giving heels.

Professional politics have often required people to look the part, and for twenty years, I did just that. I operated under this unwritten rule that guided my success. Oh, but when I turned forty, something changed! It's hard to explain, but there was a stirring inside me — a gravitational pull toward truth, a nagging nudge to "thine own self be true."

That nudge rattled me for a bit because it wasn't until that moment when I realized the darndest thing: I had become comfortable being uncomfortable all these years. The fear of no longer blending in gave me pause. If I stepped out there now and showed up with my natural hair after living a professional lie for twenty years, what would people say? Would they see me the same? Would senior execs and strangers alike now question the wealth of knowledge that I have because I wore locks?

When the first four inches of my hair fell on the floor beside me, it's hard to describe what I felt. The only word that came to mind was freedom. But when anything has been caged for a large portion of its life, there's often this moment of pause and processing that has to occur before that thing takes its first step out of what has contained it for so long.

While sitting in my beautician's chair, I stared at my feet, thinking about the journey and what it took to get here: to let go of other people's expectations of me, to be okay with not being a chameleon, and to realize that some people might reject me. It took some time to get there, but I am glad I arrived. All my years and experiences had rolled up into this big ball of courage and given me the audacity I needed to step out of comfort's cage.

After about three hours of this kind of contemplation, my loctician coiled the final twist of my hair. "Okay, we're done. It's so beautiful, too." She handed the mirror to me. This was it. My true self was about to be revealed. Excited, I held it up to reveal the new me before thinking in total shock, *Oh, my God. Oh, my God. I look like a chicken. A real chicken.*

All my hair was gone. How was I supposed to go out into the world looking like that? I guess the horror showed on my face because my loctician asked in the most caring voice, "You don't like it?" I wanted to cry, but instead I dug inside my purse and gave her eighty dollars for her services before speed-walking to my car so I could stare in my rearview mirror and cry loudly. Once I gathered myself, I FaceTimed my sister. When she logged on, her silence and hand over her mouth confirmed what I already knew.

"I look like a chicken, don't I?" I asked.

Her exact words were, "It ain't that bad" — which meant it was that bad. I cried some more on the phone with her before heading home to face my husband. That would be the ultimate test.

I am certain that his anticipation grew when he heard the garage open. Unnerved, I was shaking the keys as I tried to open the door. I walked in. "Hey, honey!" I heard him yell before I turned the corner. He was sitting at the table, and when we made eye contact, he had an uncomfortable grin on his face. We'd been married long enough for him to know that what he said next mattered. He tilted his head like a curious pet before saying in a light voice, "You like it?"

When I replied, "No, look at it," that gave him permission to breathe and be honest.

"You just gotta get used to it, is all. It ain't that bad. Give it some time." I stepped into the half-bath by our kitchen and pouted. "It's so ugly. I'm going to take it out."

My husband stood behind me and said, "Why, honey? You gonna pay that woman eighty dollars just to take it out? I say give it some time."

I sulked quietly as I headed up the stairs and straight to my bathroom. I stood in front of the mirror, trying to pin up my hair with bobby pins. That didn't work, so I resorted to trying on headbands. Nothing made it better. I showered and went to bed, trying to brace myself for the workplace the next day.

My co-workers had the good sense not to say anything. It was so awkward. Meeting. Awkward. Break room. Awkward. They darn near ignored me altogether to avoid having to say anything at all. I felt invisible, although I'm sure I was the conversation in a couple of cubicles that day.

Fast-forward a year later when my hair has loced and lengthened. There's not a day that goes by when I don't have someone at work or a stranger tell me, "Your locs are beautiful." Every time I get that compliment, I chuckle, say thanks and think about the horror of stepping out of my comfortable cage. With each compliment, I clearly think about that initial discomfort and hear my husband's advice in my head, "You just gotta get used to it, is all. It ain't that bad."

— Kimberly Taybron Lucas —

50

Upside Down and Straight Ahead

*Each time you try something for the first time you
will grow — a little piece of the fear of the unknown is
removed and replaced with a sense of empowerment.*
~Annette White

On a Saturday afternoon, my friend's eleven-year-old daughter
Jenny and I wound our way through the artery-clogging, fried-
food booths at the State Fair of Texas. Her dad, along with
my husband, followed behind. Seconds later, we arrived at the
section of the fair that I dreaded more than searching for a place to
park: the midway rides.

As the loudspeakers blared "I Will Survive," potential victims
whooshed past us like a cluster of tiny tornadoes. Jenny looked up at
the Windsurf ride, her eyes wide and her shoulder-length blond hair
flapping in her face. I was confident that she, like my children when
they were her age, would shun the twisting, terrifying, multi-story
mechanical arm on steroids and continue walking toward the games.

I was wrong.

"Will you go on this ride with me?" she asked.

"Um, sure," I answered while glancing up at the people who were
suspended upside down, their feet dangling like octopus tentacles.
"How bad could it be?" I asked.

"Not bad if rides don't make you sick," Jenny said.

I could have made up an excuse for not wanting to gamble with my
mortality. Or I could have admitted my propensity for motion sickness.

But, earlier that morning, I had challenged myself to try something new each week. I was ready to push myself out of my comfort zone. The way Jenny stared at the ride, eager to experience the same thrill as the brave group of riders in front of us, I couldn't say no.

We handed the teenager at the gate ten yellow tickets each. After climbing into our seats, an attendant reached up, pulled down the bar, and locked it in place. The ride lifted us slowly and then flipped us over like the blueberry pancakes I had eaten three hours earlier and hoped to keep in their proper place. As I stared at the concrete directly below us, I wondered if I had replacement coverage for the phone I was sure would slip out of my pocket and shatter into a million tiny pieces. I wondered why I had decided to wear flip-flops. I wondered when my new health insurance would kick in.

My stomach churned as I stared at the cotton-candy booth across from me. I thought if I found a focal point, I could calm my queasy stomach.

The ride touched down after twisting and turning our bodies like the taffy machines a few booths away.

The guys were waiting for us at the exit. "How was it?" they asked.

"Fine. No big deal," I said, even though my head was spinning like one of the other torturous machines dotting the midway.

Jenny walked ahead of us and convinced me to keep taking chances and sample more rides. Why hadn't I picked a different challenge, like filing my taxes on time? Then, I remembered my commitment to push myself — to seek new adventures.

"Oh, look at the pirate ship!" she said.

"That looks like a calm ride."

"Let's go!" she said as she rushed to join others in line.

I followed her, confident the ride would be uneventful. At the end, as the ship slowed down and my heart rate didn't, I realized my ride-judging skills were unreliable.

Our fourth and final ride was a devilish version of the Mad Tea Party ride at Disney World. Mid-spin, we felt the teacups climb several stories. Seconds later, the ride rotated us over the pavement like rotisserie chickens over an open fire.

Jenny looked over at me and mouthed, "I'm sorry!"

"It's fine. Are you having fun?" I asked, breathing deeply to calm my quaking stomach.

"Not really," she answered.

"At least it's almost over!"

After the ride touched the ground, I swayed down the ramp. When I reached the bottom, I tapped out like a WWF wrestler admitting defeat. Jenny's dad thanked me for taking his daughter on the rides, and I assured him I was having fun. He politely didn't mention anything about my left eye twitching.

On the way to the car, I texted my son a video of me on the first ride.

"That's me in the middle!" I wrote.

"LOL, no way," he answered.

"Can you believe it?" I asked.

Although my body was shaking and my brain was jumbled, I felt exhilarated. That morning, I had set a goal, taken my first step to reach it, and simultaneously made a pint-sized daredevil happy. More importantly, the next day, I revised my list of weekly challenges. None of them involve leaving the house.

— Lisa Kanarek —

51

Yes, Let's!

*Be fearless in trying new things, whether they are
physical, mental, or emotional, since being afraid
can challenge you to go to the next level.*
~Rita Wilson

I nervously walked down the aisles of the open house for OLLI, the Osher Lifelong Learning Institute, offering classes for adults fifty years and older. I studied the homemade posters and class agendas, trying to decide which class to take. I stopped in front of a table where a smiling, dark-haired woman sat.

"Improv," I said to the woman. "Now that sounds scary."

"No, it's fun," she said. "All of life, when you think about it, is an improv."

Her enthusiasm was contagious, and that was how I found myself sitting in an improv class weeks later with six other students. Although the thought of standing up in front of a room of total strangers terrified me, there was also something exciting about it.

Our teacher Randy introduced herself, explaining that she was an actress from New York who mostly performed in musicals Off Broadway. She'd moved to Miami, where her daughter and grandchild lived, hoping to find work as an extra in movies. Unfortunately, there was no work available. Two months after she moved down, the pandemic hit, and she found herself in a strange city where she knew no one but her daughter.

"OLLI became my home," she explained.

Before, during and after the pandemic, she took classes at OLLI, eventually becoming a volunteer and then a teacher.

"In this class, you have to be willing to make a fool of yourself. We'll laugh a lot, we may even cry, and, best of all, we'll have fun. Remember, there's no right or wrong in improv. This is all about thinking on your feet and keeping your mind sharp."

Next, we went around the room, introducing ourselves and telling why we took the class.

Gwen, a retired high-school psychology teacher, wearing glasses and a sweater, said she didn't know why she was taking this class.

"This isn't like me at all," she explained. "I'm very shy and reserved."

There was Norman, a Canadian, recently widowed who was tall and slim with an easy laugh. Jack, a retired doctor with a deep voice, always thought he could have been an actor if he hadn't gone into medicine.

Pam, a pretty blonde in flowing robes, had just come from a belly-dancing class and was learning to speak Arabic. Her friend Twyla, a former school administrator, was also a glider pilot and competitive ballroom dancer. To put it mildly, we were an eclectic group.

It was my turn to introduce myself. Most of the class seemed to be doctors and teachers, and I was neither. Terrified of public speaking, I took a deep breath and began.

"I was born and raised in Miami, and I was a flight attendant for Air Florida for four years. When they went out of business, I got married and had three kids. So, that was my life for the next twenty years. Then, I got divorced and re-married a widower with three little girls, and that became my life for the next twenty years. Now, all the kids are gone, we're empty nesters, and I feel like it's finally my turn to focus on myself."

I could hardly believe the words coming out of my mouth. And, despite my fear of public speaking, I wasn't at all nervous. This space, filled with strangers willing to take a risk, felt safe.

The last student was a curly-haired gentleman named Don with a gravelly voice. A retired ophthalmologist and professor, he confessed that, with the pandemic, he felt like he'd also lost the ability to socialize with other people.

"Sometimes, I can't find the words," he said.

Our teacher reassured him that many of us felt kind of rusty in dealing with other people after such a long period of isolation.

"I only talked to my cat for months," she said.

She explained that this class would help with that, as well as with interviewing and public speaking.

Our first exercise was to stand up and move our bodies, with neck circles, shoulder rolls, and shaking our legs and arms to loosen up. That was easy enough.

The next assignment was for one person to create a scenario and for another person to come in and interact with the scene, followed by a third person.

In my scene, the person was working out, and the next person was a weight. Stumped by what to do, I started pirouetting across the room. I felt silly doing ballet in front of a bunch of strangers, but I also felt light and free.

Twyla was up next. She flapped her arms and said she was a bird flying. The next student blew at her and said he was the wind beneath her wings. The third student, Gwen, screeched loudly, flapping her arms with abandon and charging at the bird.

"I'm a hawk," she said.

The scene ended, and we all clapped.

"Okay, Miss 'This isn't me,'" said our teacher.

"What, did I do alright?" asked Gwen.

"Yes, it was great. But you said you couldn't do this, that you were too shy, and then you turned into this hawk and killed it."

We all laughed. We laughed so much, in fact, that other students from nearby classes peeked into our classroom to see what all the fuss was about.

One of the final exercises had us walking together around the room. One of us was to suggest an activity, such as hopping like a bunny, and we all were to say, "Yes, let's!" and then perform the stated activity, no matter how silly.

"Do the samba!" said Twyla, the ballroom dancer.

"Yes, let's!" we answered and attempted to samba.

"Quack like a duck!" someone shouted out.

"Yes, let's!" we all said, before quacking loudly.

"Let's belly dance," said Pam, the retired radiologist.

"Yes, let's!" we said, as we all did our own version of belly dancing.

Jack, the retired colorectal doctor, stated at the end that the class was perfect. He said that the only thing missing was some cafecito, a type of Cuban coffee. He offered to bring some to the next class, and another student offered to bring snacks.

For our last exercise, we were told to close our eyes and imagine we were in our "happy place." Then our teacher went around the room and asked each of us where we were.

"Gina, where are you?" my teacher asked me.

"I'm on a beach in the Bahamas, drinking a margarita, surrounded by my grandchildren," I said.

We all had our versions of happy places: in the woods at dusk, boogie boarding on the water, at a wine tasting in Napa. But I think for the next five weeks, from 1:00 to 2:45 on Thursdays, my happy place is going to be in my improv class.

It's a place of healing, understanding and acceptance.

Yes, let's!

— Gina Lee Guilford —

52

Never the Tough Girl

*True self-discovery begins where
your comfort zone ends.*
~Adam Braun

would never be described as physically tough. By the time I was eighteen, I was fairly tall for a girl at 5'7" but weighed 120 pounds sopping wet. Even now, at twenty-eight, I haven't topped 125. My muscle mass is almost nonexistent. A friend of mine once jokingly punched me in the arm, albeit with some force, and I literally passed out.

So, when a friend asked if my boyfriend and I wanted to participate in the "Tough Mudder," an event known for testing one's physical strength and mental grit, I was completely intimidated and responded with an immediate "Thanks but no thanks." But that was not to be the end of the conversation.

My boyfriend, an alpha-male type who could bench press 400 pounds and was always looking for a physical challenge, thought it sounded like a great time. So, eventually, the two of them convinced me to sign up for the race with a promise that we could train together. I hesitantly agreed and we began "training" for the twelve-mile course that we would run while also tackling obstacles meant to test our physical and mental strength. In the weeks that followed, family and friends heard about our plans to run the obstacle course, and the reactions were less than encouraging. Each time someone heard what we were going to attempt, they echoed my self-doubt back to me. "Are you sure you want to do this?"

"You are going to try the Tough Mudder? Please be careful. You're not really built for this kind of thing. You could get hurt."

Over and over, I heard this refrain and felt my dread increase. So, I resolved that when the day of the Tough Mudder arrived, I would just aim to finish it. Even if I came in dead last, I would be happy to simply walk across the finish line.

The training started off promising. Jake and I ran a few miles around campus a couple of times a week, supplementing with trips to the university rec center where we strength-trained and I attempted to put some muscle mass on my slender frame. Unfortunately, life soon derailed our training as our focus shifted from the Tough Mudder to more pressing matters such as finishing my junior year and his senior year, studying for exams, and putting the final touches on class projects. The Tough Mudder training was pushed to the back burner.

Nearing the end of April, I flipped the page in my planner to the next week. There, in big, bold letters, were the words "Tough Mudder." My heart sank into my stomach. I had not trained in weeks. In fact, it had been weeks since the race had even crossed my mind. And now I had just one week to prepare for what no one, including myself, thought I was capable of.

I spent the next five days attempting to get my body ready for the approaching challenge while simultaneously realizing how futile the effort was. A few days before the race, the five of us who had signed up headed to DICK'S Sporting Goods to get matching outfits. I may not have been physically prepared, but at least I would look the part. I came home with a matching black Under Armour shirt and leggings, which to this day is the only Under Armour I have ever bought, and my spirits raised just a bit for that coming weekend.

All too soon, the weekend arrived, as did its many festivities. Jake's graduation from college was Saturday, as was his graduation party. Then, early Sunday morning, we were to pack up and drive nearly three hours to the Tough Mudder.

Saturday, the day of the graduation, was a perfect spring day — sunny, blue skies, and warm. I saw pictures and videos from that day's Tough Mudder race, and in spite of my fear and lack of preparation, I was beginning to get excited.

The next morning, however, my excitement was gone, as we woke to a cold and rainy day. We loaded ourselves into the car, trying to keep our spirits high, and drove to the repurposed airport where the race would be held.

When we arrived, the wind whipped across the flat land with a fury, making it feel even colder than it already was. As soon as I stepped out of the car, I was shivering.

We headed to the registration table and received our race numbers along with safety pins to attach them to our backs. Thirty minutes later, after an explanation of the course (twelve miles with twenty-five obstacles), the rules (we could skip any obstacle that we were uncomfortable with but we were highly encouraged to do them all), and a little music to get us pumped up, the starting gun sounded, and the race began.

I quickly realized that the course would be nothing like the pictures I had seen online from the previous day. It had stormed all night, and the flat land had soaked up the rain until it was covered in mud that was calf-deep in most places. The fact that it was still raining meant there was no hope of the mud situation getting any better. Even for a race called the Tough Mudder, this was excessive.

The only positive, however, was that my lack of endurance training or running ability would not be a hindrance since running was all but impossible. Every step we took required forcibly pulling our shoes out of the sticky mud, and we each tied our shoes tightly to the point of losing circulation to ensure that the suction didn't pull them right off our feet. Slowly, painstakingly, we made our way through the mud toward the first set of obstacles. I swallowed hard, trying to still the hordes of butterflies that had erupted in my gut. The obstacles were what intimidated me most, and I had heard horror stories of broken bones, electrocutions, and even burns.

We came to the first obstacle. This one required that we crawl on our bellies underneath barbed wire for forty feet. I made it through without incident and felt my first surge of confidence since signing up months prior. We labored through the mud toward the next obstacle, and as it came into view, I felt the panic begin to rise in my throat.

The Arctic Enema was one of the obstacles that had been looming in my mind since first hearing of the Tough Mudder. It consisted of hundreds of gallons of ice water dumped in a fifteen-yard dumpster, and the ice was continuously replenished so that it never truly melted. In the middle, jutting out of the water, a wooden bar stretched across the width of the container with barbed wire wrapped around it. This extended a foot into the air, and, as I was all too aware, it also extended a foot down below the surface. Anyone swimming through would have to swim under the barrier before emerging on the other side.

Jake looked at me and asked if I was ready. Before he could get the question fully out, I had summoned some courage that I didn't realize was buried within me and jumped. The initial rush of water against my skin took my breath away as I kicked against the countless ice cubes, forcing myself deeper so as to avoid the barbed-wire barrier. My lungs screamed in protest, and it felt like a thousand hot-cold needles were penetrating my skin, but I drove my body forward to the other side. As I emerged, I couldn't seem to get enough air, and every breath was ragged as if my lungs had frozen solid. I pulled myself up, sopping wet, and climbed over the rail. Jake materialized behind me, and I was surprised to see a grin on his face as if he hadn't just swum through agonizingly cold water.

My face must have communicated my confusion because he half-screamed at me, "I can't believe you just did that! I was going to offer to jump in with you because I thought you'd be scared, but you jumped in before I could!" Despite the frigid, wet fabric that clung to every inch of my body and the pervading cold that had seeped into my bones, I felt a warmth rise within me. He was right. I had done it. And he was proud of me. And I was suddenly proud of me, too.

Maybe I had underestimated myself and allowed others' opinions to become too loud in my mind. If I could take down the Arctic Enema, then I knew there was nothing this race could put in my path that I couldn't conquer. Jake and I shared a smile, grabbed hands, and took a running start so we could clear the next obstacle, hurdling over two feet of fire.

Emboldened by the Arctic Enema, we made our way through

obstacle after obstacle: crawling through muddy waters with live wires dangling on every side of us, pushing one another over ten-foot walls, and carrying fifty-pound logs for a half-mile until my shoulders ached from the weight and the uneven bark.

Not every obstacle was a success. Several obstacles required that we swing or climb over an icy water pit, but the rings and monkey bars were so coated with mud that we fell immediately into the pit of ice water below, ensuring that I remained soaking wet and chilled to the bone for the entirety of the course. As the day progressed, it got colder and windier. I watched with conflicting feelings of envy and superiority as men twice my size were wrapped in Mylar blankets and driven away on golf carts after abandoning the course.

At one point, we had to make a river crossing. When we stumbled upon the opposite bank, I noticed that my friend was bent over, with her hands between her legs and a strange smile spreading across her face.

She called out, "Pee on your hands! It feels warm and amazing!" Having just climbed out of a river and spent the past few hours soaking wet in frigid, windy weather, any chance at warmth sounded too good to pass up. So, I bent over, put my hands between my legs, and peed. The warmth was fleeting, gone as soon as my bladder was empty, but I had to admit she had been right. It felt amazing. From then on out, we guzzled as much water as we could at each water stop so that we could have a few seconds of warmth on our hands and legs whenever we had to relieve ourselves.

Finally, after hours of wading through the muck and mud, freezing, shivering and wishing I were anywhere but there, we found ourselves one obstacle away from the finish line. This time, we had to run, jumping over haystacks, while attempting to avoid live wires that hung down, ready to hit anything that touched them with up to 10,000 volts of electricity.

I watched as Jake ran through first. The minute a wire grazed his skin, he crumpled, his limbs contracting like a dying spider as all 200 pounds of him hit the ground. He stood again, a little wobbly, and made it through, stopping just feet from the finish line. He turned and beckoned me to him. My friend and I looked at each other, and I knew we were thinking the same thing: There was no way in hell we were about to let ourselves get shocked like that. We dropped down and slowly made our way through, sliding and slithering over the haystacks, keeping a wary eye on the wires that dangled just centimeters over our heads. Finally, we crawled over the last haystack, and the five of us crossed the finish line together. There we were rewarded with our "Finishers" shirt, headband, and a hard-earned beer.

I was euphoric. That was hands-down the hardest thing I had ever done, and it still is to this day. But I had done it. I was a Tough Mudder finisher, and I felt instantly different. Something deep inside me had shifted, as tends to happen when you do something you didn't think you could. I was now certifiably "tough," and I had proven I could withstand physical hardship while maintaining mental grit. I have never worn something with so much pride as I did that orange headband bestowed on me at the finish line.

It took the entire three-hour car ride home for me to warm up, and it took more than three weeks for my groin muscles to stop hurting. But, despite this, I felt as if I were walking on air.

The high of this accomplishment far outlasted the pain and was reinforced every time someone asked with skepticism how the race had gone. Each time, I proudly gave a quick run-through of the most harrowing obstacles, enjoying how their eyes widened and disbelief played across their faces. I could all but see their perception of me change. I wasn't as skinny, weak, and helpless as I looked. I had a streak of daring, mental grit, and physical endurance just below the surface.

Even when I looked at myself in the mirror, it was as though the reflection had altered, ever so slightly. The girl who looked back from the glass had resilience, tenacity, and steel in her eyes. I had never noticed it before, but now I knew those things had been there all along. It just took twelve miles, twenty-five obstacles, and a couple of times of peeing on my own hands for me to see it.

Now, I don't question if I am capable of anything that requires physical toughness or mental grit. No matter how difficult it seems, when others tell me I can't do it, I just smile and tell them to watch me.

— Andree Philpot —

53

Chicken Soup for the Soul

The Homecoming Chance

*It's always nerve-wracking to put yourself
out there. But it's the root of joy.*
~Ann Brashares

Every year, before the homecoming football game and dance, our high school had a powderpuff football game for the girls. The seniors and sophomores were paired against the juniors and freshmen.

I was extremely excited about this game because, as a sophomore, I got to be on the same team as my big sister, Susie, who was a senior. And the thought of playing the game by her side gave me comfort.

Unlike me, Susie was always outgoing. She made friendships easily and she had a date for the homecoming dance. As for me, I was the quiet and reserved sister. Don't get me wrong, I had friends, but I wasn't exactly one of the "popular" girls. Even worse, I didn't get asked to the dance. I don't think the guys at our school noticed me enough to ask me to such an occasion.

On the night of our anticipated powderpuff game, I was one of the last players getting ready in the locker room. As I was sitting down, putting on my tennis shoes, I could hear two other girls gush about their dresses and dates for the dance. They also happened to be the two most popular girls in our sophomore class.

As I was tying my laces, one of the girls, Emma, called out to me, "Hey, Sarah, who are you going to the dance with?"

I was taken aback that she even cared to ask me. Clearing my throat, I looked up and nervously responded, "Me? Oh, yeah, I'm not going. I don't have a date."

"What? You don't have a date?" her friend Taryn responded. "Who could she go with?" she asked Emma.

"Jimmy doesn't have a date!" Emma exclaimed.

"Jimmy Ray?" I responded. I knew Jimmy. In fact, we had known each other since the fifth grade, and he was currently in my geometry class. I would be lying if I said I never had a crush on him. I always thought he was cute. I was surprised to learn he didn't have a date, being one of the popular football guys.

"Yes, you should totally go with him. And, if you do, you guys could come with us!" Emma added.

Both girls encouraged me to give him a call. As the three of us were walking out to the field together, I told them that I would think about it. I must admit, I thought it was the sweetest gesture of them to invite me to go with their group. I mean, I wasn't necessarily part of the "in crowd."

We played an intense and exciting powderpuff game, and the seniors and sophomores beat the junior and freshman classes. We beat them by a long shot and were all celebrating.

I found Emma and Taryn after our game. Feeling extra pumped and excited after our big win, I told them that I would call Jimmy and ask him to the dance. I'm not sure what came over me. I would never have imagined working up the courage to do such a thing.

At home, I told my sister about potentially going to the home-coming dance with Jimmy. She encouraged me to ask him. Finally, a wave of confidence came over me, and I picked up the phone and called his house.

"Here goes nothing," I whispered to myself.

"Hello?" his mother answered.

"Hi, is Jimmy home?" I responded.

"Yes, one minute…" his mother replied, and then silence.

"Hello?" Jimmy's voice came on the line.

"Hi, Jimmy, this is Sarah… Sarah from geometry," I replied, trying to sound as confident as possible.

"Oh, hey, Sarah!"

"Hey, so Emma and Taryn told me you didn't have a date for the dance. They said that if we decide to go together, then we could join their group for the limo and dinner. Anyways, I was just wondering if you want to go to the dance with me." I hoped he didn't sense my nervousness.

"Hey, yeah, that sounds like fun! I would need to ask my parents and get back to you. Can I let you know by tomorrow?" he replied.

"Yes, no worries! I'll see you tomorrow."

"Okay, great. Thanks, Sarah. Have a great night!"

"You, too!"

Wow, what a rush. Never in a million years would I ever imagine calling Jimmy Ray, let alone any guy, and asking him to the homecoming dance. I was so nervous about seeing him in class the next day. I didn't know if I could handle a rejection.

The next day, my palms were sweating profusely in geometry. My head was turned toward the back, with my eyes on the clock, waiting for the bell to signal that class had ended. I hadn't made eye contact with Jimmy once that day. I couldn't. It was all too embarrassing.

The bell rang.

I quickly gathered my books and binder and headed for the door. As I left the classroom door, speed-walking, I heard someone call my name. It was Jimmy.

I turned around as he caught up to me.

"Oh, hey, Jimmy!" My heart was pounding.

"Hey, Sarah. So, I spoke with my parents, and I can go to the dance with you!" he replied with a big smile.

* * *

After the dance, Taryn and Emma became my best friends. I began hanging out with their group of friends, gaining confidence and new experiences. I became a different person.

Life is all about the choices we make, and these choices shape who we are. What if I hadn't worked up the courage to call Jimmy? What if I never went to the homecoming dance with him? Where would I be in my life? Would I still be the shy and quiet girl who was too afraid to put herself out there? The rest of my high school experience would have been entirely different, as well as the life I lived afterward.

It's been twenty years, and I still think back to that moment when my life changed forever with a phone call.

I am now thirty-four years old, blessed with a loving husband and two beautiful children. Jimmy Ray remains one of our good family friends.

—S.L. Brunner—

54

Singing for Strangers

To sing is to bring to the surface
all the depth of one's being.
~Marty Rubin

My mother once told me, "You sang before you could speak." I don't know if that's true, but for as long as I can remember, I've loved lifting my voice in soaring melodies. I joined my first choir when I was five and immediately fell in love with making music. As the choirs got more advanced, I reveled in the joys of harmony, counterpoint, and complicated time signatures.

As a shy child, second row in the choir was perfect for me. I could experience the thrill of singing for an audience without having to be the center of attention. No one noticed me, and that was okay. I could hide away and still be part of the music.

When I entered junior high, I joined every musical group in the school: concert band, jazz band, guitar, recorder, and even steel drums. Just like the choir, the ensembles gave me the freedom to perform with anonymity. I loved every moment!

Our choir director, Mrs. McKee, was incredibly supportive of me, musically and personally. She knew I liked hiding in the group, so her question caught me off-guard.

"Allison, how would you like to sing a solo in the Christmas concert?"

My stomach clenched into a knot. "Um, do you mean a verse with the choir?"

"No, I'd love for you to sing a whole song by yourself. You can pick the song. I'll play piano for you."

My mind started to swim. Unbeknownst to anyone, I had long dreamed of singing a solo! It was a thought that terrified me beyond measure, and yet it was my most passionate dream. I fantasized about a version of me who was bold enough to sing for crowds of people, sharing my song around the world.

But I wasn't that person yet. I was still the person who wanted to hide in the second row.

I tentatively mentioned Mrs. McKee's offer to my parents. They were thrilled! They loved music and would do anything to encourage my burgeoning self-confidence. With their support, I accepted the offer to sing a solo.

Mom and I leafed through our family's collection of Christmas music. She suggested one of her favourites, "Holly, Jolly Christmas." I started my preparations: learning the song, memorizing the words, and practicing with Mrs. McKee on piano.

Before long, it was the big night: our junior high Christmas concert!

Even though I was scheduled to perform with all the bands and vocal groups, all I could think about was that solo. On the drive to the school, I sang "Holly, Jolly Christmas" over and over to myself. Suddenly, the song was like cotton in my mouth. I couldn't make it sound good at all. I wished I'd chosen "Hark the Herald" or "Silent Night" or literally anything else.

At the school, Mrs. McKee gave me a pep talk. I'm sure I was ghostly pale, my fear visible in every pore.

The lights dimmed, and the concert began.

Finally, it was time for my solo. The emcee introduced me as I walked up to the microphone. I looked out into the darkened auditorium. I could see the outline of people but no specific faces. My legs began to shake. I held the mic stand for support, and Mrs. McKee started the piano introduction. I took a deep breath and began, "Have a holly, jolly Christmas…"

The song went by quickly. I was so focused on breathing, singing and remembering the words that I can't remember if I enjoyed it or not. The music ended, and the applause rang out. I smiled briefly and quickly left the stage.

I had done it. I had sung my first solo. I felt a quick rush of relief as I ran to join the band for the next number.

After the show, I went to my locker to get my winter coat before heading home. The halls were filled with students, parents and siblings, all chattering with post-concert excitement.

A woman I didn't know grabbed my arm.

"I'm so glad I found you!" she said excitedly. "I loved your song! You have such a beautiful voice."

I mumbled some kind of "thank you." She smiled and disappeared into the crowd.

For a moment, I couldn't move. I didn't know this woman at all. She wasn't a friend of my mom or a parent of a classmate. She was a complete stranger. She had no obligation to like my voice and definitely no reason to seek me out. And yet, something I had done had moved her to the point that she wanted to find me and compliment my singing.

I returned to the crowd. My parents showered me in loving praise. My friends cheered me on. Mrs. McKee gave me a hug of support.

But that woman at my locker was the voice that stayed with me.

A person I didn't know had loved my song. Something powerful was happening, something I didn't fully understand but something I just couldn't shake.

She didn't know it, but that woman planted a seed that began to grow.

Over the next few years, I started to sing more and more solos. Over time, the fear turned to nervousness, and eventually even that disappeared.

By the time I reached university, I knew my path: I wanted to be a professional singer.

As I write this today, I'm sitting in the rehearsal room that I share with my musician husband. Our nine albums line a shelf on the wall. Our awards sit on the mantle. Photos and posters celebrate our national concert tours.

For several decades now, I've made my living singing for strangers.

Every year, I—the formerly shy, second-row chorister—sing solos for thousands of people I've never met. The irony of it never fails to make me smile.

Performing had been my secret dream, but it wasn't until that woman gave me a simple compliment that I realized the power of sharing your voice with other people.

Now, whenever I hear young singers bravely sing their first solo, I cheer them on! I actively seek them out and give them a few words of encouragement. I pray that, for the right person, my words might be the seed that leads them on their own path of singing for strangers.

—Allison Lynn—

55

An Adventurous Grandma

Jobs fill your pockets, but adventures fill your soul.
~Jamie Lyn

"You look like my grandma."

"I am not a grandma." Mildly insulted, I scooted the cherub-faced, little boy back into place. The kindergarten class where I was substituting had yet to figure out the concept of straight lines.

Substitute teaching was just one of the part-time jobs I tried after retiring, looking for that perfect combination of stimulation and relaxation. When I was busy working a forty-hour week, taking my twins Kristen and Launa to Girl Scouts, and supporting my husband in running a construction business, I often felt as if I didn't have time to think. Now, with both girls off having their own adventures and no more forty-hour weeks, I had too much time. Who was I now that the kids were gone and I no longer had an occupation? Who was this retired woman?

I'd always considered myself adventurous. I earned my pilot's license by the age of twenty-three. I rode a Triumph 750 cross-country a year later, holding on to the back of my future husband. *You look like my grandma?* What had happened to that young daredevil? Then I realized I hadn't tried anything adventurous since Kristen and I practiced sailing on the Delaware River ten years earlier. So, when Launa called from Italy to discuss activities for our upcoming visit, I was ready for an adventure.

"We can go to Venice. Do you like gelato?"

Of course!

"There's horseback riding in Tuscany."

Everything she described sounded great.

She mentioned an Armed Forces Recreation Center at Garmisch-Partenkirchen. The Edelweiss Lodge and Resort in southern Germany was a popular retreat for military members. As in-laws of our active-duty son-in-law, we were eligible to stay.

By going to Bavaria, I would be revisiting the site of another long-ago adventure. My college roommate and I had spent a summer working in a hotel fluffing feather comforters and exploring the area.

"They have kayaking, whitewater rafting, and paragliding." My girls had inherited my adventure gene. No window shopping for us.

My heart skipped a beat. Paragliding sounded fun. At one time, I'd considered jumping out of an airplane but never took that final step (no pun intended) of making the arrangements. Paragliding was almost the same thing. You jump off a mountain. Float to the ground.

"Justin and I jumped when we visited last year. You and I can do it this time. Should I make reservations?"

The trip was three months away. Sitting on the porch of my quiet country home in central Pennsylvania, I was certain paragliding in the Bavarian Alps was just what I needed to bring back that adventurous twenty-something I used to be. "Sure," I responded, excited at her suggestion.

Arriving in Italy in September, we cruised the canals of Venice. We drank wine. We rode horses through leafy vineyards. We drank more wine. Soon, the day came for our trip north. We traveled the Brenner Pass into Austria, the same route my father had traveled as a young soldier. Concrete guard posts, or pillboxes, lined the steep sides of the narrow ravine as we drove the highway cut into the side of the mountain. I was retracing the steps of my father's adventure, although not one of his choosing.

The lodge was beautiful. At dinner, a pile of kaiser rolls graced the center of a long table. I remembered their delicious taste from thirty-five years earlier. The paragliding was scheduled for the following day. Standing in the front entrance of the resort that evening, I eyed the jagged peaks before me.

"It looks like rain. Maybe we should cancel."

My daughter shrugged. "Up to you."

Making my way to the activity office, I asked the attendant if we could get a refund if we canceled. The athletic German shook his head. "No refunds."

Scotch-Irish frugalness runs deep in my veins. This was courtesy of my World War II father, a child of the Depression who saved plastic bread bags. If I canceled the activity, one hundred dollars would go down the drain. In my head, I heard my father's voice. "A milkshake is just whipped air. Have an ice cream cone." A childhood lesson: Don't waste money.

So, I didn't cancel. That night, I lay in bed and stared out the window at the mountain. Next to me, my husband slept peacefully, but in my mind I pictured stepping off the edge of those jagged peaks and plummeting to the bottom. My heart raced.

The next day, we followed the path to a grassy field studded with tiny barns. I nodded to passersby, thinking of my early days in Bavaria when everyone went for walks in the beautiful forest. Outwardly, I was just another happy tourist. Inwardly, I was shaking.

"Who's going first?" The middle-aged man who would accompany us on the tandem jump looked from me to my daughter. I was relieved when my daughter volunteered.

Her face glowed with exhilaration when she landed. It was my turn. As we walked up to the chairlift, I noticed the guide glancing at my legs. At my questioning look, he responded, "I wanted to see if you can walk okay, but you'll be fine."

Did I look too old for this activity? We rode the chairlift to the top of the mountain. Ever higher. My heart pounded at the thought of that first step. On the grassy slope outside the gondola, the guide spread out the orange-and-white chute, the ropes stretching to a chair harness. No cliff, just a grassy slope leading into a rocky area.

Strapping me into the harness, the guide climbed in behind me. "Run as fast as you can and, as soon as we're airborne, sit back in the seat."

I wondered how secure the straps were. Before I knew it, I was running, and we lifted off into the air. I was so entranced by the feeling of flying through the air that I didn't even notice the ground disappear beneath my feet.

Through the rain clouds, I glimpsed the field, tiny barns, and my husband far below. As usual, I had anticipated a worse scenario than what actually happened. I didn't step off into space. I ran down a slope and floated into the air. What an adventure!

Back home, I studied the bulletin board next to my desk. My pilot's license in a plastic sleeve hangs from a thumbtack next to certificates certifying a sailboat class and a hot-air-balloon ride from ten and twenty years ago. Yes, I'm getting older. Yes, I'm retired. But I'm still adventurous.

A few months later, our daughter Kristen texted me. She had sent an email to my husband. "Open it together," she informed us. As soon as my husband opened it, I knew what was coming: a sonogram picture.

A different kind of adventure. I became a grandma. An adventurous grandma. So, yes, you can call me Grandma. I don't mind a bit. In fact, I love it.

— Tanya McClure Schleiden —

56

Don't Think, Just Dance

When you dance, your purpose is not to get
to a certain place on the floor. It's to enjoy
each step along the way.
~Wayne Dyer

The butterflies multiplied in my belly and made it difficult to breathe. I was on my way to a dance competition. Wheelchair ballroom dance was one of my passions, but illness and transportation issues had caused me to miss several competitions in the previous few years.

There was a time when I couldn't imagine doing this at all. However, that began to change in 2007 when I decided to compete for the title of Ms. Wheelchair Kansas. It was not a choice I made lightly. In fact, when I first got the application in the mail, I laughed. For as long as I could remember, I had bought into the stereotype that people with disabilities simply were not attractive. Even if the carriage that carried me to Prince Charming was an accessible van that had a lift, once the clock struck midnight, my wheelchair would be waiting, and he would turn away.

As I read through the application, though, I came to learn that the Ms. Wheelchair America pageant is not a beauty contest. Instead, the program strives to empower women who are wheelchair-mobile to advocate for themselves and disability rights. The state titleholder gets to travel and speak to audiences about issues affecting the lives of people with disabilities.

That was right up my alley. I have a passion for advocacy and was hoping to be a motivational speaker someday, so I thought this platform might give me some much-needed experience. Therefore, a few weeks later, I found myself as a contestant competing for the crown. Even though I thought this pageant would be a good thing for me, I was nervous because crowns and sashes are not at all who I am.

Over the weekend, we attended various workshops, and then Sunday was the crowning ceremony. When I got to the pageant, I was told that, during the crowning ceremony, the contestants would be performing a wheelchair dance routine.

I was so gobsmacked that I wondered if I had heard correctly.

"You want me to do what? Dance? You do see my wheelchair, right? Dancing is not at the top of my list of abilities." It felt like I was being asked to climb Mt. Everest in the rain.

Since I was a toddler, I've been fascinated by dance. The elegance. The beauty. The way people could get their bodies to move to music was enchanting to me. I knew doing it well took talent. I also knew it wasn't for me. I thought that, in my life as a wheelchair user, dancing was like kissing your elbow—a really cool idea but impossible to accomplish.

I gave it a shot after learning some moves over a couple of hours.

In a word, I hated it. Okay, that's three words, but you get the idea.

My spastic muscles didn't move in time to music, and rhythm doesn't mix with my reality. To me, at that time, dancing only underscored everything I feared. I was slow. I was awkward. I was not "able." The whole premise of the pageant was to prove those myths wrong. I told the people in charge that I didn't want to dance because I thought it was a disaster, but somehow I went on to win the crown.

Little did I know that on the journey of being Ms. Wheelchair Kansas, I would have to do what felt impossible: I would have to learn to dance.

First dance step: Move. Naturally quiet and introverted, I'm not used to approaching people to make conversation. But that wouldn't do. Lorraine could be shy; Ms. Wheelchair Kansas couldn't be. Turns out most people open up if they are asked the right questions. I also learned that using my advocacy skills didn't mean I was being obnoxious; it meant that I was fighting for my rights. Being quiet about that wasn't something I was comfortable with.

Second dance step: I learned to pay attention and focus on the good. There is power in being positive and beauty in every situation. Focusing on negatives doesn't get me anywhere and makes most situations feel worse than they are. If I truly seek the silver linings, most of the time I don't see the clouds.

During my reign, I traveled around the state and spoke out about discrimination, disability etiquette, and living your dreams.

Third dance step: Flow with the music. I had to change my mindset. I had to believe nothing was impossible and redefine the reality I thought of as routine. What did I want? I wasn't sure, but I did learn I was doing myself a disservice if I put limits on it. Other people could put me in a box with a label if they chose, but I wasn't going to help them tape it up and put a bow on top. I had seen that things could be different. Box-busting became my specialty.

In 2008, my reign as Ms. Wheelchair Kansas ended, and I attended the pageant ready to pass on my crown to a new titleholder. JoAnne, a former Ms. Wheelchair Kansas who had started a dance company, was there with her instructor. They were going to perform a wheelchair ballroom-dance routine. Considering what happened when I tried to dance the year before, I wasn't prepared to be impressed.

Instead, I was mesmerized. I had never seen anything like it, and it moved me in my soul. Poised. Flowing. Pretty. Magical. Wheelchair ballroom dance. What I never thought I could do.

With tears streaming down my face, I asked JoAnne how I could learn to do what she just did. A few weeks later, I started meeting with the same instructor on a regular basis. Over time, I relaxed and learned new moves.

A few years later, I was on my way to my first dance competition in a very long time. The doubts abounded. That is where the butterflies came from.

Would I forget the moves? Would I mess up the timing? Would people laugh? Was I kidding myself?

About thirty seconds before we were to perform, my dance partner leaned over and whispered in my ear, "Don't think. Just dance."

Then, he confidently led me out to the floor. With every note of music, my insecurity fell away. I trusted myself. I took a deep breath and smiled as we started our routine. It would be okay. We were dancing. And I had learned to love it!

— Lorraine Cannistra —

Chapter 7

Follow Your Dreams

57

Middle-Aged Mermaid

Be a mermaid. Swim fast, wear a crown,
and dream big.
~Author Unknown

'd always been a positive person, but the stuff of life was wearing me down. In my twenties, I struggled to be like the women on magazine covers but was never pretty enough, thin enough, or ambitious enough. In my thirties, I had children but never managed to be the kind of mother the parenting books said I should be — homemade organic baby food, a daily routine, a clean house. Not me. In my forties, my children became teenagers, and I felt old. As their store of knowledge grew, I felt as if mine was evaporating.

I didn't know who I was anymore. That all changed when, at the age of fifty-three, my best friend presented me with a mermaid tail. We didn't normally exchange Christmas gifts, so I was a little surprised when she handed me a bright-red gift bag. I was more surprised when I pulled out a rubber monofin and a tube-shaped garment made of shiny, green Lycra.

"I got you a mermaid tail. You can swim in it!" Her smile stretched from dimple to dimple.

I held the bag in shock for a moment. Then, my own smile worked its way up the corners of my mouth. "I love it!"

My friend looked me in the eye. "You have to promise to try this in shallow water first. I won't be responsible for you drowning in your mermaid tail."

I promised to be careful and then looked out at the snow-covered lake. It would be a while.

During the long winter, I imagined being a mermaid, swimming through the ocean and frolicking with dolphins, my long hair flowing behind me.

My friend knew that I'd wanted to be a mermaid since my first glimpse of the ocean at age four. I still remember the smell of the salty sea air, the sound of the waves crashing on the shore, and the full moon's white reflection on the mysterious dark water. I was sure there was a mermaid out there.

I grew up reading stories about mermaids. Mermaids are strong, even fearsome at times. Mermaids never compare themselves to others. Mermaids wear whatever they want or nothing at all. Mermaids don't do heels or hairspray or worry about keeping everyone happy. They know how to say no to children, over-volunteering, or housework. When they've had enough, they dive deep into cool ocean waters.

But mermaids are fantasies, and I was all too human. Would some rubber and a piece of Lycra manufactured on the other side of the world provide me with the magic I longed for?

Finally, the snow melted, the sun came out, and it was time to try my mermaid tail. I walked down to the lake (Michigan lacks an ocean), clutching my monofin and shiny fabric sleeve. Sitting on the dock with my legs dangling, I put my feet into the monofin. Then I took out the fabric that was intended to hold my legs together and make the tail. After sliding the fabric over the monofin and securing the Velcro fasteners, it fit perfectly — until I had to pull the fabric the rest of the way up over my legs and hips. I squished and I pulled, and then it ripped.

Luckily, my tail was intact despite the small rip. Now, my problem was being stuck on a dock with my legs melded together, wondering what the neighbors were thinking.

I tried to pull down the tail, but it wouldn't budge. The circulation in my legs and my confidence waned at the same time. I thought about calling for help, maybe dialing 911, but what would I say?

"Excuse me, but I seem to be stuck in a mermaid tail. Do you have any marine biologists on staff?"

And what if help did come? Would they cut me out of my tail like they cut people out of cars using the Jaws of Life? My dream was coming to a humiliating end. I had to think.

Staring at my big, beautiful tail fin, I realized that a mermaid wouldn't care about the neighbors. She wouldn't panic. And she certainly wouldn't ruin her tail by cutting it off. A mermaid would be brave, take a risk, and sink or swim. She'd live with the results. But first, she'd take a plunge.

I rolled off the dock and into the cool, clear water. Sinking at first into a cluster of lake weed, I leaned back with my arms out and tail extended, letting my body relax. My legs shifted, the fabric loosened, and I pulled the tail up the rest of the way. All it needed was water, like a mermaid. With a few kicks of my tail, I glided into the deep, open water, clear of the weeds. After diving under and flashing my tail, I floated on my back and stared at the puffy clouds overhead. I continued to splash, dive, float and, dare I say, frolic. If the neighbors happened to have taken a peek, they would have seen joy.

In that moment, I wasn't a worn out, middle-aged mom. I was a fearless, fun-loving mermaid, without a care in the world.

—Julie Angeli—

Mom the Intern

Be fearless in the pursuit of what sets your soul on fire.
~Jennifer Lee

rogramming Intern. I wasn't sure why this job announcement popped up on my feed. I was looking for a real job, not an internship. That ominous fiftieth birthday was looming in just a few months, and I needed to get my act together — to finally figure out what I was going to do all day for the next twenty years or so. An internship? No way! I was way past that point in my life.

The past five years had passed in a frenzy. Our oldest kid was married and out of the house, but we still had two young kids at home. I also helped my mother through three joint-replacement surgeries and planned more funerals for various family members than I cared to count. After fifteen years of homeschooling, my youngest two were now attending school, and I knew I needed something more. Somehow, I felt that life had passed me by and I hadn't accomplished a single thing.

I couldn't help but read the description on the job board. "Interns will create an educational program for their local national wildlife refuge. They will take a leadership role in designing youth environmental education curriculum at the site by authoring activity booklets and website content around the refuge."

Create an educational program for a national wildlife refuge? We had spent the last three years visiting national parks all over the country with our boys and participating in programs exactly like this. It sounded too good to be true, exactly the type of writing I'd love to be doing on a regular basis.

Then, I looked at the qualifications. "Enthusiastic people who are great at written communications." Check. "Previous experience in environmental conservation or any science coursework." Uncheck. I had absolutely none. I doubted my food and nutrition science classes from thirty years ago in college were going to count for anything.

Not a single aspect of my job or educational experience matched these requirements. I figured I was too old, too unqualified… It's funny how strong that inner negative voice can sound. I dismissed the internship and continued looking at the "real jobs" on the job app.

Two days later, I was hiking at the local park near my kids' school. I hiked most days to avoid the rush-hour traffic going back home. It was either walk three or four miles or sit in my car for an extra thirty minutes in traffic. As usual, my thoughts were scattered. I had been in a transition period for over a year, looking for a part-time job and making no progress at all. Overeducated forty-nine-year-olds who have been out of the traditional workforce for fifteen years are not a hot commodity on the job market.

That morning, I couldn't concentrate on the bird sounds or pray like I normally tried to do. All I could hear was one thing: *Apply for the internship!* It was so loud and demanding that I felt like I was probably going through some sort of mental breakdown and dismissed it as "mind gossip," the name I had given the crazy thoughts that tended to race through my head when I spent too much time by myself.

I went home and started yet another load of endless laundry. *Apply for the internship! You are going to get it.* Really? Clearly, the long days of silence had led to some mental disease or defect. *Apply!* I tried to focus on some other projects around the house, but that same thought kept pounding at me until I decided to open the job app to look at the announcement one more time. It asked for a brief description of my relevant experience.

I had no idea what to write. *We like to travel to national parks, and my kids have over twenty badges from completing the educational booklets? Last summer, we came in first place in the first-ever Great Outdoor Scavenger Hunt and visited twenty-two state parks throughout Texas in three months?*

I like to hike? None of these things sounded like real experience. Yet those are exactly the things I put down as experience. I sent in my application that same morning and promptly forgot about it.

Two days later, I got an interview request for the next day. It was a video interview, something I had never done before. I couldn't believe I was contacted at all, so I figured I needed to do a little research. A quick search of the organization revealed it was founded by a young environmentalist from California and run by volunteers and interns, all who appeared less than half my age. I figured it was such a long shot that I didn't even mention any of it to my husband, friends or family.

I changed my shirt four times before the call. I tested the camera angle in numerous spots in my house, trying to decide which lighting made me look less old. No amount of make-up could hide the lines under my eyes. The founder could guess my age based on my graduation dates anyway. I took a deep breath and waited for the founder of the organization to appear on screen.

"Hi, Denise! We are super excited you applied to intern with us. A real writer! Your résumé is just fantastic," Lynnea welcomed me warmly. She was so kind and enthusiastic, and I immediately felt at ease with her. "Tell me why you applied with us."

"Well, I love national parks and lands. My family and I spend all our spare time visiting parks and participating in educational programs. I want our kids and all kids to appreciate these amazing places and take care of them for future generations. And this internship just sounded so perfect for me. I would love to create a program like that."

"Can you explain a common concept in nature, but for kids?" she asked.

Now, this I could do. "Leave No Trace. It means you take nothing from the public lands when you visit, and you leave nothing behind either. You pick up all your trash, even things like orange peels or peanuts. And you don't take anything, even flowers or rocks. It's important to take care of our parks and lands to keep them intact for many years to come. I'm pretty passionate about it, actually. My kids know these rules backward and forward."

Lynnea then read me a couple of sentences to edit, a task that seemed pretty effortless.

"We will be letting you know very quickly," she stated before we ended the call. There was something about our conversation that gave me the feeling I would be hearing back.

That same night, I received the email. "Congratulations! We would love to offer you the position as Programming Intern with our team."

It was time to tell the husband and kids. Maybe I would leave out the part about the persistent voice that encouraged me to apply. Perhaps an internship at my age wasn't so ridiculous after all.

— Denise Valuk —

59

Getting My Wings

Believe that you can and you will.
~Annette White

tried to calm my nerves on the train to Philadelphia International Airport. Following directions, I found a large sign in front of a conference room that read, "UE Flight Attendant Interviews." I was applying for a job with U.S. Airways Express, at age fifty.

What had I been thinking to answer this open call at my age? Here, I was practically invisible among the crowd of eager young women. Most of them were manicured and stylish in a way guaranteed to catch an interviewer's attention. The new, sensible black suit that I'd been so proud of this morning seemed dowdy by contrast.

I considered leaving. The chances of making the cut were tiny. But on the other hand, this was my last chance to pursue this dream. As a child, I'd been fascinated by movies about flight attendants. Though shy, I wanted to wear a trim suit and be part of that elite group who strolled casually through airports.

Throughout the day, we were broken into groups, rotating from one task to another. The purpose of some was obvious, such as taking turns reading a script aloud. After a lunch break, I noticed several empty seats. Had some participants failed? Hope bloomed inside me. After individual interviews, the room became noticeably emptier. I met another woman in her fifties, Helen. We whispered in shock that we were among the last applicants. But we weren't convinced that we'd be chosen, considering the remaining young and beautiful women.

When I was offered the chance to attend flight-attendant training, my heart pounded with joy. I took a train home, eager to share the news with my family. Two days later, I headed to the training facility in Virginia. Cliques quickly formed among my twenty classmates. I made friends but decided that studying was more important than socializing. Every other day, we were tested on comprehensive FAA regulations. If we scored below ninety, we were allowed only one make-up test. This job wasn't primarily about serving beverages but about passenger safety.

During our last week, one of my gorgeous new friends, Mia, along with her roommates, surprised me with a makeover. They straightened my curls and taught me how to apply make-up. My new look definitely boosted my confidence. Presenting a polished image was my final step toward handling this new career.

When I graduated, I reverently held the silver wings in my hand. I traced the insignia and then pinned it on my blouse. Tears stung my eyelids as I thanked my teacher. I'd gotten my wings. I hadn't completed my college education. Life had thrown me a few curveballs. Ten years earlier, I'd applied to a major airline and chickened out of the interview.

Now, finally, I'd overcome my fears and gone after this particular ambition. These wings had become a badge of honor, my trophy for winning a personal race.

The next day was Thanksgiving and my first trip. I was sure that the pilots and passengers could see my heart beating with fear. However, my wings gave me courage. After a day of negotiating strange airports and doing my job, I was more than ready for a quiet night. After checking into the hotel, I discovered one of my classmates, Lauren, staying there for her overnight. Since we were far from home, we decided to have dinner together. To our surprise, our captains invited us to share their Thanksgiving dinner. My stress disappeared as I enjoyed the evening. After coordinating a morning wakeup call with the front desk, I headed to my room and made a phone call. My daughter answered. "Mom, how are you doing?"

I shrieked, "I did it! I'm a flight attendant."

My confidence grew with every trip. I haven't achieved all my dreams, but this career made me proud. I'll forever cherish my flying days, when I wore my silver wings with pride and joy.

— Karla Brown —

60

Olympic Pride

Dare to dream, but even more importantly,
dare to put actions behind your dreams.
~Josh Hinds

"Hello, is that Rebecca?"

"Yes." My heart raced.

The woman continued, "I'm pleased to tell you that you've been hired to work at the 2010 Winter Olympics."

At just nineteen years of age, this was something I'd dreamed about since hearing the Olympics were coming to Vancouver. To actually work at the Olympics in my own country, let alone in my own city, was going to be amazing.

I hadn't actually thought I'd get the job. There were an extremely limited number of openings for university students. And, prior to the interview, I had been told the spots were already full. Despite this, I'd decided to go for it.

I remember the night before orientation, laying out my uniform — the ocean-blue colours of the Olympic jacket and shirt standing out against the navy pants — and wondering what tomorrow would bring.

As I walked up the steps into the Vancouver Convention Centre, the main media centre (MMC) during the Olympics, I could hear the excited crowd growing louder and louder the closer I got. I took a deep breath and walked in. A sea of blue uniforms covered the entire seating area. Everyone was talking to each other. I stood at the bottom of the stairs for a moment, looking for an empty seat, finally spying a few near the top of the auditorium. The sharp smell of coffee hit my nostrils as a few more people came in clutching mugs, and I hurried to find a seat.

I remember seeing a girl, a couple of seats over, sitting alone with a chair gap between her and the people next to her. I took a chance and sat beside her.

"Hey, do you know what we're supposed to be doing?" I asked, trying not to sound as nervous as I felt.

She gave me a big smile. "Hey, I'm Callie. And I have no idea."

We both laughed.

I found out she was from another university nearby and had just turned twenty. We seemed to share the same sense of humour as we chatted.

I took a deep breath and said, "Do you want to get in the same group for orientation?"

"Sure." She laughed again. "I was going to ask you the same thing!"

I'd forgotten what it was like to have to put yourself out there to make friends. I was glad I didn't have anyone I knew with me because I wouldn't have met Callie otherwise. Taking the risk of sitting by her and talking started a great friendship. I still keep in touch with her.

Two days later, we had our first shift — the day of the opening ceremonies, which we'd all been waiting for. I remember seeing droves of people in red and white proudly brandishing their Canadian flags and red Olympic mittens, walking the Vancouver streets. Accents from all over filled my ears, and I couldn't believe how many people had come from around the world. The games seemed to unite us all.

As night fell, I was stationed just outside the MMC. Suddenly, I could see hundreds and hundreds of people running down Canada Place toward the harbour. Someone shouted near me, "I think it's this way!"

I turned to Callie and said, "Isn't that the way to the torch?" I could feel the ground vibrating under my feet.

"Yeah! You want to go down and see?"

We looked at each other and started to run.

My heart pounded as I sprinted. The air seemed charged with everyone's excitement like a kind of electric energy pulsing through us — the same energy that fed my adrenaline as we wove our way through the crowds. I'd never felt an atmosphere like it before. It felt surreal.

Then, fireworks exploded into the air above us. Their bright colours glittered against the dark sky. I could not stop smiling. I had watched the lighting of the torch many times on TV, but to actually see it in person was amazing.

When the last of the fireworks died down, there stood the Olympic torch unveiled in all its glory with its flames licking at the night sky.

Even now, I can still remember the heat from the torch on my face as I walked beneath it. The glass arms of the cauldron were cool against my fingertips. I had been one of the lucky MMC staff to walk underneath it while it burned. A beacon of hope.

I stood for a moment right under it, listening to the excited voices of my new friends, and I knew I'd made one of the best decisions of my life.

— Rebecca Franklyn —

A Second Chance

*Don't just be a dreamer, create goals for yourself
and follow them to the end.*
~Nathan Ergang, Big Life Change

"What is there to think about? You have five children and no life insurance! Of course, you are going to have the surgery!" Those were my panicked words to my husband as we sat in the cardiologist's office. He had been diagnosed with a congenital heart defect when he was eleven years old, but until about ten days before that visit, it had not been an issue. The pressures of life, though, finally broke through, and he ended up in the hospital.

The doctor told us that my husband, Jim, was playing Russian roulette with his life. He needed heart surgery. He had stubbornly said he had to think about it.

At that time, I worked where my children attended school. It felt more like a volunteer position considering my meager paycheck, but it helped a little. With the possibility that I might become a widow and the sole provider for my children, I was shaken to the core. How could I care for my family? I had no education beyond high school, no special skills or training. My husband had never wanted me to work outside the home. He wanted me to be with our children. Great idea in theory, but my reality was telling me I needed to do more, be more.

In the months that followed, while Jim thought about the doctor's dire warning, I enrolled in classes at our local community college. He argued that I was wasting my time and was needed at home. His words stung, but I argued that life was uncertain and I needed to be prepared for the worst. In truth, I was terrified he was right about wasting my time, but I just had to take the chance.

I had not been a stellar student. Growing up, my brothers and I would bring our report cards home from school and dutifully place them in our parents' hands. Dad would take my brothers' reports and go over every grade carefully, discussing what the boys needed to do to make the best of their education in preparation for their future. When he looked at my report card, he checked to make sure I was passing everything and then wordlessly handed it back to me.

He always told me that I wasn't going to go to college. It would be a waste, and there weren't enough resources to go around. My brothers needed the money for their education. I was supposed to bide my time until I could marry a man who would take care of me. My interpretation: I wasn't smart enough or valuable enough to use any of those precious family resources.

However, as I began classes at the ripe old age of thirty-four, I discovered that I was indeed smart enough. I found that I could not only hold my own in an academic setting, but I could excel. I loved it! Although Jim balked at first, he couldn't help but realize that going back to school was meeting more needs for me than just attempting to insure our family against financial disaster. I had something to prove. I needed to know that I was a competent thinker, an intelligent, capable individual.

Jim finally consented to have the heart operation, and we set up the consultation appointment. The doctor walked in to tell us he had changed his mind! He said that the surgery was proving ineffective in other patients with similar defects. He suggested a less invasive heart-catheter procedure to determine the actual risk of a heart attack, and then he would discuss the best course of action.

We followed his suggestion, and what he discovered made all the difference in our lives. I won't go into the medical details, but the bottom line was that my husband's version of Wolff-Parkinson-White syndrome was not critical. Although it could throw him into an arrhythmia, it would not cause a cataclysmic failure. Since then, we have discovered that WPW is not nearly as uncommon as we had originally been told. At that moment, though, the doctor's discovery felt like a miracle. Breathing a sigh of relief, we moved forward.

It didn't take long before the argument once again arose about my continued education. It was unnecessary, my husband argued. He was fine. He would provide for us all. It was an expense we would be better off without. My children needed my full attention. I was being selfish. I thought my head would explode with the pressure and guilt. Yet, I liked who I felt myself becoming. I loved learning. I also wanted to contribute in a bigger way, not only to my family but to the community beyond. I wanted to teach. I wanted to continue and reach that goal. And, I realized, I wanted to prove my father wrong.

Jim, hearing my heart in the matter, eventually threw his full support behind me. He became the single parent while I pored over textbooks and labored to perfect an essay. His help and encouragement were icing on the cake. I would have pushed through without it, but it sure made things sweeter.

When I walked across that stage and received my diploma, I felt like I could fly. I looked out at the crowd and saw my family beaming up at me. They were also clearly proud of my accomplishment. Returning to school had been a risk. It was terrifying. It could have torn my family apart. It could have proven my worst fears: I was not smart enough, good enough, valuable enough.

In truth, I realized that I had buried a number of my dreams. Our family's circumstances forced me to take another look inside, and the steps I felt forced to take to an uncertain future exposed hidden potential. I got the chance to find out who I could be and what I could do. It just took courage to grab hold of it.

— Marcia Wells —

62

Finding My Fire

Though she be but little, she is fierce.
~William Shakespeare

nervously rolled the colorful brochure in a tight circle on my lap as I closed my eyes and tried to fall asleep to the hum of the engines. After a tearful goodbye with my parents, I had stuffed it in my pocket to serve as my pep talk on the red-eye flight to London. "Study Abroad: Theater in Britain" was written in calligraphy above a picture of Shakespeare. The brochure described the program that I'd signed up for with great anticipation.

My dad had shown it to me, ecstatic about this elite program. Studying in London and seeing eighteen plays over five weeks was a dream for a theatre lover. My parents' enthusiasm was contagious, and before I could change my mind, I enrolled.

Now I was traveling across the ocean with students and a professor who were strangers. Desperate for reassurance, I opened my travel book to a dogeared page about The Minack, one of the world's most spectacular theaters. The sea was a breathtaking backdrop to an exquisitely carved stone stage at this open-air venue constructed on the edge of a cliff on England's southern coast. I couldn't wait to see it in person.

We arrived to learn that our summer-abroad home was nothing out of a travel guide. New Cross, a working-class area of southeast London, was not the picturesque place I had envisioned. We each had our own flats, which only made me feel more alone. Filled with regret,

I stared at the steel bars safeguarding the windows. I buried my book of fascinating destinations under clothes at the bottom of the drawer as I reluctantly unpacked, praying the time would pass quickly and safely.

The weeks that followed were filled with nervous excitement. My classmates and I learned new names for foods and how to convert dollars into pounds. We navigated the railways and the Underground "Tube" subway system. After class, we'd venture to the West End to see theatre and experience this remarkable city. On weekends, we visited Wales, Scotland, Ireland, Bath, Oxford and Shakespeare's birthplace, Stratford-upon-Avon. Each adventure fueled my ambition for another.

One memorable day, *The Winter's Tale* was performed at the new Globe Theatre, and I was thrilled to see one of Shakespeare's great works in a replica of his famous venue: a beautiful, circular, standing-room, open-air space on the bank of London's River Thames. At intermission, my group moved near the exit to beat the rush home. I didn't want to lose my view and thought that, if I moved quickly after the curtain call, I'd catch up. But they were gone. It was the 1990s, so there were no cell phones to call or text, no GPS to help find my way.

My heart raced as I searched for the Underground station. My palms were drenched as I prayed I was getting on the correct train. I ran home from the New Cross station and finally exhaled when I closed the door to my flat, vowing never to stray from the group again.

At five feet tall and 100 pounds, I was well aware of my physical vulnerabilities and never wavered from safety rules. I was always with my sorority sisters on our small college campus in Pennsylvania. At home, every outing was with family who joked that I had zero sense of direction because I even got lost in the mall.

Our final week, I convinced some of the other students to travel five hours south to see the glorious Minack Theatre. My classmate Tim and I were finishing our coursework while the rest of our group took an earlier train to Penzance to reserve rooms at the youth hostel.

When we stepped off the train, I was shocked to see them at the station. "We're heading back to London. That theater is too hard to find. You have to take buses to a dirt road and walk. We're not getting lost in the middle of nowhere."

Assuming I'd join them on the next train back, Tim shrugged apologetically and rushed after them.

I sat on a steel bench, struggling with self-doubt and battling a burning desire. Each time a train to London was called, I was tempted to return to the safety of my flat.

Finally, I walked out of that train station into the coastal town of Penzance. I didn't look back, afraid I would change my mind.

My heart pounded as I grabbed maps at a kiosk and asked questions of the locals as I walked the mile up Alverton Road to the youth hostel to book my room.

I bunked with Japanese students who invited me to join them at Land's End to watch the sunset on England's most southwestern tip. We sat on a grassy hill as the scorching sun faded into the sparkling sea and talked about life at home and adventures abroad. They giggled at the "tiny American girl" traveling alone and marveled at my ambitious plans to find The Minack.

The next morning, the driver gave me the same look: a startled gaze with a mix of awe and concern. When the bus pulled away, I was completely alone in the English countryside with no way to ask for help.

I took a deep breath as I followed the dirt road leading to a steep hill. When I reached the top, I could see the spectacular Minack Theatre overlooking the water, and it was like nothing I had ever seen.

I rested on the gorgeous granite seating carved into the side of the cliff. I walked slowly across the stone stage with the deep blue sea as the backdrop, joyfully reciting my favorite Shakespeare monologue to myself. This vivid picture is forever etched into my memory.

The Minack was no longer a wistful page in a travel book; it was a part of my story. It was exhilarating to walk back down the steep hill, along the dirt road to where the bus would return. Instead of going to the railway station to return to London, I booked another night at the youth hostel and mapped out a journey to the next page in my travel book: St Michael's Mount, a magnificent castle surrounded by water.

I carried my shoes as I walked barefoot on the ancient cobble causeway to reach the tidal island. The tide was starting to come in, so the stones were grazed with delicate waves just below my ankles.

Soon, the castle was majestically surrounded by water. I explored for hours and, as I left by boat, the sun's fiery rays illuminated the tower's brilliant stone.

Today, a portrait of a woman staring out to sea at St Michael's Mount hangs in my office. Over twenty-five years later, it serves as a daily reminder of a tiny American girl sitting alone on a bench at a railway station in England who, on her way to finding The Minack, found her fire.

—Jennifer Kennedy—

63

Called to Write

Don't tell me the sky's the limit when
there are footprints on the moon.
~Paul Brandt

t was a few days after my fifteen-year-old daughter, Cassandra, died following a three-year battle with lung disease. I was alone in my house when I felt a strong urge to write a book. I truly believe it was divine intervention.

Although I had been writing most of my life, I never did anything serious or attempted to be a published author. Most recently, I had been writing Facebook posts and keeping journals to process my feelings; it was an outlet. My family and friends followed the Facebook posts and offered support and prayer. A few months later, I took a GriefShare class and did a lot more journaling and processing of my grief. Despite the rather constant divine reminders, I was still too lost in my grief to pursue writing seriously.

After a few years, I knew I had to honor the call to write, but I didn't know where to start. About the same time I was trying to figure this out, one of my friends mentioned a retreat center in Montrose, Pennsylvania where she accompanied the youth from her church. I was drawn to find out more about it. I found their website and saw there was a writers' conference there every year. I didn't even know there was such a thing as a writers' conference.

Nevertheless, a trip to Pennsylvania was out of the question. It was four hours away from my home, and the trip would involve — horror of all horrors (at least to me) — bridges! I could imagine all the cars honking as I slowly made my way across the bridge and past the toll plaza. I had never driven more than fifty miles from my home, no less over a bridge, and I did not intend to start.

Despite my fears, I could not overcome what had now become an overwhelming urge to go to the conference. The more I thought about it, the more I knew I had to go. But how was I going to get there? "El, I can drive you," my husband John offered.

"It's not practical for you to drive me. What are you going to do while I am attending the conference for a week?"

"I'll find something to do."

"For a week? If I am going, I have to get there by myself. Also, the cost of the conference, food and lodging are not in our budget."

"If you are supposed to go, it will work out."

I took another look at the conference website and saw they had a scholarship contest. It required the submission of a written piece on being called to write. I wrote about my calling and my fear of bridges and submitted it to the contest. A few weeks later, I was notified I had won second place in the contest. I won a partial scholarship. One by one, the excuses not to go were being eliminated. I accepted the scholarship and started to plan my trip. I also began to accept that I had to drive over two bridges each way.

The day of the trip arrived. It was a sunny day full of promise. My car was packed and I was ready to go. I had a lot of conflicting emotions as I drove away from my house. Even though I felt I would be protected as I followed the call, I still stiffened and tightened my grip on the wheel as I got closer to the bridges. I prayed my way through it and felt fine. The trip took a little longer than I thought it would, but I made it safely over the bridges and all the way to Pennsylvania.

I arrived at the conference center and saw that Montrose was more beautiful than the pictures on the website. There were elegant Victorian buildings on the grounds, a gazebo surrounded by plantings, and a large field of daylilies. As I walked to the main building, with its inviting porch featuring rockers and hanging flowers, I immediately felt a sense of belonging.

The writers' conference was a week of great growth and revelation. I was able to talk (albeit through tears) about my daughter and my call to write. Everyone was understanding and supportive. One speaker, who was a frequent contributor to Chicken Soup for the Soul, encouraged me to start by telling some of my stories and submitting them.

As I attended classes during the week, it quickly became obvious that one doesn't just write a story or book and, voilà, they're an author. A lot of hard work goes into the finished product. There were terms and requirements that I never knew existed: one sheets, elevator pitches, query letters and book proposals, to name a few. It seemed I needed all of these to evolve from writer to published author. I came home humbled but energized.

I have returned to the writers' conference every year, even during the Covid crisis. I look forward to visiting Montrose and seeing my writer friends each year. It seems like no time has passed as we pick up where we left off, catch up, encourage each other and celebrate our victories.

Between my trips to Montrose, I read, write, laugh, and cry. Many of my memories bring me joy, and I am grateful I have them to hold onto. Other memories make me cry. It has been difficult for me to relive life events and put them on a page in painful detail. I have had to revisit times and days that were bleak. I am grateful I have my journals and notebooks where I recorded what my mind would not allow me to fully grasp and hold onto.

Writing has helped me to heal and process. It has given me a new journey to encourage and comfort others with my writing while giving me a wonderful group of friends whom I would never have met if I did not follow the call to write.

— Eleanore R. Steinle —

64

A Picture Worth a Thousand Wishes

If you are working on something that you really
care about, you don't have to be pushed.
The vision pulls you.
~Steve Jobs

My family always had the basics, but there was little money for much else beyond food and shelter. Everyone in our small town lived the same way, which is why I was pleasantly surprised when my mother came up with the money to purchase my fourth-grade class picture. Twenty-two students lined up in three rows and faced the camera with goofy smiles. My teacher, Mrs. Cornell, a fiery redhead, stood to the side. She kept strict rules, but I loved her as I did all my teachers. I clung to my one-and-only class picture like a new teddy bear. Ever so carefully, I wrote all my classmates' names on the back.

I was the nerdy kid who loved school. Every subject engrossed me as I absorbed knowledge. Schoolwork was never a burden. Even when I was sick, I still wanted to go to school.

"Mom, I don't feel that bad."

"Your temperature is 102! You're not going!"

My teachers were my heroes. They all left life-long imprints upon my life.

As the years passed, I would run across that fourth-grade picture

from time to time. It always reminded me that I had wanted to become a teacher. I had married right out of high school, though, and my focus was on building a family. Every so often I would feel that longing for the teaching career I never got to have.

Once my children were in school, I had some time to myself. The yearning to teach was still there, but I was now forty-two years old. It would mean going back to college. I had not been a student for over twenty years. Were there any brain cells left after raising three rambunctious children? Having only my husband's income made money an issue as well.

After much internal debate, I managed to come up with enough money for my first semester, a total of nine hours, but I had no idea how I would pay for anything beyond that. With a step of faith, I moved forward. Standing in line with baby-faced teenagers to register for classes, I questioned my ability to do it all. Could I be a student, mom, wife, and homemaker simultaneously? But here I was, deciding between Women's History or British Literature.

College proved to be a blessing and a challenge. It came as no surprise that my essay-writing skills were more than a little rusty. I was back in the thick of it, attending classes and challenging myself to learn new things. My days and nights were spent reading and rereading difficult textbooks. I wrote, marked out, revised and scratched out essays on seventeenth-century authors.

I watched as kids half my age aced tests while I studied for hours to make a passing grade. After the initial first weeks passed, however, I found myself starting to relax and enjoy the classes. Who knew that Henry VIII was so interesting or that women had served the nation well during World War II?

The majority of students in my classes were twenty-something. There were, however, a handful of moms like me who were giving a Hail Mary pass to their never-forgotten dreams. We shared class notes and childrearing secrets between classes. We brought our kids to class during their summer break. There was never a more determined group trying to fulfill their long-awaited careers.

One day, a professor mentioned that grant money was available to those going into education with bilingual or ESL certification. I mused over this thought. Would they even consider giving grant money to someone my age? I had a few good years left in me, but I couldn't compete with the youngsters who had a lifetime of teaching ahead of them. Feeling I had nothing to lose, I began the tedious application process followed by an interview. All I could do was wait and hope.

Several weeks later, I received a call from my professor telling me that I had been selected as a candidate for the grant program. I would have to invest some volunteer hours as required by the grant, but the remainder of my college expenses would be covered. I hung up the phone with teary eyes. I couldn't believe that my dream to teach was becoming a reality. My faith had been rewarded.

For another two years, I continued taking summer sessions. The professors were amazing and encouraging through the entire journey. Graduation day loomed. My family sat in the audience as I, a graduate with gray-tinged hair, crossed the stage. I wanted to jump in the air and click my heels, but I knew that would embarrass my teenagers.

For the next eighteen years, I taught fourth grade, with a brief three-year foray into third grade. I began each school year by telling the students about myself. I prepared a bulletin board that showed pictures of my family, vacation souvenirs and, yes, my fourth-grade class picture. I told them the story of how I had wanted to be a teacher all my life; it just took me a while to get there. That old class picture that I had hung onto was my encouragement that I would finally get there.

— Vicki Pinkerton —

65

My Momma's Hair

The need for change bulldozed a road down
the center of my mind.
~Maya Angelou

ecause I grew up in foster care, I wanted to repay the kindnesses shown to me by becoming a foster parent. I promised myself that, if circumstances ever allowed, I would try it. Having had no real role model for proper parenting, however, I could not convince myself to actually take steps to foster children.

My husband and I often discussed the possibility, and he was completely on board. He loves children as much as I do. Still, when it came to making that first move—a simple phone call—I would freeze up. I finally overcame my fears of inadequacy because of an incident I experienced at work. I was employed by Child Protective Services as clerical support to the two nurses and numerous social workers in my department.

One day, five children came into the nurses' office, all from one family. I was asked to come into the room and help take photos of each child and record physical notes of lice, bruises and such. Each child had a pillowcase with a few personal belongings such as clothes or toys.

Suddenly, I was reliving my past. I was one of five children taken from our parents and never returned. I was ten when we were all split up and placed in different homes. Two of my younger sisters were adopted by separate parents, my brother went to an orphanage, and my older sister and I went to one of many foster homes and were eventually separated.

Seeing these five children and reliving my own experiences convinced me not only of the dire need for foster homes but my need to give back as well. I soon took that first step, enrolling my husband and me into the necessary classes we had to take for six weeks.

No matter the circumstances, my goal was to be a loving and kind foster parent. We wanted to take in siblings who would otherwise be separated. Touching moments happen often while caring for neglected or abused children. Sometimes, it just broke my heart to see not only the physical suffering of these children, but the silent, mental suffering that only the astute sees. Child abuse/neglect is a touchy subject that most of society wants to ignore. For me, it is a passionate subject that I have fought hard to share since becoming a foster parent.

Our first two children were Daniel, age four, and his sister, Susan, age three. Every time these two little ones returned from a visit with their mother, they were so sad. Because they were hurt, angry, and confused, they tended to act out for at least a day or two, which is pretty much the norm for most of these children.

At the breakfast table after such a visit, Daniel appeared to be sad. His head was down, and his favorite breakfast of biscuits and gravy sat before him untouched. One hand covered his forehead and eyes, so we could not determine whether he was upset or sick. Noticing, my husband inquired, "Say, buddy, aren't you hungry this morning?"

Daniel remained hidden and silent for a moment. Then, in the broken language of his youth and a speech impairment, he replied so softly it was difficult to decipher. "Hair."

Puzzled, my husband asked him, "Is there a hair on your food? Just brush it away, buddy, and eat up!"

"Face…" was Daniel's reply.

My husband and I exchanged puzzled glances. Then, suddenly, from an inner intuition, the realization came to me. Somehow, I knew exactly what he was saying, the reason why he was sad and unable to eat.

"Daniel, did your mother hold you on her lap yesterday and give you lots of hugs and kisses?" I asked.

He dropped the hand from his lowered head, looked up at me

with pools of unshed tears in his eyes, with his lower lip quivering, and said, "Momma's hair. On my face…" And, as he spoke, his little hand brushed the side of his face ever so gently.

My heart almost broke. Barely holding back tears of my own, it was all I could do to speak. "Come here, precious, and let me hold you for a minute."

The sobs were released at last as he jumped from his chair and ran around the table and into my arms. As I engulfed him in a fierce hug and lifted him onto my lap, I rocked him and whispered in his ear how special he was to us and to God.

I said a silent prayer of thanks for being allowed to help this child in some small way. I prayed for this child and all those innocents who so badly needed their families. I also gave thanks for the day when I relived my own confusion and fear, which made me decide to step out of my comfort zone and foster children.

The boy's tears were spent in a short time, maybe five minutes, but his pain would never completely go away. James and I could love him and try to reassure him that he matters… that he is special. Our motto to always be kind would help. But we couldn't give him what he really needed and craved so badly: to be with his mother. Oh, that she could know the longing of her precious son and daughter. Would she try harder to get her act together and gain back custody of her children? This was my wish and daily prayer — not only for this little boy but for all the special children who remember the simple touch of a mother's hair on their cheeks. I still remember it myself.

— Christine M. Smith —

Go Far Away

An Uncomfortable College Initiation

A journey of a thousand miles begins with a single step.
~Lao Tzu

Take a moment to conjure up memories of your first month in college. Maybe you recall dorm parties and reckless behavior uninhibited by anyone with a fully formed prefrontal cortex. Perhaps you visualize yourself locked away in a library, hardly seeing the light of day in the name of higher education.

I would venture to guess no one is imagining living off the grid deep in the woods with a group of strangers. If you are thinking of such things, I would love to form a support group with you because that's exactly what I did.

I attended a small liberal arts college near Green Bay, Wisconsin called St. Norbert College. Located twenty-five minutes from my house and boasting just over 2,000 students, it hardly seemed like an exciting launch into independence. My mom, dad, and brother had attended St. Norbert, so it was my destiny whether I liked it or not. My grandpa, two aunts, and a cousin had gone there, too. My mail carrier probably went there for all I knew.

My attitude improved when I was accepted into St. Norbert's Gap Program — an experiential learning program in which I could travel (to the Boundary Waters, Albuquerque, Chicago, and Guatemala) throughout my first semester while also earning sixteen college credits.

This sounded like the opportunity of a lifetime (which it was), so I committed to the program and didn't think much of it... until I thought a whole lot about it the night before I left.

You see, I didn't think it was important to consider that I would be away from my family and friends, and any contact with them, for a month, living in the woods and sharing tents with strangers. I was the kid who struggled with being away from home for a mere sleepover, had never been camping, and was an extremely independent introvert. Like I mentioned, a college freshman's prefrontal cortex is not yet fully developed, so I blame that.

In any case, my stomach was in knots the whole night before the adventure started. I struggled to sleep in my bunk bed located in the basement of my college dorm where they parked the Gap students before our departure. There was a lump in my throat the next morning as I said goodbye to my parents (and civilization) and embarked on the seven-hour drive to Ely, Minnesota. Before I knew it, we had arrived at Outward Bound's base camp, and it was going to be sink or swim for me (literally... we did a lot of canoeing).

The first few days were filled with an abundance of learning: how to set up a tent, build a fire, tie special knots, steer a canoe, navigate waters that all looked the same, carry a canoe on your back without tipping over, and sleep with a rock wedged underneath your spine. I was really bad at most of it.

We carried everything we needed with us, in ginormous bags called "mandos," which I could hardly hoist onto my back without assistance. We canoed all day for just over two weeks, breaking only for lessons from our instructors and food, which was usually some variation of peanut butter and jelly. Sometimes, we would have "Voyageur Starts," which is just a fancy way of saying that we had to wake up at 4:00 A.M. to start paddling as the sun came up. When we were done paddling for the day, we summoned our (nonexistent) energy to set up camp, find wood, build a fire, cook our dinner, and have a team meeting before curling up on the rock that was always under the tent and drifting off into sleep, bordering on comatose.

At the end of our canoeing leg, we exchanged our mandos and

canoes for backpacks and our own two feet as we began the ten-day hiking portion of our expedition. We hiked from five to twelve miles a day, which actually gave us more downtime for naps, taken in odd places, like simply on the ground or cuddled into a tree root. However, it did not come without its own challenges, like asthma attacks and a highly infected ingrown toenail. (Luckily, neither of them applied to me.)

As a team, we learned to weather the tumult of Mother Nature's—and our teammates'—emotions. Whenever there was a thunderstorm (which was often), we had to stop what we were doing (which was usually sleeping), put on our smelly rain gear, disperse ourselves throughout our campsite, and kneel on our life jackets in hopes we wouldn't be struck by lightning. It was really an odd sight to behold.

As we were pushed to the edges of our mental and emotional resilience, we learned to navigate others' and our own emotions. There is no shoving feelings aside when living in an intricately interdependent community. Assertive communication, even if it had to do with another group member, was a must. The physicality of our expedition was challenging but natural to me; assertive communication was a whole other story. I am from the Midwest, after all. It scared me tremendously to show emotions I had previously viewed as weakness and share parts of myself I rarely, if ever, allowed to see the light of day. But I did. My group and I laughed together and cried together. We had difficult conversations and saw each other for who we were. We were a community.

Something happened as we continued on our journey. The more our muscles ached from paddling or hiking, the stronger we felt the next day. The more we encountered difficulty, the more we laughed (perhaps maniacally). The more we felt hunger or stress, the more inclined we were to share food or a word of encouragement. The more voluminous our armpit hair and unibrows became, the less we cared about our appearance or anyone else's. The more connected we became with the elements, the less we desired to return to lives riddled with technology. Somewhere amidst the long days and cold nights, we changed.

Our Outward Bound instructors stressed the importance of venturing into "The Land of the Uns,'" meaning the realm of what is unknown to you. As you move into The Land of the Uns, you move outside of your comfort zone. But moving outside of one's comfort zone expands it. You become comfortable with experiences that were previously unknown and uncomfortable.

Being uncomfortable is a muscle that needs to be strengthened and stretched so as not to be atrophied. When that muscle is strong, one feels empowered to take on more challenges and therefore reaps more rewards. That is exactly what I gained from my first month of college. I had never felt so empowered to accomplish anything I desired.

I reflect on my experience whenever I face difficulty, knowing I can overcome it just as I overcame the myriad obstacles from living in the woods. And I rise to the challenge every time.

— Natalie Bradish —

Miracle in the Highlands

We travel not to escape life,
but for life not to escape us.
~Author Unknown

It was an impulsive decision. I was off to ride horses in Iceland for ten days.

My husband had died seven months earlier, and I was lost, staggering through my life like a zombie. I had no idea what to do next. I'd retired from my high-school English teaching job after a thirty-year career so as to be home for my youngest son, a sophomore in high school. So I didn't even have work as a distraction.

One sunny May day, I found myself flipping through a *Travel + Leisure* magazine while sitting at my kitchen counter, looking out at the same view I had been looking at for twenty years. And I hated it.

I hated the tourists laughing on their way to the ice cream parlor. I hated the surfers with surfboards under their arms. I hated the happy beachgoers, laden with beach chairs and coolers, making their pilgrimage past my house to enjoy a sunny day on the beach.

I needed to get away — out of my house and out of my head. I continued flipping pages when my eyes suddenly stopped at a tiny ad at the bottom of the page looking for adventurous women to ride horses in the Icelandic highlands.

Iceland? Really? I asked myself. I had never traveled alone and hadn't been out of the country in years due to my husband's health issues. I didn't even know how to book a flight or get to the airport by myself.

But I was desperate. I dialed the number, took the one spot that was left, and texted my sons.

"I'm going to Iceland."

On the third day of the trip, as my riding group navigated through rough Icelandic terrain, my horse, Máni, decided to race at top speed to keep up with the guide's horse. He was galloping, I think, unless there is something faster than galloping, and I could hear the shouts of the other guides and women behind me, instructing me on how to slow him down.

Far from being an expert equestrian, I could feel myself starting to slide out of the saddle. I thought I was going to fall off the horse and die. I pictured my body being flown back to the United States. The image of my three grown sons at my funeral was so clear that I could hear church music. Strangely, I couldn't help but wonder what horrifying frock my family would dress me in for my funeral. I decided that if I got out of this, I would add a codicil to my will that I was to be buried in my Nicole Miller sheath.

Then, in one split-second, it happened. My head cleared, and the tight ball of fear that I had nursed and protected for twenty-five years burst open in my chest. The fear spilled out all over that volcanic patch of land, and as I looked up into that Icelandic sky, I knew my life would never be the same.

My heart and mind relaxed, and my body followed. I pressed my knees against Máni's flanks, gained control of my arms and the reins, and got him under control.

The person I became that week would have been unrecognizable to anyone who had known me before. Without fear, anger, worry or guilt, my heart was able for the first time in my life to operate from a place of joy and bliss. I remember getting very quiet, but my travel sisters remember differently. They remember laughter, chatter and singing.

I sang?

So, I did not die that day; rather, I found life. And when I returned home, as I began to exist from a place of pure joy and gratitude for the first time in my life, good things began to happen. I was careful to avoid those whom I felt would pollute my happiness, so out went the dysfunctional. Out went the hateful. Out went the greedy, the pretentious, the vapid. I protected my happiness and huddled around it to shield it from aggressors.

In those highlands, I opened my heart for the first time in my life, and love crawled in. Gratitude. Acceptance. Bounty, riches, grace.

—Mary Oves—

My Irish Adventure

*If we were meant to stay in one place,
we'd have roots instead of feet.*
~Rachel Wolchin

had graduated from college eight months prior with a degree in journalism and no fulfilling job prospects in sight, even after countless interviews. I was working a job I hated, where I was just a number, and it caused me endless anxiety every day.

My romantic life wasn't much better. I was painfully shy most of the time and a bit chubby. It took me a while to come out of my shell, and I felt like I was never anyone's first choice. People whom I was interested in always seemed to like me until someone better came along. But I was used to it and thought that was just how it was. I accepted the fact that I wasn't good enough.

Then, one fateful day in March, the course of my life changed forever. I got yelled at by customers at work all day, and that night the person I liked chose someone else. I knew I needed to leave my small town behind, at least for a while. If I could just go somewhere where no one knew me, I could do anything, be anyone, and maybe finally get out of the rut I had dug myself into.

That night, I went online and signed up to be an au pair for one year. I had an interest in a few different countries and hoped that I'd end up where I was meant to be. Oh, that night how I dreamt of what life could be for me! I didn't expect anything to come of it, but two days later I was contacted by a family in Ireland looking for an au pair.

I immediately called my mom and told her everything. I'm sure she was apprehensive. How could she not be? She didn't convey any of that, though. She seemed excited for me, for this potential new path in my life, and confident that I would make the right decision.

A day later, I was video-chatting with this adorable family of four. I loved them right away. After talking some more, I felt good about the prospect of going to live with them. They had an American au pair currently, whom I also talked to, and she helped ease a lot of my fears. They offered me the job at the end of the interview. The catch? They needed me in two weeks.

I felt my heart race. As someone who had basically lived in the bubble of my small town all my life, with my safe group of friends that I saw every weekend, I started to panic a little. Could I do this? Could I leave everything behind in two weeks for a whole year? I told the family I would think about their offer, talk to my mom, and call them back.

I called my mom and told her they had offered me the job. Her only question was, "Do you want to do this?" I told her I was scared, but I felt like going was the right decision. She booked me a ticket right after our call for a flight two weeks later.

I had some really great send-off parties, and then it was time. I think the fact that I only had two weeks to stew about my decision was a blessing. I was so busy preparing that I didn't have time to overthink this life-changing journey I was about to embark on.

My plane landed in Ireland, and it felt like a weight had been lifted off my shoulders. I was so ready for a new place, new people, and new job. I decided right then that I would make the most out of the year. I would put myself out there. I would start conversations with strangers. I would make friends, explore and find myself. I would not be the shy, timid version of me, but the person who deserved to be someone's first choice. I was going to live like the main character of my story instead of being too afraid to do anything new.

And I did.

The year I spent in Ireland was glorious. I went on sightseeing trips and to pubs and clubs all by myself. I don't think I ever left a place without having made at least one friend. By the time my year was up, I had many new life-long friends, and I feel like part of my "au pair family" too. I still visit them as often as I can.

By the time I came home, I felt like a whole new me. I was able to put myself first. Instead of thinking that I wasn't good enough, I was able to reframe my thinking into *they* weren't good enough for *me*. I deserved love, happiness and friendship, and I wouldn't settle for less.

Three months after I came home from Ireland, I met my now husband. I was able to start a conversation with him and keep it going, which is something I used to struggle with a lot. He was so easy to talk to. Before I went to Ireland, there's no way I would have been able to chat so easily and freely with him. I knew he was the one for me that first night we met.

Eventually, we moved from Pennsylvania to Seattle together. He proposed while on a hot-air-balloon flight, and we were married at a courthouse three months later. Eventually, we moved back to our small town to start a family. We now have an adorable daughter who we'll be taking to Ireland with us this St. Patrick's Day to visit my au pair family and friends.

I have always believed that everything happens for a reason. I was meant to find my Irish family and come alive in Ireland so that I could live my life to the fullest, change my view of myself, and find my confidence. I'm not sure if I would be with my husband if I hadn't changed for the better during that year and had so much practice talking to new people. I still get shy sometimes, but now I'm not afraid of breaking out of the box I had put myself in when I was younger. In Ireland, I found the person I was always meant to be.

— Brittany Cernic —

Shedding the Load

Wherever you go, go with all your heart.
~Confucius

Following the sudden death of my partner, my own existence had become miserable. I couldn't see a reason to carry on. With time, my grief subsided, and I was comfortable living in my apartment. Although my job was tedious, it was safe. But I couldn't shake the feeling that I should be doing more. I was blessed to be alive, and I should truly live that life rather than experience nothing more than survival.

I asked myself what I would do if money were of no importance. The answer was easy: I would donate my time to animals in need. I searched online for charities requiring volunteers and found a place in Sri Lanka. Within a week, my application was accepted, and after a course of vaccinations, I took a flight to a new life.

It didn't take long to adjust, and the natural way of life suited me. I lived at the rescue center in a village in the jungle. No longer could I take the basics for granted. Running water wasn't always available, and the electricity was often cut off with no guarantee to return anytime soon. Even stepping outside, it was imperative to keep an eye out for vipers and cobras, and more people are killed by falling coconuts than anything else in this country. But nothing beat waking up to the heavenly sunrises and the sounds of the jungle: monkeys chattering, parrots and peacocks squawking alongside the music of the monks chanting in the nearby temple.

Life was simple. There were no ready meals or pre-packaged fruits and vegetables. Sugar and spices were housed in large canvas sacks. Eggs were considered a luxury and sold individually. Bread was baked at a street kiosk, and fish was usually bought fresh from the boats lined up along the coast.

People in this part of the world are poor. Some have never owned a pair of shoes, and many are bow-legged as a result of childhood malnutrition. They don't have beds, so they sleep on stone flooring. Most Sri Lankan villagers wash using an external tap, and they cook outside with wood. Yet, they are the most giving of souls. They happily share the little they have. They are generous of spirit, and cheerful and pleasant to be around. I didn't come across incessant moaning and complaining. Depression and anxiety disorders were not prevalent. The people in the village have lived alongside each other for all their lives just as their ancestors had. In fact, some of the older folk have never travelled more than five miles away from their homes.

I loved living alongside the Sri Lankan people and working at the rescue center. At times, it was heartbreaking due to so much animal suffering. Dogs and cats were brought in from the street with an assortment of illnesses, diseases, and appalling injuries. With good veterinary care, most managed to make it. I threw myself totally into the work. After three months, I was promoted and became the manager. I secured a resident visa and stayed in Sri Lanka for two years.

I didn't realize how much this country and its way of life had changed me until I returned. In fact, I found the adjustment back to our first-world country far more difficult than adopting a humble and natural life. I became overwhelmed. On my first trip to the supermarket, I stared in awe at the options. I wanted a loaf of bread and could not choose among the immense assortment. Wandering among a plethora of different laundry soaps and powders, I questioned the need for so much choice. Of course, for most of my life, I had considered this to be normal. My apartment was home to around twenty-five cups and mugs, seven sets of bedding, fifteen pairs of shoes, and seventeen coats and jackets. I had saved up for my lilac-colored leather sofa, and whether it was really necessary had not occurred to me.

None of these material possessions had made me happy, but I had never questioned it before. In Sri Lanka, I learned that the pursuit of personal property is nothing but a burden. I knew that I could not go back to a materialistic way of life. I learned that it isn't what I have that is important but what I do and with whom I spend my time. I decided to devote my life to friends, family, and animals rather than work long hours to afford inanimate objects.

I cleared out all my unnecessary belongings and even donated that leather sofa. These days, I don't care what I sit on. Even the floor will do. And I most certainly would no longer buy a leather product of any kind. I have kept the items considered to be basics in our Western world, such as the washing machine, microwave, and refrigerator. But when I see the cost of things today, I still think of what that money is worth back in Sri Lanka. An enormous smart TV, a fancy barbecue, or an all-around sound system would most likely feed those living in a Sri Lankan village for six months.

Freeing myself from all that was familiar and diving into the unknown was the best move I could have made. I think I have become a nicer person. Sri Lanka altered my priorities and values, and my belief system has changed for the better. I now have far more resilience and have become less selfish. I have further compassion for others and live in peace and tranquility, with complete respect for the natural world.

— Caroline Caine —

70

Confessions of a Reluctant Traveler

Until you step into the unknown,
you don't know what you're made of.
~Roy T. Bennett

I swear I'm the last person in the world who'd have voluntarily chosen to be traveling in an oxcart through a Vietnamese rice paddy.
Yet, there I was, eight thousand miles from home. Even the ox
seemed surprised.

World travel was never high on my priority list. I was forced to
attend three different high schools in three different states because my
father was always changing jobs. That left me with a strong preference
for staying put. I've lived in the same apartment for the past quarter
of a century. My idea of a fun trip is going to Trader Joe's for Persian
cucumbers.

Plus, multi-national sightseeing can be expensive, and I rarely had
a lot of disposable income. And when my two children were young, I
just didn't see long-distance expeditions as a practical option.

Needless to say, the regular news reports of bombings, kidnappings
and terrorist attacks didn't exactly whet my appetite for hopping on
a plane for distant parts. I was pretty sure that if something terrible
were to happen, I'd be the one whose frantic family would receive the
ransom demand. It was understandable, then, that by my mid-sixties,
the closest I'd come to using my passport was dinner at HU's Szechwan

restaurant in Los Angeles.

So, I was as surprised as anyone else to find myself at the age of sixty-seven, a year prior to the current pandemic, on an All Nippon Airways jet, winging across the Pacific to kick off a seventeen-day trip to Thailand, Cambodia and Vietnam. Okay, granted, I took a boatload of cautious traveler precautions: a hepatitis-A vaccine, malaria tablets, typhoid medication, mosquito lotion, sun protection, and the antibiotic, Cipro. If I was going to come down with something, it wouldn't be for lack of preparation.

The last time I'd even thought about Vietnam was as a college student in the 1970s. I spent many a sleepless night envisioning myself being snatched by the U.S. government directly from my Introduction to Shakespeare class and dropped into the perilous jungles of Hanoi.

Why in God's name then was I now heading back to the scene of my nightmare for a supposedly fun vacation? For the same reason, of course, that so many men do so many things that may not have been their first choice — to please their romantic partner. Oh, yes. How many members of my gender have found themselves cleaning their homes, grooming their bodies, attending "chick flicks," writing thank-you notes, and chewing with their mouths closed — solely out of fear that Love Lake would dry up?

So, that's why, when my girlfriend indicated on more than one occasion how enchanted she was by visiting new places, how much she wanted to explore the world with me, and how very important this was to her, little cracks began appearing in my lifelong aversion to venturing outside the comfort zone of my zip code. Love conquers all, the wall crumbled, and one day I found myself reluctantly agreeing to a Southeast Asian adventure.

And you know what? The expedition wasn't nearly as traumatic as I'd feared. In fact, keep this to yourself, but I'd even go so far as to say that, well, I kind of enjoyed it — the food, cultures, people, educational aspects, and so much more. I took tons of photos. I ate things I couldn't pronounce. I attended a drag queen show where the men were the most beautiful women I'd ever seen. I had a two-hour foot massage for $22. I became addicted to fresh papaya served on banana leaves, with a side of passionfruit. I didn't even come down with anything, other than a little jet lag. And the great news is that I never once had to fight my way out of a jungle with a machete.

Experiencing this strange and wonderful part of my world also gave me a new appreciation for other people and cultures. And don't think I'm not grateful for the best part: It has reinvigorated our love life. I even took the lead on suggesting some possibilities for our next exploration — Rio, Barcelona, or Mykonos — especially if one of them is on sale.

You might think from all this that I've learned to face my fears head-on and continually challenge myself for the sake of personal growth and enlightenment. You'd be thinking wrong. I'm not about to start hang gliding, trying LSD, or eating steak tartare — unless, of course, my sweetie makes them deal breakers. After all, I'm nothing if not reasonable.

— Mark Miller —

71

A Magical Transformation

A mind that is stretched by a new experience
can never go back to its old dimensions.
~Oliver Wendell Holmes

had lived in my suburban home in Syracuse, New York for my entire life, surrounded by family. Even when I went to college, I commuted to school every day with my mom, who worked at the university. Thus, I barely made friends. My home was my comfort space, a place where I felt safe no matter what was going on in the world.

After graduating college, I had two options. I could continue to live at home and work at my stable job at a local grocery store, or I could move all the way down to Florida and participate in the Disney College Program. It was an incredibly daunting prospect. I mean, how could I just pick up and leave my comfy home and family to go to a land where I knew no one?

The day finally came when I gathered up all my personal belongings and packed them into my Honda Civic. Still doubting that I was making the right decision, I said goodbye to my mom and hopped into my lonesome car. I then drove away, bawling my eyes out as I waved goodbye to everything I had ever known.

Over 1,000 miles later, I arrived at Flamingo Crossings, the Disney College Program housing complex. I met my roommates and resolved that I would make the most of the experience, particularly in the realm of making long-lasting friendships. My roommates and I spent many moments together, from playing games in the Commons to relaxing by the pool. All of us eventually had to start work, which was another adventure in and of itself.

I worked at the Riverside Mill at Disney's Port Orleans Riverside resort. Day one, everyone was extremely friendly. However, it was not the type of work I was accustomed to. We'd have to fry French fries and chicken, cook pizzas, and assemble burgers, among other things. The day would be hectic, and I'd get out super late every night smelling like greasy food.

A week after my training at Riverside began, right when I was starting to get somewhat comfortable with the role, I decided to take another leap and pick up a shift at a different food-service location. I took my co-worker Hannah, whom I had begun to get to know, and we worked a night shift at BoardWalk Ice Cream. This was much more pleasant since we were dealing with desserts, and though it was busy, it was pretty fun.

While working at BoardWalk, I met a guy named Albert who also happened to be picking up a shift at the location. We joked back and forth most of the shift, and at the end, he asked for my number. We went out a few days later, and after a month, I had my first boyfriend. Albert and I went on many day and weekend trips, which allowed me to experience Florida to the fullest. Without him, I'm not sure I would have left Flamingo Crossings very much, let alone explore Florida all the way down to Miami. Similarly, I wouldn't have had him continue to push me outside my comfort zone all the way back home in New York, where we now reside.

In addition to Albert, I met some amazing people during my time in Orlando. I made friends whom I know are going to be in my life for the long haul. And, for those who aren't, we'll always have those shared memories that we made. From visiting the parks on a daily basis to going to the local Wawa every night after work, those moments will always be there. Had I not done the program, I wouldn't have had all these amazing people and experiences in my life.

Taking that step and participating in the Disney College Program truly changed me. Not only did I learn that I was capable of living on my own and successfully forming relationships with people other than my family, but I also found a new passion for exploration. It made me realize that I can do whatever I want to do, even if it may seem daunting at first.

There were many times during the program when I wanted to quit and go back home, which made succeeding at the program that much more special. I am not the same person I was before I moved down to Florida — or perhaps I am but finally realized my potential. I would not trade the discomfort of leaving my family for six months for anything, as it has made me the person I am today.

— Nicole Perrigo —

72

Restoration

*All journeys have secret destinations
of which the traveler is unaware.*
~Martin Buber

The small ad was in the back of a fashion magazine that I was flipping through while waiting for a haircut. It showed a picture of a turtle swimming in a square of blue, with the imperative: Help Save Sea Turtles. It invited the reader to join a volunteer expedition to Costa Rica for a week at a research station to help with sea turtle restoration. It would cost only $1,300 plus airfare.

I have to do this, I thought. And then, *Are you nuts?* I was not an adventure traveler. I didn't go to exotic locations but to places with major museums and clean hotel rooms. Nonetheless, I wrote down the phone number listed in the ad, and on Monday I called it from my office.

The packet of information that came in the mail a few days later only reinforced my sense of inadequacy. It described the research station, located in a wildlife refuge on the Pacific Ocean, and what would be involved for us volunteers. Getting there — and being there — would be challenging. The remote village had no electricity. I was a poor candidate. I was not physically fit, I hadn't spoken Spanish since ninth grade, and I liked to blow-dry my hair every morning.

Two months later, I disembarked in San José, Costa Rica and took a taxi to the rundown hotel where I was to meet up with my travel companions. There would be eight of us: our leaders, Gwen and Steve, who knew Costa Rica and spoke Spanish, and five other women who were more or less like me. My confidence notched up a bit.

Early the next morning, we boarded a bus and headed west toward the Nicoya Peninsula. We crossed emerald hills of banana trees and bumped along unpaved roads that became increasingly rough and muddy. When the bus got stuck, all the passengers except the elderly got off and pushed it out of the mud. In the afternoon, we reached a small town where we were met by the truck that was supposed to take us the rest of the way to the village — until it stalled crossing a shallow river. We climbed down and waded to the other side, backpacks over our heads. Another truck picked us up and took us on to Ostional.

We were way off the grid. The research station was a cinderblock building painted white, just steps from the Pacific Ocean. We were welcomed in Spanish by Jorge, the resident researcher, and two cooks/housekeepers from the village. They handed us our bedding and a mosquito net and directed us to our rooms. Steve and Gwen got their own room, while ours had bunk beds. We chose our bunks and hung up our mosquito nets. I was grateful there were flush toilets, and I would almost get used to cold showers.

That first evening, we ate a classic Costa Rican dinner, complete with rice and beans, by the light of kerosene lanterns. Afterward, Steve translated for Jorge, who gave us an introductory lecture on the work of the research station. The beaches near Ostional were a preferred nesting site for the olive ridley sea turtle, which sometimes arrived by the thousands during the nesting time of year. Adult turtles tangled in nets were given medical treatment and tagged before release. Turtle hatchlings fell prey to crabs, seagulls, and vultures. But the biggest threats to the turtles of Costa Rica were the humans who believed that consuming turtle eggs increased a man's libido. Villagers were paid by the government to patrol the beaches at night and protect the nests from poachers and dogs. Our job would be to help turtle hatchlings make it from their nests to the sea.

Close to midnight, Jorge summoned us, and we walked to the beach by the light of the moon. He spotted a sea turtle making her nest. We stood by quietly and watched her fling sand with her flippers until she had carved a deep hollow, into which she deposited maybe 100 eggs. She carefully covered the nest with sand and tamped it down with her shell, rocking over and over until it was solid. When her nest was complete, she made her way back to the sea and disappeared into the waves. She would never know whether, weeks later, her hatchlings would join her in the ocean.

It was well past 1:00 when we returned to our bunks. At dawn the next morning, only Steve, Amy from Minnesota, and I got up to head back to the beach. The women and children of the village were already there with plastic bowls, huddling over nests where there were hatchlings from previous nestings. As the babies emerged from the sand, they were gently lifted and placed in the bowls. Once the nests had emptied, the bowls with their wriggling contents were carried to the edge of the ocean. Each hatchling was placed on the wet sand a few yards from the water so it could imprint and return as an adult to that beach. The little turtles got their bearings and scrambled to the sea, diving in without hesitation.

By mid-morning, the gang from the research station was on the beach, and the hatching that would occur that day was finished.

We had a full but leisurely week of morning activity followed by afternoons in the surf of the Pacific. The mayor of Ostional — a woman — talked to us about the village's important work in conservation and what might change within months when Ostional finally got electricity. Would turtles still come to a beach that was partly illuminated by the glow of electric lights? We visited the primary school and were welcomed by polite children in crisp uniforms. One evening, we walked up the road to the cantina, which had a generator, and ordered cold beers. Hens rambled undisturbed, clucking quietly in the schoolroom, at the cantina, and in the small village store. Everything tasted good: the fresh pineapple juice, the coffee, the pico di gallo. And, everywhere we went, we were eaten alive by insects. My bunkmate Charlotte dubbed us "Las Malarias."

Late one afternoon, I sat outside the research station with Charlotte's *New Yorker* magazine, hoping to finish an article on Sylvia Plath before it got too dark to read. I realized I was the happiest I had been in a long time. I was sweaty, covered in mosquito bites, and at peace. I had thought my routine at home made me safe, when, in fact, I was just stuck. I was numb from a bad breakup, the untimely death of my boss from breast cancer, and then the loss of my dad. A crushing job had robbed me of my confidence. Like the sea turtles, I needed restoration. Whatever impulse had led me here was the right one.

On our last morning, Steve paid a local man who was driving toward San José to give us a lift in his flatbed truck. For three hours, we stood in the back of the truck, clinging to the wooden rails as we passed through the beautiful countryside. I thought, *Boy, this is the way to go.*

— Fran Baxter-Guigli —

73

Chopsticks and Challenges

I am not the same, having seen the moon shine
on the other side of the world.
~Mary Anne Radmacher

My stomach was grumbling, so I was thrilled when my friend Shizuka motioned me to the dining room table for dinner. It was our first night staying at her aunt and uncle's house in Osaka, Japan. Shizuka's aunt and her grown daughter had prepared a meal for us while we were upstairs unpacking and getting settled.

We gathered around the table. Shizuka sat to my left, and her aunt, uncle and cousin sat across from us and at the head of the table. The fancy layout impressed me: a beautiful tablecloth spread across a wide table, with tasteful decorations and colors. Everyone had their own bamboo food tray set in front of them.

Their Japanese conversation flowed around me like a river while I looked at the food. When I realized what it was, I suddenly lost my appetite.

Sushi.

There was no food I hated more than raw fish. I struggled to eat even cooked fish in America, but uncooked fish made me sick to my stomach. I sat nervously, pushing away the nausea, and didn't talk as everyone else picked up their chopsticks to dig in.

The sushi sat in neat rows on the wooden platform, with varied colors. I knew this was an expensive, gracious treat, but I couldn't help but find it unappetizing. I slowly picked up my chopsticks and poked around the pieces of raw fish on my tray. This was my nightmare and one reason why I had told my friend no when she mentioned taking me to Japan with her.

We first met in health class when we were sixteen years old. We struck up a conversation after finishing our worksheets on the first day. I learned how much she loved chocolate, how she hated English, and that her little sister drove her crazy. I understood because I had a little brother at home, too.

We became fast friends. I had fun drawing little pictures in the margin of our homework to explain English words. She made me laugh and wrote me notes and stuffed them in the slots of my locker between classes. At the end of the school year, she talked about going to Japan to visit her family for the summer.

"You should come with me!"

I laughed. "No way. I can't go to Japan." It seemed absurd. I wasn't even working at the time except for babysitting.

"Why not?" she probed.

Oh, gosh, I thought. *She's serious.*

"Well… I don't like fish."

Now, it was her turn to laugh. I should have realized I was stereotyping her culture and being insensitive.

"We eat good food! Not just fish. You will love it."

One month after graduation, I flew from Grand Rapids, Michigan, to Osaka to stay for two weeks. The money for the plane ticket came entirely from my graduation gifts.

But I almost didn't get on the plane.

In the terminal before boarding, I got scared, so I called home.

"Mom, I can't do this." I stared at my shaky hands. I had transformed from an adventurous high school graduate to a panicky little girl.

My little brother got on the phone. He told me to get my butt on the plane because it would be worth it. He gave me the courage to face my fears. With his encouragement and a whole lot of praying, I boarded the plane.

Shizuka was my tour guide and only friend, and we were having a great time together. The food was different, but as good as she had described, and I somehow survived the first week without eating fish of any kind.

But now my lucky streak had ended. I sat staring at eight pieces of innocent fish, picking at the white rice in the middle of the sushi rolls. My chair squeaked as I rose to my feet and walked away, hiding my red face from our generous hosts.

On a trip overseas, there is bound to be a breaking point. The culture shock had been slowly building and was now blowing like a volcano. We had spent the week walking miles each day, and I relied on Shizuka for everything from communication to keeping track of our money and learning how to bathe with a handheld showerhead and a bucket.

I ran upstairs like a wimpy American and cried into my pillow. I missed home. I missed hamburgers.

Shizuka came up after me and apologized.

"I didn't know what they would cook. They wanted to give you a traditional Japanese meal to welcome you. I am so sorry."

I told her I missed home. That I felt stupid for not being brave enough to try the fish. That I wasn't used to Japan. She looked at me with kind eyes.

She understood all too well. She lived in America and missed home desperately the entire school year. Only on trips back to Japan did she really feel like herself. In one night, I was getting a glimpse of what she felt like all the time. I never realized how brave she needed to be just to make it through the day.

We didn't talk about the incident again. I was embarrassed, but Shizuka worked her magic with her aunt. The rest of the week, I had the best meat, rice and sauce bursting with flavor, egg rolls, potato dishes, and dessert. I ate with gusto and poured out my thanks incessantly. Their faces lit up when I said, "Oish !" Delicious!

One sushi dinner broke me, but not for long. I learned to look for "udon" on the menus when we went out to eat. I enjoyed the warm, brothy soup filled with doughy noodles while everyone else happily ate their sushi and shrimp eyeballs.

More importantly, I learned more about Shizuka and Japan. She convinced me to come to her country because she knew I would love it. She was right — but only because she was right by my side, the best tour guide ever. And we had adventures in the streets of Japan together, arm in arm.

As friends from two different worlds, we shared the best thing in common: courage.

— Kim Patton —

74

Ashes and My Bucket List

Man cannot discover new oceans unless he has the
courage to lose sight of the shore.
~André Gide

I carefully scooped spoonfuls of ashes into little baggies, talking to my husband the whole time. I had always talked to myself, frequently planning conversations I might have with others, so talking to him didn't feel weird.

My husband had died six weeks after he was diagnosed with metastasized pancreatic cancer. Since then, I had been learning how to manage on my own, doing the chores he used to do for us, cooking in smaller quantities so I wouldn't eat the same meal for a week.

Now, I was going on my first solo trip, visiting Egypt and Jordan and taking him along for the ride. After all, this tour was number one on our travel bucket list.

Travel was our passion. We always joked that we didn't need a fancy house or cars. We saved our money to buy plane tickets. Forty souvenir T-shirts from all the places we had traveled hung in the closet. I lovingly touched each one as they brought back memories of our wonderful adventures. Smiling, I remembered racing to see the great migration of wildebeests and zebras in Tanzania, talking to kids practicing their English in Vietnam and Chile, and finding the duck's head, beak and all, in our soup in Shanghai. These shared experiences enriched our lives. How would I make new memories as a solo traveler?

I decided my trip had two challenges. The first one was finding people to talk to. Professionally, I had always talked to students, teachers, or parents every day. However, socially, I always said I didn't talk to people I didn't know. It wasn't hard when traveling with someone who would strike up a conversation within five minutes with the person sitting next to him in a bar or on a tour. Once that door was opened, I had no problem joining in. I knew I'd be terribly lonely if I spent two and a half weeks on a trip of a lifetime and never talked to anyone.

So, as I planned for this trip, I started practicing. At an outdoor mountain concert, I claimed a seat. My husband and I would have enjoyed a beer while listening to the band. Dilemma. If I left my chair, I'd lose it. It took me thirty minutes to find the courage to ask the woman next to me to hold my seat. Then, I had my beer and talked to a stranger. Baby steps.

I had a script of conversation starters. "Where are you guys from?" "Have you been to Egypt before?" "Where have you traveled?" In my head, all those questions sounded just fine, although I couldn't bear to practice the answer for when people noticed I wore a wedding ring and asked about my husband.

I always organized our travels with input from my best friend. Organizing this time was easy; figuring out how to change my mindset, not so much. I knew I would continue to talk to my husband, but doing that seemed pretty eccentric.

The thought of walking into the dining room for breakfast the first morning gave me a moment of anxiety. Should I go early, late, or sometime in-between? Where should I sit? Under Covid protocols, the dining room manager took my temperature at the door. Good thing he didn't check my heart rate. My husband's voice in my head said, "It's only breakfast, not a commitment." Armed with my pre-planned script, I asked a couple if I might join them. Soon, we were discussing the food and other places we had traveled. I could do this. I had found people I liked to talk to. Step one, accomplished.

That moved me to challenge number two. I've learned there is a big difference between being lonely and being alone. We liked traveling independently so we could plan our day, whether it was visiting museums and sites or just sitting on a park bench watching people.

We always enjoyed the "free time" to explore on our own if we were on a tour. Could I enjoy doing that alone?

Moving away from the crowds at the Giza pyramids and wandering farther down the path at Petra, I found I actually liked the alone time. It wasn't the same as sharing the walk with my husband, but at dinner I could share the experiences with other travelers.

I found quiet places to sit and spread some of the ashes at each site. From the veranda of my stateroom on the Nile, I sprinkled more ashes. Each time, my mind said, "It isn't supposed to be like this." If traveling was going to bring me joy, my thinking needed to change. I reminded myself that my husband would have loved this trip. It was comforting to know that he was with me in some way.

When we traveled with a group, we never joined in on costume or dress-up nights. It just wasn't our thing. The ship's Egyptian theme party was my next test. What would the "new me" do? I bought an Egyptian dress at the street market. Would I actually wear it? I put it on. I could always leave if I hated the party. I sat with some of my new friends. Then, the games and dancing began. I sat gripping my drink as others moved to the floor. Maybe I wasn't as "new" as I thought. Then someone grabbed my hand, pulling me in to the line dance. I smiled — not a phony "I'm supposed to be having fun" smile, but a real one. I was having a good time and a new experience.

I have changed. I always saw myself as a strong, independent woman. But I now recognize that I have strengths and courage I didn't know I had. I met interesting people to share adventures with. People did ask about my husband, and I learned I could talk about him without falling apart. I learned I needed to change how I thought about travel to have a great time in this new chapter of my life. Each time I spread the ashes, I felt a huge sense of loss. But I knew there were many more adventures in my future. Armed with ashes and a new perception of myself, I planned my next trip.

— Sue Harris Sanders —

Just Say Yes

☑ Try avocados

☑ Go ziplining

☐ Sign up for art class

☐ Make a new friend

☐ Run a 5K

☐ Buy a bathing suit

75

Yes Day

Continuity gives us roots; change gives us branches,
letting us stretch and grow and reach new heights.
~Pauline R. Kezer

My besties and I were savoring our leisurely breakfast at a Mexican resort while enjoying the sea breeze and gorgeous views. The sun was shining, and it promised to be another relaxing day in paradise as we welcomed the respite of a short vacation from the daily grind.

We were looking over the list of daily activities the resort offered, and we each had things we wanted — and didn't want — to do. After trying to negotiate with each other so we all got our needs met, I finally said, "You know what? Let's just have a YES DAY! Let's just say yes to it all, every activity, whether it's in our comfort zone or not. Let's eat all the unique food, whether it's something we like to eat or not. Let's have all the ice cream and French fries we can. Calories don't count on Yes Day. Drink the fruity drinks. Let's challenge and enjoy ourselves in unexpected new ways."

For that one perfect day, we put our personal preferences aside and embraced each moment with anticipation and excitement. We challenged ourselves and each other throughout the day and found ways to support and encourage one another. Instead of picking and choosing, we tried every activity.

My friend Sarah doesn't like guns and had never held or shot one. They had BB guns and target shooting, which we went to first.

She started off nervous and uncomfortable, but by the end she was holding the gun like Queen of the South. She was a good sport about the whole thing and smack-talked the pros like she knew what she was doing. She never hit the target, but she was sure glad she tried.

I'm not a huge fan of heights, but the zipline over the resort was next. I was scared when I climbed to the top of the landing and peered the long way down to the ground at what I was sure was my impending doom. I wanted to back out when they put the harness on me, but my besties were at the bottom, cheering me on the whole way, and waiting for me with hugs and a drink. So, I took the leap off the platform and screamed my head off the whole way down. But I was so glad I did it because I was exhilarated from the adrenaline and my courage. I also appreciated the amazing views from up high, which I would have missed if I followed my normal impulse of saying no to heights.

My friend Katie didn't want to do karaoke and dancing. But since it was Yes Day, she had to face her fears of being the center of attention. We danced and sang the night away, laughing the whole time. We were even uncharacteristically bold enough to crash the tail end of a wedding party and danced on the glass topper over a swimming pool! We were literally walking on water, feeling elated and fulfilled in ways we had never experienced before.

We still talk about our epic, magical Yes Day! When those pictures pop up, the three of us are so happy in them, with smiles reaching ear-to-ear. We would have missed so much if we had stuck to what we were comfortable doing. I believe we all need random Yes Days.

— Tory Wegner Hendrix —

76

Tickled Pink

If I was not a dreamer, I would have achieved nothing.
~Clint Eastwood

I entered the theater via a red carpet that my friends and family had brought. Sure, we were in Augusta, Georgia, not Hollywood, but for us this was the premiere!

When seated, I was super nervous. My scene might have been cut during editing, and this could all be for nothing.

I knew which scene I was in, so I was elated to see the main character pull up in his truck and enter the hotel. I watched anxiously as he walked down the hall, interacting with characters. And then, much sooner than expected, he was at the table, passing out the flowers. Then, lo and behold, there I came through the crowd, shaking hands with and speaking to the man himself, the incomparable Clint Eastwood! My fans in the theater cheered. I was in complete disbelief!

We watched the film, which was a much more interesting story than I had expected. There were some racy parts that made me blush. And then the credits rolled, and there was MY NAME! It was eighth on the list. It was in order of appearance, so I was above Clint's own daughter! It was truly amazing and one of the greatest moments of my life.

How did all this come to pass?

After caring for my dad through his terminal cancer, I needed to heal. When I saw that Clint Eastwood was coming to Augusta to film his next movie and was hiring local extras, I figured, what the heck.

After all, Dad had always been a big Eastwood fan, and I had always wanted to act.

I applied and provided some photos. And then I was called for a costume fitting! I brought the only items in my closet that fit the role, including a pink short skirt I had bought the previous week at the local thrift store for five dollars. I remember arguing with myself about whether a woman of forty-five should wear such an item. But it was cute, and I had lost a few pounds, so I went for it. I am not a super "girly girl," so I didn't have many shirt options. At the fitting, they made me try several items and settled on a shirt I can only describe as obnoxious with huge hot-pink flowers. I was mortified! I am not a small woman, and I was plenty self-conscious wearing it. Sure enough, they called me for the shoot and said I would wear the hideous flower shirt.

I went to hair and make-up, and then it was time to hurry up and wait. If you have never been on a movie set, I should tell you that it's incredibly interesting. There are so many things going on. Things get done, then redone, and done again. The attention to detail is fascinating. It has made me much more aware of the perfection that goes into setting even one scene. It is truly an art.

So, we sat and sat and sat, and finally a guy walked through and asked if we had been "used" yet. We told him no, and he led us out into the lobby where all the activity was happening. We were supposed to be attending a flower convention, and they shot several scenes of us looking at daylilies from about 900 angles. Then, the big man himself, Clint Eastwood, who was starring and directing, walked in. I tried not to fangirl because he was closer to me than I am to my television right now. I couldn't help but think of my dad and how giddy he would be to watch this. Again, we shot several scenes, and his assistant director came over and said, "Ladies, this guy is your hero. I want you to rush the stage like he is a rock star."

In that moment, I got braver than I have ever been. I could see my dad's face and his big smile. I pushed through the crowd (which, in my memory, parted like the Red Sea) and stuck my hand out while grabbing and shaking Clint's.

If you have never been starstruck, let me tell you, they call it "struck" for a reason. Eighty-eight or not, that man still has star quality and the prettiest blue eyes that will make any woman of any age melt. I shook his hand and said, "You rock, Earl," which was the character's name. He grinned with his whole face and said something that I did not hear because CLINT EASTWOOD WAS TALKING TO ME!

I said it again, and he said, "No, say, 'Is that Jimmy Stewart?'" I said it in my flabbergasted, wide-eyed way, and he laughed. They yelled, "Cut!" Then, they took me by the hand away from the crowd and told everyone to go to lunch.

At this point, I decided I must be imagining this and pinched myself. Nope, that hurt. It was real. They put me at a table and had me give them some information. Then, Eastwood walked back and reviewed the scenes we'd just shot. The other director walked up and said it was "a crack-up," and then Eastwood came back and said, "Thanks for doing that. It was great." I stuttered and said some form of, "No... thank YOU!" I got the million-dollar grin again before joining the line for lunch. I was literally shaking at this point and could not think at all.

I sat down, and a friend I have known since high school came over and said, "I have been doing this for twelve years. You walk in the first day, and Clint Eastwood gives you a speaking role." I think I apologized, but I wasn't really that sorry. From then on, Eastwood was cutting up with me like we were best friends. As the day ended, I thanked the lady who made me wear the hideous shirt because it had clearly worked in my favor.

Two weeks later, a woman called and asked how I wanted my name listed in the credits. I laughed and decided to take my one and only life opportunity to be a diva.

"Yes," I said. "I want McClintock with a small c and then a big C."

— Christine Powell McClintock —

77

Eat Your Oyster!

Life is either a daring adventure or nothing.
~Helen Keller

Sitting at the bar overlooking my in-laws' kitchen, I nervously eyed the slimy, gray blobs staring me in the face. Saltine crackers, pretty lemon wedges, a bottle of Tabasco and a small bowl of horseradish sat innocently nearby. I had never eaten an oyster. I loved seafood, though. I'd never had any seafood or fish that I didn't like, and I love to try new things.

But the sight of that gooey, shapeless thing... Ugh. I just couldn't do it. Timidly, I stuck one with a tiny fork and lifted it onto the saltine in my left hand. There! That was something at least. I'd put the thing on a cracker. I moved the saltine to my right hand and brought it close to my mouth. It smelled salty. "Do I bite into it or just put the whole thing in my mouth? How do you do this?" I asked. Everyone else just kept popping the darn things into their mouths while they teased me for not trying them. I'm no chicken. Why was this so hard?

Nowadays, it's a different story. I gobble them up as fast as the waiter can keep them coming! But not that day — not the first time. I sat there staring at the cracker in my hand topped with that weird blob of goo. I could almost feel it in my mouth, wanting to spit it out but knowing I couldn't. That would be rude, and, more importantly, I'd never live it down. No, I had to eat the thing. Those were my thoughts as I cautiously brought it up to my mouth and then pulled it back away over the next forty-five minutes. Yep, you read that right. I sat there and stared at an oyster for nearly an hour before I could work up the nerve to actually put it in my mouth. Meanwhile, everyone else was snacking on them like popcorn at the movies!

The average female in the United States lives approximately seventy-eight years or just over 683,000 hours. And, once they're gone, they're gone. You don't get to hit rewind, and no one brings you another round. I wasted one of those fleeting hours trying to psych myself up to gag down an oyster. Oy vey!

I finally had to do a mental "1... 2... 2½... 2¾.... 3!" in order to get it in my mouth. But once I did? Oh, man! It was the most delicious thing. Could it be? These gray, slimy blobs were actually good. I wanted more! By then, of course, everyone else had long since eaten my share. Lesson learned.

That time, it was an oyster, but there've been too many times I've let that happen in my life—waited too long to try or do something. And then, once I did, realized not only that it was not terrible, but it was something I really enjoyed... a lot! Oh, what fun I could have had if only I'd been brave enough to try things sooner!

The oyster incident, as it's referred to in our family, changed how I view so many things—and not just food. When something comes along that pushes me outside my comfort zone and I'm feeling hesitant, I remember that day. It helps give me the nudge I need to get out of my own shell. Obviously, I'm not advocating being reckless, but when opportunity knocks, now I say, "Eat the oyster!"

—Sara Todd-Stone—

78

Volunteered

To be outstanding — get comfortable
with being uncomfortable.
~Alrik Koudenburg

O h, this was horrifying. "Thank you for volunteering to coach soccer..." the letter began. Coach? Soccer? Me? That was insane. My knowledge of the sport began and ended with you-can't-use-your-hands. Later that afternoon, my six-year-old son informed me that goalies are allowed to use their hands. Who knew?

Data entry. When Community Sports asked for volunteers, I signed up for data entry. Keyboards, I knew. Coaching? Impossible! I quickly called the head coach about the misunderstanding. It did not go well. He had been transferred out of state and would not be coaching at all. Great.

As panic ensued, I called the other assistant coach. In broken English, he explained, "We just arrived from India. I know nothing. But I have time. I can learn game with my son." Mercy!

I phoned the Community Sports Commissioner about our dilemma. "I am sorry," he said. "Not enough parents are willing to volunteer. If you cannot coach, we will call your team and let them know they will not be playing this season." Seriously, that was his solution?

"Okay," I surrendered. "I will figure out something. Sure, put me down for coach."

"Good," he said. "We have a coaching clinic on Saturday. You might want to attend. It would help." Click.

With determined resolve, I picked up my son at school. He glanced through the coaching packet, intrigued by the pictures of drills. Then he laughed. "Hey, Mom! The word 'coach' is by your name. That is so funny."

Funny. I had to agree with his assessment. "Yes, son, I get to be your soccer coach. Since I don't know much about soccer, I need to learn. Let's start at the library." (This was the pre-Google era.)

At home, my husband looked at the stack of books and videos under one arm and the soccer ball in the other.

"What is all that?" he asked.

"Well, if I am to coach soccer," I responded with more confidence than I felt, "I will have to learn about the game, rules, and some practice drills."

"Okay. Sounds like a plan. And what about that?" He pointed at the soccer ball.

What a dumb question, I thought. "If I am going to teach a bunch of first graders about soccer, I think it best if I practiced the drills and ball handling myself. So, we stopped at Walmart and bought a soccer ball."

"Uh, coach," came his hesitant reply, "that there... is a volleyball."

I am happy to report that I can now tell the difference between a volleyball and a soccer ball. The books and videos helped. I recruited our neighbor to assist in the endeavor. He had missed the registration deadline and asked if his youngest son could join our team. I asked the commissioner whether a player could register late if his dad volunteered to assist me as a coach. The commissioner responded, "Sure, but that is not how we normally recruit coaches."

Yeah, I know. You usually wait until they volunteer for data entry and then trick them into coaching. But I didn't say it aloud.

My newly recruited assistant coach convinced his older son — a high-school varsity soccer player — to join us as well. Our Saturday morning practices and scrimmages were quite interesting.

Our varsity player showed off his skills while our pint-size team practiced theirs. My assistant coach from India sometimes blended the two languages in his excitement, which produced some comical action on the field.

Although progress was evident, I was frustrated that our drills and games did not resemble the ones in the books. My neighbor provided a much-needed perspective. "Remember, these are first graders. This is a game. It is supposed to be fun. If our team is running in the same direction, at the same time, and it is toward the correct goal... then, hey, we're doing good!"

I was not qualified to coach soccer for seventeen first graders, but because I stepped over the comfort zone boundary, they got to kick a soccer ball on Saturday mornings. My son and assistant coaches were the only ones who knew how unqualified I was. With their support and encouragement, I was able to overcome my biggest obstacle: my fear that everyone would find out I didn't even know how much I didn't know.

Along the way, I learned that success isn't measured on a scoreboard. However, the lesson I treasure most from that endeavor is this: When I stepped out of my comfort zone with a volleyball in my hand, I made a difference. Nowhere is that difference more evident than in me.

— Marie T. Palecek —

79

Riding Shotgun in a Semi

When we say yes, we do more, create more, live more.
~Author Unknown

"Mom, please, just go and have a good time! We'll be fine!" My daughter was becoming more and more emphatic, virtually dragging me from the car toward the huge yellow Freightliner.

Each time I think back upon that night so many years ago, I am consumed with myriad emotions: sadness, serenity, love, grief — but, above all, gratitude.

Larry and I met and began dating when I was a senior in high school and he was nearing the end of his military commitment. We married young, bought our first home, and began to raise a family.

Several years down the road, Larry decided to switch from driving trucks locally to taking a job driving an eighteen-wheeler cross-country. It was the only way we could achieve our dream of owning a house in the country. Although the decision was mutual, it wasn't easy. I had been a stay-at-home mom since the day our first child was born. Now, there were five, and my husband was on the road more than he was home.

I was running every which way to get them where they needed to be for their sports activities, making certain their homework was done, putting meals on the table, and ensuring they had clean clothes for school.

But we did manage to move to our brand-new, large, two-story home in the country where we felt safe, settled, and happy. The kids kept me profoundly busy, but I loved being a mom.

I served on soccer and gymnastic boards, and fulfilled parental volunteer obligations with football, basketball, cheerleading, baseball and track. Their dad was awesome and attended the kids' activities whenever he was home and called to check on things every night when he was on the road.

Ultimately, Larry became discontented working for large trucking companies as a team driver and considered buying his own tractor-trailer. This would give him the freedom to choose the runs he wanted, possibly allow him more time at home, and permit him to take family members on the truck with him.

I was exceptionally excited about the idea of tagging along on future trips across the country — that is, until the opportunity actually presented itself!

"Hon, I've got a good run to Miami. Ready to go?"

"I… I was thinking… Maybe I should wait until the kids are on summer break," I stammered with panic. In truth, I was scared to venture from the comforts of home — the kids, the routine, the only life I'd ever known.

Although the thought of a relaxing getaway with my husband was certainly enticing, I felt my place was at home with the kids. My emotions were all over the place, from anxiety, fear, confusion and regret to guilt.

It would be different if it were only a single week, but I feared one trip would lead to the next, and I'd be away from home most of the time just as my husband had for years.

By late spring, the kids had convinced me that, with one of them already out of school and the next two only a year away from high school graduation, they would be perfectly fine without me.

When the big day arrived, our daughter drove me from our home in Sandy to Portland to meet Larry.

Along the way, my thoughts ricocheted back and forth between elation and anxiety. I had never traveled far from Oregon, where I'd lived my entire life, having only briefly visited the four bordering states: Washington, Idaho, California and Nevada.

For the umpteenth time, I rattled off countless cautions for my daughter to keep in mind while I was gone. No wonder she was overly eager to get me out of the car and into her dad's truck.

When Larry jumped down from the driver's side and greeted each of us with a huge hug, a warm feeling of expectation enveloped me. It had been a long time since we'd been able to spend time alone together. This was going to be an enchanting adventure!

Larry had picked up a load of lumber in Vancouver, BC, earlier in the day, and we were headed to Atlanta, Georgia. How exciting! I'd always wanted to visit the southern states.

That first trip did not disappoint. It was nice not having to think about my usual daily responsibilities. Instead, my thoughts were focused on the breathtaking, diverse landscapes.

Cities, states, highways, rivers and special points of interest that were once simply symbols on a map came to life, as did the locales I'd only encountered through reading books or watching movies and television shows.

I felt free and energized, much like the warm, gentle breeze blowing through the open truck windows. Larry seemed remarkably happy that I'd decided to tag along, and I was happy, too!

By the end of our trip, I had, for the first time in my life, traveled through twenty-four new states, splashed in the warm ocean water on the East Coast (our West Coast ocean water is icy cold), eaten several unbelievably delicious truck stop meals, and slept ten nights in the truck's comfy sleeper next to my husband.

Although I was happy to be home, it was sad watching Larry leave on the next trip. However, during the summer, the kids took turns going with him and thoroughly enjoyed themselves.

We had decided that I should try to alternate between staying home and joining him on the truck.

Eventually, we were able to buy a brand-new Mack truck with a huge walk-in sleeper, which made it convenient to take our two little grandsons along. This was always a good time for all. The boys especially loved our side trips to Disney World. Obviously, they had Grandpa wrapped around their little fingers.

It may have taken a semitruck to get me out of my comfort zone, but I have zero regrets about the years I spent with my husband on the road. We met wonderful people, took in some amazing sights, and made a multitude of memories as we traveled back and forth throughout the forty-eight contiguous states and into parts of Canada.

It proved to be a good decision for us and our kids. While Larry and I were able to spend more quality time together, the kids learned the importance of being there for each other. While I managed to broaden my world perspective, they learned to take on more responsibility and become more independent.

As a family, we became more understanding and appreciative of each other.

Although it had crossed our minds that we'd have time together after Larry retired, it was a blessing that we didn't wait. Sadly, I lost my husband when he was in his late fifties, years before he would have retired.

Since tomorrow is never promised, I continually encourage my children and their spouses to spend as much time as possible together — even if it means riding shotgun in a semi.

— Connie Kaseweter Pullen —

80

Downhill All the Way

Do one thing every day that scares you.
~Eleanor Roosevelt

I stood straddling a yellow road bike, dressed in the matching Day-Glo jacket and pants provided by the tour company, and felt the trepidation of elementary-school gym class return in all its stomach-churning glory. Only I wasn't a kid anymore. I was thirty-four, married, and had paid good money to do this.

It was 4:00 in the morning. Earlier, about a dozen of us were picked up at our hotel in Maui and driven by van to a location 6,500 feet above sea level. We were now gathered at the edge of the dormant Haleakalā volcano and staring into its crater, which was large enough to hold Manhattan.

My husband and I had signed up for the Maui Downhill with our friends, another couple who had done the sunrise bike tour on a previous vacation. More than a decade older than me, neither was particularly athletic, so I believed them when they assured me it wouldn't matter that I hadn't been on a bike since I was fifteen.

The sky was dark, and as we looked down on layers of clouds, my breath formed smaller puffs in the frigid air. The guardrail separating the blacktop from the drop-off into the crater was ridiculously short — knee-level at best. Would the clouds catch me if I went over?

The athletic dude leading the tour called out instructions to our group. We were to ride behind him, single file, and keep our eyes toward the center line of the road.

"Your bike goes where your eyes go," he told us. Another tour guide would follow in the van.

True to its name, this was a downhill ride. It didn't demand strength or endurance, but it did require a comfort level on the bike, which I quickly determined I didn't have.

One by one, we climbed on our bikes and began following our leader down the volcano's winding road.

It's just like riding a bike. Remember that stupid expression? No one tells you that you *can* forget how to ride. I wasn't used to navigating hairpin curves and was trying to steer the front tire into each turn, gripping the handlebars with shaky hands. Afraid to go faster and careen over the cliff, I quickly ended up at the rear of the pack. My husband hung back to keep an eye on me, which only added to the pressure I felt.

I was the kid who hated gym class, who couldn't run fast or climb a rope. Team sports and relay races made me anxious that I'd cause my side to lose. As an adult, I'd mostly managed to avoid embarrassing situations in which I appeared weak or inept.

Our leader waved us all to a stop at the side of the road to allow a line of cars to pass. Really? Traffic, this early? On a volcano? Why on earth had I agreed to this?

"We ride as fast as the slowest rider," he announced. "If anyone here feels uncomfortable or like they can't keep up, raise your hand."

I glanced around. The rest of our group, a mix of ages and genders, looked unconcerned as they stood astride their bikes. I knew it would soon be obvious to everyone that I didn't know what I was doing. I imagined each person's annoyance as I slowed the pace and ruined what should have been the highlight of their trip. Without looking at my husband or friends, I sheepishly raised my hand.

"Come up front behind me," he said.

For the rest of that ride, I was second in line. I started out awkward and wobbly, a newborn foal learning to stand. Then, I gradually gained confidence. The leader showed me how to lean into turns instead of steering into them. I mimicked what he did, and, amazingly, once I relaxed, my body remembered how to ride. It was just like riding a bike.

The road through Haleakalā National Park was a breathtaking tour of terrains. Once below cloud-level, we passed through lush green forests, red earthen fields, and groves of eucalyptus trees that filled the air with their invigorating fragrance.

We stopped at a restaurant partway down, and I shared my exhilaration with my husband and friends. I couldn't wait to get back on my bike. As the sun rose higher, the temperature did, too. We peeled off our windbreakers, pants and gloves, and tossed them into the van.

Hours later, the final stretch of our ride took us directly onto the white-sand beach. By then, I was coasting at top speed in shorts and a T-shirt, with my sunglasses reflecting the sharp blue sky and a huge grin plastered on my face. I felt triumphant.

That experience stayed with me, and I began questioning my risk-averse nature. I'd always been careful to stay in my lane, stick with my strengths. I thought about all the adventures I'd missed because of my own insecurities. How many times I'd sat on the sidelines rather than chance looking foolish? No one had batted an eye when I raised my hand and admitted to feeling uncomfortable on my bike.

I would continue to draw courage and inspiration from my Maui Downhill ride.

Months later, I received a postcard advertising a tennis club in my area. I recalled how much I'd enjoyed taking lessons as a teenager — one of the few sports I liked playing — and signed up for a private session. I had so much fun that I began signing up for weekly clinics with other beginners. I'd recently left my corporate job to launch my own freelance business (another adventure) and had a flexible schedule. If I could ride down a volcano, surely I could handle tennis lessons.

Tennis became a major part of my life. My husband started playing, and we bought a Friday night doubles contract, rotating in a handful of women and men who fast became friends. I joined a women's team and clicked well with one of my teammates. One day, we tried testing our friendship off-court. Years later, we replaced Friday-night tennis with weekly double dates. We're still best friends.

My bike ride inspired me to say yes to other experiences, too. Once I let go of the belief that I had to be good at something in order to participate, new possibilities opened up. I discovered I like the feeling of learning, of challenging myself to follow my curiosity and lean into the discomfort of being a novice—much as I leaned into those hairpin turns.

At forty, I drove my daughter to a skating party. Instead of sitting with the other moms, I rented Rollerblades and had a blast. I later bought my own.

At forty-four, I said yes to Hoop Camp, a three-day gathering of (mostly younger) hula hoop enthusiasts among the California redwoods.

At fifty-three, I registered for a writing course and began sharing my stories, summoning the courage of my much-younger self as she timidly raised her hand and admitted her vulnerability on a bike.

Each new venture has added another layer to the story I tell about myself.

—Abby Alten Schwartz—

81

A Pilgrimage to the New Me

Walk slow, don't rush. That place
you have to reach is yourself.
~José Ortega y Gasset

On Tuesday, June 13, 2006, I dropped my backpack to the cobblestones, gave a shout of joy, and hugged my daughter-in-law Marina and her mom, Iris. We had just completed a 194-mile trek along the Camino de Santiago (Way of Saint James). It had all started a year earlier when Marina and Iris suggested we tackle a portion of the ancient pilgrimage. My son had hiked the entire 490-mile Camino Frances route from the Pyrenees mountains to Finisterre on Spain's western shore soon after graduating from college. He'd raved about his trek and had been urging us three women to experience the adventure.

I shook my head and laughed. "Are you kidding?"

Marina, age twenty-seven, had youth and energy. Iris and I were both fifty-eight, but she walked several miles every day and had even participated in a half-marathon. My idea of exercise was an occasional turn on the treadmill or a stroll around the subdivision. For me, tackling the Way of Saint James seemed like scaling Mount Rainier.

However, as I neared sixty, I made a decision to say yes to opportunities more often. Could I walk across Spain with Marina and Iris? Maybe. We discussed the possibility for several months, and the idea grew in my imagination. On February 1, I started working toward that goal. I walked the hills of my neighborhood, included more vegetables and grains in my diet (and fewer sweets), and faithfully swallowed a daily multivitamin supplement. I bought a pair of hiking boots and a backpack. Weeks passed, and I grew stronger and more confident.

With only three weeks available for our adventure, Marina, Iris, and I researched the pilgrimage route and determined how much of the Camino we could cover in the allotted time. The segment from León to Santiago de Compostela in northern Spain seemed the most logical itinerary for the time available to us.

I checked out books from the library and learned that the Camino retraced the route followed by the Apostle Saint James across the Iberian Peninsula. It had been a pilgrimage route since the ninth and tenth centuries, with the first Camino guidebook written in 1139. I read online journals posted by modern pilgrims who had recently made the trek and imagined myself walking alongside them.

On May 27, I flew to Spain with Marina and Iris. After a short train ride from Madrid, we arrived in León, spent the night in a hostel, and took our first official steps as pilgrims the next morning. The red numbers on a nearby thermometer gave me pause: 3.5 degrees C (38 degrees F). Had I packed warm enough clothes? I shivered. Even worse, the route out of town was not well-marked. What if we got lost? Farther on, we were afraid we'd somehow missed Hospital de Órbigo because the sign on the main road had conflicting messages. Should we go left or right? To our relief, other hikers we encountered were happy to share their knowledge, and signs, yellow arrows, and shell markers (the Camino's symbol) became plentiful.

Seventeen days later, the three of us stood in the square outside the Cathedral of Santiago de Compostela and whooped with joy. On our shortest day, we had walked 13.2 km (8.2 miles); on our longest, 22.5 km (14 miles). We'd crossed plains, clambered up rock-strewn hills, sweated, and shivered. We'd eaten bocadillos (sandwiches), chorizo (pork sausage), and tapas. I'd even tasted pulpo (octopus) at lunch in Galicia. It was delicious but definitely not my usual diet.

We'd spent nights in hostels (albergues) with varying degrees of comfort. They ranged from dormitories filled with dozens of bunk beds that squeaked with every movement to a luxury room with only three twin beds. Every evening, my muscles ached, and moleskin covered the blisters on my toes. But, after a day of physical exercise, insomnia was not a problem.

My endurance and self-assurance had grown with every step. I'd made friends with fellow pilgrims from around the world — Swedes, Spaniards, Germans, Japanese, Australians, Americans, young and old. It seemed every pilgrim had a story and shared them as we covered the miles. Their hopes and dreams weren't very different from my own, and I felt a connection I hadn't expected. Best of all, I came to know Marina and Iris very well. We formed a bond and relied on each other in a way that we probably wouldn't have achieved under normal day-to-day circumstances. When we reached the cobblestones surrounding the cathedral, I felt as thrilled as Edmund Hillary must have been when he reached the summit of Mount Everest.

On our hike from León to Santiago de Compostela I felt a kinship with those who had made this walk before me. I swelled with pride at my accomplishment. To commemorate my achievement, I bought a pair of silver earrings in Santiago and carried them home.

Now, at age seventy-five, I routinely hike with a group from the senior center in my small town. When I first registered to participate, I wasn't sure of my abilities. What if I couldn't keep up? What if I became injured? Then, I thought of my Camino adventure and the souvenir I'd purchased. I looked in the mirror as I fastened the silver earrings to my ears, reminded of the pilgrimage in Spain. Shoulders back, head lifted, earrings glistening in the sun, I joyfully stepped out of my comfort zone again, bolstered by the knowledge that I could achieve more than I'd anticipated and fueled with the energizing spirit gained when I said yes to a walk along the Camino de Santiago.

— Sandra Nachlinger —

82

Where Are You Supposed to Be?

*Change is the law of life. And those who look only to
the past or present are certain to miss the future.*
~John F. Kennedy

t was Day Four of summer break. I sat alone on the front porch, hoping the warm morning sun would melt away my fear. I had only one more paycheck before I was no longer contributing to the household budget. And I was the steady paycheck. Every time I panicked I would second-guess the decision I'd made three months earlier to resign from my private-school teaching position.

I thought about the peace I felt when I did the "Where are you supposed to be?" trick. I learned this from my beloved grandmother, our family's beautiful matriarch and wellspring of simple and profound wisdom. No matter what dilemma I faced, she would sit with me and ask, "Where are you supposed to be?" I have to say this question had a 100-percent track record of helping me make the right choices.

When it was time for the question, my grandmother and I would sit down where there were no distractions. First, I would imagine myself making the decision one way. I would close my eyes and sense what would happen if I followed that path. I remained in that moment for one minute without opening my eyes. Then, I would open and reclose my eyes and imagine making the decision a different way. I would consider what it would be like to go that way instead. Every time I used that question I would sense which direction was more positive for me, and I would make my choice with calm assurance.

Suddenly my phone rang. "Are you available for an interview next Tuesday at 10:45?" I couldn't believe my ears. One of the most sought-after public-school systems was calling me for an interview. This was an incredible opportunity! Word on the street was that there were more than fifty people applying for every open position. I thought there was absolutely no way that I would ever even get an interview, let alone be hired. Now, they were calling me to schedule an interview!

"Tuesday? As in next Tuesday, the ninth?" I asked. *Please don't say the ninth. Any day but next week.*

"Yes," the administrative assistant replied.

She said the ninth. Okay, calm down. Just ask for another date.

"I'm leaving on an anniversary cruise on Sunday with my husband, and we will be gone all next week. Is there an option to schedule an interview for the following week?"

"No. We are making a decision on Tuesday the ninth."

My heart sank. "Then," my voice broke, "I'm sorry, but I will have to decline the invitation to interview."

"Okay," she replied. "Thanks so much. Good luck on your job search." The phone clicked.

Now I was frustrated. Ever since I was a little girl, my dream was to work in public schools as a music teacher. This phone call was my chance to make that dream come true and teach where my children would attend. Yet here I was turning it down because of a cruise. My face fell into my hands, and my fingertips firmly rubbed the tension in my forehead. I had worked so hard to get the degree and certification, including holding down a full- and part-time job while raising two kids. Why was I choosing to walk away from the best opportunity I ever had to get the job of my dreams?

Where are you supposed to be?

That question was prompting me. But I didn't have a choice. Or did I? Maybe I could postpone the cruise and go to the interview. Wait, no. That idea was simply ludicrous. My (then) husband would be furious with that decision. I always seemed to make him angry. Canceling a cruise would surely be a whopper to add to the list. Besides, it was too late to cancel and get any of our money back, and

I had already declined the interview. It was too late to call back and take the interview. Or was it?

Where are you supposed to be?

I felt the urge to close my eyes and imagine myself at the interview. Suddenly, I saw myself talking to people… smiling… answering questions better than any other candidate… feeling excited to share how my experiences would be a great asset to the school… my dream of being a public-school music teacher coming true… I opened my eyes and felt happy, elated, and filled with purpose. I took three deep breaths and closed my eyes. This time, I was on the deck overlooking pristine blue waters… eating an omelet… drinking coffee… listening to steel-drum music… and I'm just… sitting there. When I opened my eyes, I was not as happy, elated, or filled with purpose as I was when I opened my eyes after imagining the interview. I knew what I had to do.

"Um… Hi. Yes, we just spoke," I stammered. "I wanted to call you back and let you know that I canceled the cruise, and I will be there at 10:45 on Tuesday the ninth."

"You what?" she responded. "You canceled a cruise to interview for a job you may not even get?"

"Yes." This response was the most confident I had felt all morning… actually, in years.

"See you on the ninth," she said, surprise still in her voice.

Ten of the most wonderful years of my life were spent working in music education in that public-school system. I was named Teacher of the Year in 2012, named Grammy Semifinalist for Music Education in 2014, and also one of the Top 25 Music Teachers in the United States by Music and Arts in 2016. And now, I have returned to this wonderful school system in hopes of completing my career as a music educator. This incredible life journey all began one June morning when I faithfully acted on the answer to the question, "Where are you supposed to be?"

— Dana Lamb-Schaubroeck —

83

A Leap of Blind Love

Love is not something you protect.
It's something you risk.
~Gayle Forman

"**C**an one of you guys drive me home?" Angie asked. Our social time after the weekly Bible study was coming to a close, and most of the young singles were leaving. As usual, I hesitated and couldn't look her in the eye. Should I say yes to this pretty girl? Or should I say no and stay in my safe place, getting enough sleep before my early job at Disney?

My friend seemed to realize I wouldn't answer, so he offered her a ride. Now, I was thankful and depressed. Tonight was Angie's last night at our church before moving back to Ohio in a few days. That she'd asked me for my address only ten minutes earlier could be life-changing. In the early 1990s, social media was yet to be, so writing letters would be the only way we could keep in touch.

We talked and laughed a few more minutes, and I couldn't resist reaching for a hug. She had flowing auburn hair, playful brown eyes, and an engaging personality. To put it mildly, Angie was stunning.

For the past three months, we'd chatted briefly, but only at church when we'd both been there. I liked her but lacked the confidence to ask her out. The close group of twenty-something singles at our Orlando, Florida church had become almost second family. Although we'd go out after services as a group, my social awkwardness had held me back from real dating.

Angie wrote to me first, I wrote back, and we started writing each other almost weekly. Having Asperger's syndrome made sharing my thoughts and dreams easier on paper than face-to-face.

"I got another letter from Angie," I casually said to a few of the usual gang as we sat in our favorite diner after another Bible study.

After two months, our letters were still platonic, but two of the guys started humming the "Wedding March," grinning. I took it as a joke. The following month, I couldn't shake the butterflies in my stomach because of one line in her latest letter: "Forgive me for being so bold, but I hope the man I'm to marry is a lot like you."

Was this a hint? I responded with something similar, for the thrill was unstoppable. In her next letter, I already thought of her as mine. Soon, she wrote, "I really do hope you're the one for me." I'd always wanted a serious girlfriend but never had one because I was an introvert. In the following two or so weeks, we affirmed with each other that we felt we were meant to be together.

I was astounded that we were already talking about vague wedding plans before we even talked on the phone. This had all happened via letters, a blessing for me given my fear of dating. Proposing would be a breeze. Life was beyond good.

Then, two unnerving thoughts blindsided me. Of course, I was thrilled she was coming for a visit when we'd get engaged, actually date, and attend my cousin's wedding near Washington, D.C. But she'd probably try to talk me into riding Space Mountain at Disney, which I dreaded. I could get her into the parks without charge, so I knew we were going. I'd either have to deal with motion sickness or have her think I had no courage.

I ended up choosing the first option, prayed like crazy, and actually enjoyed the ride.

The bigger issue was how good I'd made myself look in my letters and recent phone conversations. She was gung-ho about us leading church youth group when we got married, hopefully a year from now. I had no leadership skills and feared speaking in front of people. But I hadn't told her that. "Sure, that sounds great, hon," I think I responded.

Watching for Angie at the bus station, while the ring lay in my car's glove compartment, I feared I wouldn't recognize her after our seven months apart.

My romantic proposal at flower-filled Leu Gardens, near Orlando, had gone just as planned. And, yes, we had our first dinner date ever after getting engaged. Angie was easy to get along with, and we had a few fun weeks. I did work up the nerve to tell her I didn't think I'd make a good youth leader, and I'm sure I must've shattered some perfect image of me in her head.

My biggest moment of courage came at my cousin's wedding. My family kept begging Angie to join the giggling, single girls lined up to catch the bouquet. She stood at the far side, not even trying.

It landed in her arms. My heart pounded. This meant I'd have to catch the garter to keep some other guy from putting it on her leg. I resolved to jump in front of the drunk guys to grab it — even reinjure my knee — if I had to.

I stared down my fears, claimed my position front and center, and ignored the joking guys behind me. I eyed that cloth garter soaring over the dance floor like a football player eyeing the winning touchdown pass at the Super Bowl.

Something supernatural took over me, and I caught it. Maybe it was fate.

Angie didn't know of the garter tradition. And I struggled to keep her calm while putting it on her, trying also to relish the roaring crowd. She laughed and cried at the same time, obviously embarrassed as I slipped it over her knee. I had to be okay with my family staring at us as we only had room to dance near their table.

Over the years, life has often been like Space Mountain, stepping out in fear. But it's been worth every minute. Angie and I recently celebrated our twenty-fifth anniversary.

— Norbert F. Markiewicz —

Put Yourself Out There

84

Planes, Trains, and Automobiles

Travel doesn't become adventure
until you leave yourself behind.
~Marty Rubin

wanted out. The year was 1998, and I was a University of Michigan undergrad who was tired of working the night shift at the graduate library. It wasn't the job itself that I had grown weary of, however. (During my four-hour shift, I checked out a handful of patrons on average, which hardly qualified as manual labor. Boredom was a far greater threat than exhaustion, but I digress.) No, I wanted out because I was tired of being broke.

I had expensive tastes that involved a hankering for omelets at an upscale café, impromptu trips to the record store, and the hope that I would eventually carry a black, nylon Kate Spade tote (because, again, it was the late 1990s). Also hanging over my head was the notion that I should get busy growing a nest egg for life after university.

Suffice it to say, my measly checks from the library did little to bring me closer to any of the above. Little did I know, my luck was about to change — but not in a way that I could have possibly imagined.

The summer before my senior year, I snagged an internship at a quaint yet established public-relations firm. Despite its respected and well-connected clientele, the company's day-to-day atmosphere was unbelievably casual. The owner, Marcia, even treated us to Friday evening happy hours at a local golf course.

One morning, I arrived to find Marcia engaged in a rather lively phone conversation with someone I would later learn was her cousin Pam, a modeling agent. When I quietly slid into my chair and attempted to disappear behind my computer monitor, Marcia grew quiet.

"I think I have someone," she whispered into her receiver before taking a long drag from her cigarette. "I'll let you know. Okay. Bye."

The next thing I knew, I was sitting in the lobby of Pam's agency.

If someone had told me earlier that morning when I was pouring my cereal that I would be auditioning for the International Auto Show tour by lunchtime, I would have told them that they had the wrong girl.

If you've never frequented an auto show before, here's an illustration of what the cost of a ticket buys you: Envision roughly 1,000 never-before-driven cars, trucks, and SUVs basking under the glow of bright recessed lighting and elaborately displayed throughout 700,000 square feet of exhibition space. Innovative kiosks punctuate the landscape, and hundreds of attentive, well-manicured representatives who represent every automotive brand (foreign and domestic) are on hand to answer any and all questions. Like a casino, windows and clocks are nowhere to be found, which endorses the illusion of time standing still.

In short, an auto show is car nirvana for gearheads as well as a fun escape for those looking to be entertained.

Three grueling interviews and two long weeks later, I was offered a narrating position with Honda. (I was joining the ranks of the men and women who stand on turntables and give spiels about the car.) And, after a month of thorough training — and getting my upcoming absences excused by my professors — I was ready for my first show in Boston, Massachusetts. I don't know what excited me more: performing live before thousands of people or receiving a check worth several times more than what I could have ever earned at the library.

Looking back, I now refer to that time of my life as The Autumn of Firsts because there were plenty, starting with how I would get to the show in the first place. I was twenty-one years old, and while I had flown before, I had never boarded an airplane alone. Parking my car, nabbing a shuttle, and then navigating the airport infused me with a sense of confidence that I found exhilarating.

After a refreshing flight — mind you, this was back when meals were provided for free — I took a taxi to the luxurious Copley Plaza Hotel on St. James Avenue. When I finally pulled up to the curb, my eyes traveled upward to take in my home for the next ten days. Then, I encountered another first: my very own hotel room. *Pinch me,* I thought.

My first day on the show floor was a blur and, at times, overwhelming. By the end of my shift, my toes were screaming for an escape from my pricey Stuart Weitzman pumps, and I resisted the urge to stand barefoot as I rode the elevator back to my room. I was beat, yes, but not so fatigued that I couldn't recognize valuable information when I heard it.

The words "Filene's," "big," and "sale" were what stood out when I tried hanging on to every word from the two impeccably dressed women in front of me. I called the concierge as soon as I reached my room. Apparently, Filene's Basement, a department store, was the destination for those seeking high-end clothing at a deep discount. And it was just a subway ride away. I hung up and calculated the time it would take to make it there and back tomorrow morning before my afternoon shift. If I skipped breakfast, I would have a decent shot.

The next morning, I made my way to Filene's, driven by adrenaline and the prospect of unprecedented bargains. And here's another first: I had never ridden mass transit before. I sat eagle-eyed by the window to ensure I wouldn't miss my stop. When I finally crossed the threshold into the store, I was certain that skipping breakfast was a wise choice. I was (and continue to be) that girl who carefully digs through clearance racks for any whiff of a juicy markdown, so I needed all the time I could get.

I was rooting through a bin of Emilio Pucci bikinis when I saw it. At first, I thought I was seeing things: the Kate Spade tote of my dreams.

I took that sucker to the checkout so fast that I nearly tripped over my own feet.

The purchase ate up what remained of my per diem and killed any prospect of ordering room service for the remainder of my stay, but I didn't care. I was a tremendously happy camper.

Oh, the places that tote has been since that day.

It accompanied me to every auto show I worked from coast to

coast and served as a back-up diaper bag after the birth of my first child thirteen years later.

John Lennon said, "Life is what happens while you're busy making other plans."

I have another way of putting it: Life is also what happens when you're tired of working at the library and wind up seizing the chance to travel the country with a bunch of cars instead.

—Courtney Conover—

A Sportscaster's Advice

Because if you take a risk, you just
might find what you're looking for.
~Susane Colasanti

When a nerdy teenager (me) joins a youth group at her parents' urging, the adventure can evolve in a lot of directions. My adventure brought with it a powerful lesson from a man I respected but didn't expect to meet.

St. Mark's Community Center sat on the edge of the French Quarter in my native New Orleans. I had attended the Girl Scout program there until it ended. My parents didn't want to see me slip back into my bookworm ways, so they encouraged me to join the teen group at the center. Wait, boys and girls in the same group outside of school? That sounded scary. I was ready to run back to my hideout at the neighborhood library, but my parents insisted.

The first meeting I attended marked a new activity year and featured an ice-breaker program based on a scavenger hunt. We were divided into teams, given our lists, and sent out into the neighborhood to find our target items. I followed my assigned group from a position a few paces back. Most of them seemed to know each other, and I felt like a total outsider.

We roamed up and down the local streets as we accumulated our prizes. A couple of boys seemed to know all the best spots to look for the items and we ticked them off the list one by one.

Time was running out on our quest as we came to the only item missing: a political button. None of the houses we'd called on in the neighborhood had one. The team was about to call our task done when I finally found the courage to speak up.

"How about the television studio?" I asked. One of our local stations, WWL-TV, had a studio a block away from the community center. "They might have one. They have lots of politicians as guests."

Our leaders conferred and decided the new girl might have a decent idea. We made our way to the studio.

"You go in and ask," one of them said, and pushed me forward.

Well, it was my idea, so I guess it was my job. I took a deep breath and headed into the lobby. A young man looked up from his position behind a big desk.

"Can I help you?" he asked.

I explained I was part of a group from St. Mark's on a scavenger hunt and in urgent need of a political button. "Please, would you happen to have one you don't need?"

He smiled and then rummaged around in his desk for a few minutes.

"Sorry, I don't have one." He seemed genuinely sad to have failed.

"Thanks for trying," I said and turned away.

"Wait a minute," he said. "Let me see if one of the staff might have one." He disappeared into the depths of the studio, leaving me there to peruse the artwork in the lobby.

A few minutes later, the door he had used opened again. The figure coming through the door was not the young man. Oh, no. This was an icon of New Orleans television and one of my heroes: Hap Glaudi. Mr. Glaudi was my favorite sportscaster, the man who related our school team's scores each week and cheered us on with his comments. I stood in speechless amazement.

"So, young lady, tell me why you need a political button this evening. You impressed our desk clerk, and he really wants us to solve your problem." His voice sounded every bit as friendly and kind as he did on the air.

"Mr. Glaudi, I'm so sorry to bother you. I'm in the youth group over at St. Mark's, and we're on a scavenger hunt. We haven't found a button, and we're running out of time. I thought if anyone in the neighborhood would have one, it would be the station. Please, would you know if there is one around?" I could feel the heat creeping up my face. Did my request sound as stumbling and bumbling as it felt?

He paused for a moment and looked me in the eye.

"Are you afraid of me?" he asked.

"No, sir, but I know you must be busy, and I'm interrupting you. Please forgive me. I'll just leave."

He held out his hand. Nestled there was a colorful circle, a campaign button from the previous year's presidential election.

"Always remember one thing. If you respectfully ask for help, you give the other person a chance to be a good guy. You're giving as well as getting. Don't ever apologize or be embarrassed to be part of that process." He handed me the pin and smiled. "Thank you for letting me help."

I smiled back and thanked him. When I brought the button back to the team, they whooped at my success. We ran back to the Center to check in.

Our team won that night by one item. We had the only campaign button in the competition, a nice coup. I wish I could say my contribution got me "in" with the group, but my innate nerdiness overshadowed my accomplishment. I dropped out within a few weeks. But my life course was changed.

More than half a century later, the encounter lives clearly in my memory. Although I can't remember any of the kids in the group, there's one thing I've never forgotten: Hap Glaudi's kindness and advice. Thanks to him, I've found the courage to approach people for interviews as a journalist; ask for donations or volunteer time as a fundraiser; and experience myriad other opportunities when a polite, respectful request opened the door. Most of the time, the people I've approached have responded favorably. Thanks to a great man's advice, I've had some amazing adventures. I've also tried to live up to the other side of the equation: to follow his example and help where I can.

—Mary Beth Magee—

86

Hola, Confidence

If you look confident you can pull off anything—
even if you have no clue what you're doing.
~Jessica Alba

finally landed in Chicago and caught a cab to a hotel that I could barely afford. As I checked in, an uncomfortable nervousness overcame me. How had my mother convinced me to attend this conference alone?

"It will be an adventure," my mother had said.

An adventure it was.

I had just completed my first year of law school when the Hispanic Bar Association advertised its yearly conference. Being only one of two Hispanics in my law school class, I could not find anyone interested in joining me. Although I considered myself outgoing, I didn't like doing things alone.

I unpacked my suitcase, changed into business casual attire, and headed to the hotel's top floor to attend the preliminary events for the conference attendees. As I stepped off the elevator, I thought of my mother's words, "Many people attend these events alone. You'll be fine." At that moment, a young Hispanic woman walked past me with her eyes wide open and a big smile as she and another woman embraced. "Maria! So, nice to see you again!"

I cringed and started to get dizzy.

My mother had made me a promise. "If you feel anxious, call me." I felt comfort in that promise. The sound of her voice always calmed me.

Mom answered after the first ring. "Mom, people know each other. It's like a reunion," I said.

"Just be yourself. You'll meet people," she said.

I hung up the phone and attended a series of seminars for the next two days. Mainly, I engaged in small talk with whoever sat next to me. At every break between workshops, I called my mother to keep me moving forward. Each time, she answered on the first ring. My mother was my lifeline in an unfamiliar world of accomplished attorneys, judges, and only a sprinkle of law students who dared to attend.

The last day of the conference came — the gala. I was terrified. It was a semi-formal event to close the conference, an evening of cocktails, dinner, and live entertainment. I felt anxious as I put on my little black dress.

I took the elevator up to the ballroom. Before I took the plunge, I called my mother. Hearing her excitement gave me that last nudge I needed.

I approached the dinner table closest to the entrance just in case I needed a quick exit. As I was about to sit down, I heard someone at the next table call me over to join them. It was a New York lawyer whom I had met earlier that day at one of the seminars. Instantly, I began to feel less nervous.

The lawyer introduced me to all the attorneys at the table. I was the only law student. Dinner was fabulous, and the conversation flowed, with each lawyer giving me advice. After dinner, lawyers and judges walked around the ballroom, mingling with each other as salsa music played in the background.

As I looked around the ballroom, the New York lawyer motioned me to follow him. He wanted to introduce me to a judge from the U.S. Court of Appeals for the Second Circuit.

The judge was gracious and soft-spoken. I recall her striking, red power suit. I also fondly remember how kind and perceptive she was. I did not hesitate to ask if we could take a photo together.

I met many lawyers that evening, from prosecutors to corporate counsel. Upon returning to my room, I immediately called my mother and shared with her all the wonderful people I had met, especially the kind judge who took the time to talk to me.

That lovely Second Circuit judge I met now serves as the first Hispanic judge on the nation's highest court — Supreme Court Justice Sonia Sotomayor. And that photo we took together is my favorite souvenir of the legal conference that forced me out of my comfort zone over and over again, setting me on the path to being the confident woman I am today.

—N.L. Zuniga—

87

The Reluctant Entertainer

The shell must break before the bird can fly.
~Alfred, Lord Tennyson

I glared at my husband David. "I can't believe you're making me do this. Thanks to you, I'm going to make the biggest fool of myself I've ever made in my entire life! You know I hate being the center of attention."

"Just act like you know what you're doing," he said. "You'll be fine."

"Right!" I snapped. I got out of the car, grabbed my tip basket, slammed the car door and marched into the country club to meet my fate. A crowd had gathered in the banquet room for a romantic Valentine's dinner, and they awaited their entertainer for the night: me. I'd been hired to play love songs for the next several hours while cozy couples ate their dinners.

Granted, I was a seasoned musician; but I was also one of the biggest introverts on Earth. In my younger days, I'd played in a band, but with other band members. Throughout the years, I'd accompanied singers and played piano in church on a piano tucked in the corner. My husband and I had even performed a vocal duet, but he'd stood right beside me. In my wildest dreams, I couldn't imagine playing piano all alone where everyone would see and hear me.

How did I end up with this job? Well, David had been asked to play Valentine's night at two different places. Instead of turning down one of the jobs, he'd decided that I could play the extra gig for him. We were deep in debt, and he figured the money would come in handy and I wouldn't mind helping out. Boy, was he wrong. I did mind but felt I had no choice in the matter.

Valentine's Day was six weeks away, which meant I had to learn a hundred songs in all genres ranging from tunes our parents enjoyed to the latest hits for the younger generation. I'd have to learn to play them by ear since there wasn't time to find and buy music. It didn't help that I hadn't touched a keyboard or piano in years.

Surprisingly, the romantic dinner at the country club went okay despite a few goof-ups. Taking my husband's words to heart, I acted as if I knew what I was doing and even managed to make a decent amount in tips to add to the money the club paid me. I survived. Barely. And I swore I'd never do anything like it again.

Once we got home, I made us sandwiches, and we sat down to eat.

David took a bite, swallowed and looked me in the eye. "The country club wants me to play at their Sunday brunch," he said.

I stared at my sandwich and felt sick. I knew exactly where this was heading, and I wanted no part in it.

"It seems a shame to let all those songs you learned go to waste. You could play my usual brunch, and I could play the country club. It would bring in some much-needed money."

"I can't do it," I said. "You're comfortable performing solo in front of people. I'm not." But it didn't matter how I felt; David was right. We were in debt up to our eyeballs.

The first few times I played on Sunday, I was so angry with my husband that I sat at the piano like a dud and pounded out my songs while watching the clock. I also didn't make many tips.

One Sunday, David got off early from his brunch and showed up to listen to me play. "You'll never make any tips if you sit there with that dead-looking face," he said. "You need to connect with your audience, or you might as well not even be here."

After that, my anger melted away, and my attitude changed. I opened my heart to this uncomfortable situation and realized I was there for one reason: to give the customers a great time so they would enjoy their meal and want to come back. And they did.

Eventually, my jitters disappeared, and I started looking forward to entertaining each week. I got to know all the customers who came each Sunday and greeted them by playing their favorite songs. I gave them hugs and got to know their families. I gained a large following, but they were no longer customers; they had become my dearest friends.

My co-workers at the restaurant were so caring and supportive. I couldn't have asked for better people to work with.

I played every Sunday plus extra performances for holiday brunches and also got booked for private parties and weddings. Little by little, the introvert who wanted to hide in the corner and not talk to anyone disappeared.

For thirteen years, I got to work at a job I loved with people I enjoyed seeing and talking to. And while the money helped a lot, stepping out of my safe, secure hole was the real reward.

—Jill Burns—

88

My Challenge List

The only way out is through.
~Robert Frost

"Six slick slim sycamore saplings and five thrifty fun fifty-somethings..." I chanted along with the rest of the group as I tried to slow my breathing. We finished our warm-ups and lined up behind the door. Somehow, I ended up at the front of the line, placed my shaky palm on the doorknob, and prepared myself to open it and walk on stage.

Three years ago, I found myself with my hand on another doorknob, on my dorm-room door, trying to gather the strength to turn it. Every weekend, I told myself that this time I would open the door and join in with the students merrily chatting and laughing in the hallway. But, instead, I would put an eye to the peephole and watch the brave people who weren't afraid to leave their rooms.

After a semester stuck behind my door, I decided that something needed to change. I started to look online for advice on how to make friends at college. I felt embarrassed because it was a skill that I thought most people had developed in kindergarten. But as I looked at online forums and articles, I found stories of other people who had the same struggles. And as I read these stories, I started to see the words "social anxiety" appear over and over.

When I looked up the term, I found that the definition suited me perfectly: a disorder characterized by feeling fear in social situations and of being judged by others, which often causes anxiety and avoidance of social interaction. Check, check, and check. And while I wasn't thrilled that I seemed to have a mental-health disorder, I was relieved that my thoughts and feelings had an explanation, and that I wasn't alone in feeling this way.

Further reading on websites devoted to social anxiety helped me to learn that having social anxiety wasn't a life sentence. I learned that I could change my anxious thoughts and feelings through cognitive behavioral therapy. This type of therapy involves exposing yourself to situations where you feel fear and anxiety and learn through experience how to deal with these situations and how not to fear them. It was scary to think about facing my fears, but I decided I might as well try.

At the top of a page in my journal I wrote the words "Challenge List," and I started writing down all the things that I wanted to do that made me scared. I called them challenges for two reasons. One was that I never backed down from a challenge. I always did the hardest problems on my math homework first and even went to middle school at a place called The Challenge School. The second was that these things may not be challenges for most people, but they were for me. They spanned everything from "saying hi to people I know when I pass them" to "asking someone to eat lunch with me" and "starting a conversation with a stranger." And while they were my challenges, I believed they weren't insurmountable.

I chose a new challenge to be my goal every week, so I could begin to face my different fears. For the first week, I decided to say "hi" to everyone I knew. Whenever I passed someone on the sidewalk, I briefly considered looking down and walking by, but then I thought about my challenge and how I wanted to complete it. I would look up and greet them. That first week, I learned that simply saying "hi" meant that I got into many more conversations than I expected. Even when it didn't go further than saying hello, it felt good to be friendly and make little connections. No one thought I was strange or rejected me. They were happy to greet me back.

I moved on to the harder challenges. When I asked people to have lunch with me, I found that they were excited to talk to me and get to know me. And when I had conversations with strangers, I found that I made more new friends. Even when I didn't, I enjoyed talking more than staying silent.

Soon, I started going beyond the challenges — starting conversations with strangers even when that wasn't my challenge or just going out of my way to engage in social situations. It became second nature to do these challenges. At the end of the semester, I no longer needed to pick a goal for every week because I was challenging myself daily and seeking out ways to push myself every moment I could. I found that these challenges weren't so challenging anymore, and they just became part of my everyday life.

Now, I readily take actions that used to make my stomach tense and my mind fret for days. I always try to meet as many new people as I can. I often initiate going to meals or events with friends. And my job as a radio producer means I talk with people all the time, and I record pieces that are broadcast to audiences every week. Yet sometimes I still need a reminder to get out of my comfort zone, so I flip to that journal page with the list I made four years ago. I remind myself of the challenges I've overcome and remember to keep striving.

And that's what I was doing behind that stage door: preparing myself to tell a story in front of a live audience of my peers. It's something I've always wanted to do since I saw the storytellers perform my first year, but I never believed I would make it up on that stage. Now, it's one more challenge I decided to complete in my final year at college. I took another deep breath and thought about my resolution to keep facing my fears and how proud I am that I've gotten this far. Without another thought, I turned the knob, rushed out onto the stage, and began to speak. When I finished the story, the crowd began clapping and cheering, but the loudest cheer I heard was my own.

— Molly Magid —

Can You Count to Three?

Don't step backward toward nothing,
step forward toward something. Better awkward
steps forward than coward steps backward.
~Victoria Addino

Mom drummed her fingers on the small restaurant lounge table. Her lips were pursed. Her facial expression was either disgust, annoyance or both.

"It's a good band, don't you think?" I asked.

She shrugged. "What use is a good band when no one is dancing to it?"

I laughed. "You know how to fix that."

Mother gave me a deer-in-headlights look, indicating she had no idea what I was talking about.

"The 1990s are nearly over," I said. "Why don't you just get up and go ask one of these guys to dance?"

"Janet Marie!" my mother hissed between her teeth. "A lady always waits to be asked."

I rolled my eyes. "Well, then, I guess the ladies always sit and watch others out on the dance floor."

Her expression turned into a definite scowl.

"You know almost everyone in here," I said, "but it's for sure no one is going to ask you to dance when you're displaying such a welcoming look!"

My mother finished the last of her diet soda and abruptly stood up. "Let's go."

I sighed and followed her to the parking lot in silence. So much for our anticipated girls' night out.

I slid behind the wheel and waited for her to say something.

"What are you waiting for?" she asked.

"Do you want to go to another country-western bar, or are you finished listening to live music for the night?"

She turned to face me.

"I was really looking forward to your visit. You don't come to see me nearly often enough."

"I'm here now, Mom." I started the car. "Is there someplace else where there might be more people dancing?"

"I'm not about to look like the poor little old lady who showed up without a dancing partner."

"Number one," I said, "you're not that old. Number two, maybe nobody knows what a good dancer you are. Number three, as I said before, the world has changed, and it's perfectly okay to ask a man to dance."

"Harrumph," Mom replied. "I like to waltz, and that band was playing a lot of waltzes. But none of those unattached guys know how to waltz. They all just do some offbeat, ridiculous, hug-and-sway thing."

I laughed. "There's the answer right there!" I shut off the car. "You can teach them to waltz, and then you'll have plenty of guys to dance with!"

My mother shot me an incredulous look, and her lips puckered up once more. "Just take me home."

"It's Friday night," I replied. "I'm only here for the weekend."

"Then, you teach them to dance! You're the teacher in the family!"

"Mom! Have you forgotten that it was you who taught all four of your children to waltz? You told us that if we could count to three, we could learn to waltz. Why not create your own dancing pool of single men? You'll end up being the most popular dance partner in there!"

Mom shook her head. "Not happening."

I sighed. "Well, fine." I sighed again just for the heck of it. "Do you want a burger or something?"

Before the words were even out of my mouth, Mom was on to me. "I'm not going back in there."

"Suit yourself." I shrugged. "It will probably be a wait of a half-hour or more. Do you want to just sit in the car while I go in and order us some food?"

"Janet Marie..."

"What's with the use of my middle name twice tonight? You only do that as a last resort to get my full attention."

"Fine," said Mom. "I'll go in, but just so I can listen to some more good music while we wait."

We walked back through the door, found a tiny table close to the kitchen, and placed our burger orders. Then I excused myself to go to the bathroom.

"I'll go with you," said Mom.

"I'm not a child anymore," I reminded her. "I'm old enough to go all by myself. And besides," I added, "we don't want to lose our seats."

I took my time walking to the bathroom, saying hello to a few of my mom's friends, waving to the band members she'd introduced me to, and generally chatting up the room. I may have even mentioned that my mother was a former dance-school instructor, and she was willing to help out some of the men who'd like to learn to waltz.

Then I took my time combing my hair, washing my hands, and generally stalling for time, hoping Mom was still speaking to me when I returned.

I waited until the band started playing a waltz before I exited the bathroom and discovered that my plan had worked even better than I'd dare to hope! Mom was out on the dance floor, counting loudly to the man she was attempting to dance with: "1-2-3, 1-2-3, 1-2-3, 1-2-3…"

And, at the end of the night, Mom admitted she'd had the best time ever and had plans to dance again the following weekend with several of the gentlemen she'd "taught to waltz."

The following Sunday afternoon, Mom called to tell me she was having such a fun time dancing that she'd changed her email address from "eMom2000" to "WaltzinLady."

It doesn't get any better than that!

— Jan Bono —

90

In the Spotlight

Art can never exist without naked beauty displayed.
~William Blake

The classroom is dead silent except for the sound of pencils scratching furiously on paper. Eyes peek out from behind large wooden easels, studying every inch of my flesh. A navy-blue robe lies twisted on the floor beside my hairy calves, but I'm surprisingly comfortable for a first-time undraped model. For a long time, I was able to count on one hand the number of women who'd seen me naked post-puberty. Now, at age thirty-five, the number is doubling.

Two thoughts bother me as the women continuously eyeball my manhood. First, I pray the cool November air seeping through several aged windows doesn't cause certain body parts to be misrepresented. Second, it's incredibly difficult to imitate a statue. Sitting on the edge of a chair, with my chin resting on my fist in a thinker pose, muscle fatigue quickly sets in.

Ten minutes of silence is broken by a single bell chime, and the instructor yells, "Switch." A moment after shaking out my limbs, I lie back on a chaise longue. The caffeine I ingested before class starts activating my bladder but does nothing to keep my eyelids from growing heavy and collapsing. I'm not sure how I'll stay conscious the next forty-five minutes. Lying motionless, counting tiny holes in the ceiling tiles, I remember something that Steve Jobs said: "You can't connect the dots looking forward. You can only connect them looking backward. So, you have to trust that the dots will somehow connect in your future."

Those words arouse my curiosity. How did I become comfortable enough to engage in tasteful public nudity? Working backward, the dots of my life connect from one experience after another stepping outside my comfort zone.

***

First dot, age eighteen. "Let's go dance in there," Tammi yells over the music, her shoulder-length, blond hair bouncing to the beat of the music in the Roadhouse. "Come on, let's go to the cage."

My only concern is not being drunk enough for that kind of high jinks. Not far above my head is a 150-square-foot, rectangular cell overlooking the dance floor. Spiral staircases on both sides lead up to the enclosure. I've been to this bar enough times to know what goes on inside: a public display of intoxicated gyration. I'm not even comfortable where I am now, anonymous and camouflaged amongst a hundred or so horny young adults. The dance floor is dark and rambunctious, and an occasional white light sweeps across grinding bodies. The room reeks of sweat and cigarette smoke, while my shoe sticks to what I believe was an orange-flavoured rum cooler.

"Fine. I'll go without you," Tammi says, turning and wiggling away.

The sex hormones coursing through my veins silence the part of my brain screaming to cease all further action. Excess levels of testosterone and dopamine hijack my body and propel it through the crowd to the base of a spiral staircase. We ascend through a cloud of fog and secondhand smoke into the belly of the beast. I keep my eyes focused on Tammi, not wanting to peer through the bars at the horde below. I can feel their gaze on me, the masses taunting and judging me.

Perhaps it is my blood-alcohol level finally rising above the legal limit, but after several minutes my inhibition is just low enough to view the Roadhouse from that altitude. To my amazement, looking through the cage is like looking through a pair of prescription glasses, a clear picture from a new perspective. Hardly anyone is looking up. The odd person takes a brief gander and then quickly carries on.

I come to the sudden realization that no one cares I'm up here. Even if someone notices, chances are they won't remember details in the morning. For years, I walked around thinking a giant spotlight followed me around, highlighting every flaw, causing me to grossly overestimate the number of people observing my every action. I will later learn that social psychologists referred to this phenomenon as the "Spotlight Effect." And what happens now? Well, in that suspended, steel contraption, I say that my small comfort zone triples in size.

***

Let's look at the second dot, which happens early in my college years.

The Media Communications class is comparable to a clown car with thirty-six students stuffed inside its tiny frame, all waiting to take centre stage. The assignment: get in front of our peers and tell a two-minute story about anything. Going alphabetically by last name puts me in the middle of the pack. I have about twenty-five minutes to work out my anecdote. Instead, I use that time to envision ridiculous scenarios of tripping over a desk or getting a nosebleed mid-story.

"I, uh, took this trip, um, over the summer," I manage to get out. "I went to, uh, Egypt."

Thirty-six pairs of eyes focus on me, and, like sunshine through a magnifying glass, I feel their concentrated stares scorch my skin. I heat up, I sweat, and my face turns red.

"If you, um, stand in front of the Sphinx," my mouth is drier than the Egyptian cotton I handled on the trip, "turn around, uh, and there's a Pizza Hut like three blocks away."

I stumble through a few more stories about being stung by a jellyfish in the Mediterranean Sea and some guy trying to hold my hand in Alexandria. Unbeknown to me, that's normal cultural behavior in the Arab world. At the end of two minutes, the butterflies in my stomach are on the verge of bursting from my belly like a scene from *Alien*. By the time I sit down, everyone's attention is focused on the next presenter, and I'm a distant memory. As the awkwardness and embarrassment cools off, I realize that, although extremely uncomfortable, being the centre of attention won't kill me. A crucial revelation for someone working towards a diploma in Broadcast Journalism.

* * *

Sixteen more years pass, and dots keep connecting, each one growing my comfort zone enough to try the next venture. My first broadcasting job evolves into public speaking, community theatre, working as a stand-up comedian and even skydiving. The milestone events of my adult life, at first glance, appear random and insignificant. But once I connect the dots, it's a finely crafted story of growth and development.

Years after first discovering the Spotlight Effect, I'm now lying naked on a couch with an actual spotlight on me. The bell chime offers sweet relief from a near hour-long pose. I have to pee, my forehead is itchy, and my right leg is asleep. But I smile, knowing my comfort zone has just expanded its boundaries again. I thank the ladies, put on my robe, and leave.

— Steve Krysak —

91

The Reluctant Diva

It's never too late to reclaim your inner diva
and reclaim your inner strength.
~Michelle Visage

I am shy, so it took a lot of gumption to make myself walk into a roomful of seventy strangers and try something completely out of my comfort zone — joining a seniors' choir that sings rock songs from the 1960s and 1970s. Luckily, several of the singers were friendly to newcomers. Although I was invited to sit in the front row with them, I chose to sit in the last row so I could hide among the throng and avoid being heard by the choir director who I was told liked to walk up and down the aisles, listening for sour notes.

One afternoon in rehearsal, our director, Holly, announced that we were going to perform "The Shoop Shoop Song" in our year-end concert. She advised us to watch the version made famous by the singer Cher as shown on her YouTube video.

The next week, Holly asked the "Divas" to stand together to perform Cher's part, while the rest of the choir was assigned the background part, sung by Cher's dancers. As I was not a Diva, I prepared to sing in the background, happy to remain invisible.

After the Divas had sung their first line, Holly called out, "Wait. Where's Christine?"

Surprised, I answered from the back row, "I'm here."

"Why aren't you standing with the Divas?"

I was stunned. "I'm not a Diva."

Holly shrugged. "Sorry. I guess I forgot to e-mail you. Now, you're a Diva."

While I was pleased to be selected, I was also nervous to be singing next to the experienced "stars," who had powerful singing voices. I could sing on key, but I couldn't belt it out, which was needed for this song. Why had she chosen me?

I felt anxious as well because it is a very fast-paced song, and my timing had to be perfect in order to join in at the correct moment. If I came in a second too soon, I would be the only one singing, which in a choir is a faux pas equal with disaster. On top of that, the Divas would be standing in front of the choir, and I would be seen by the entire audience. No more hiding in the crowd.

At the next rehearsal, Holly announced that the Divas could not stand in front of the choir on stage, as was previously planned. After measuring the stage in the concert hall, they discovered that when the microphones and band were in place, there would be no room for the Divas to stand together in front of the choir.

She told us the Divas would now have to leave the stage and stand on the floor in front of the audience. Furthermore, as we would then have plenty of room to spread out, we would learn the dance steps seen on Cher's video and dance while we were singing!

Holly's announcement sent waves of shock and fear through me. At that moment, I resolutely wanted to resign my position as a Diva and return to the comfort and anonymity of the choir.

Driving home that night, I had a full-out mental battle with my inner self, listing all the reasons why I couldn't be a Diva.

I can't be a go-go dancer! I could never dance and sing at the same time! My balance is not good. I might stagger while doing those fast, sideways steps and make a fool of myself. I hate people looking at me. I like to hide in the background!

However, there was another quiet, little voice underneath the loud one that kept urging me to go for it.

I've never tried, so how do I know I can't? If I practice enough, I might do a good job. Fear of failure can only be beaten by dancing through it!

Realizing that life often gives us unexpected opportunities to grow,

I ultimately decided to quit whining and make an effort to strut my stuff! By the time I reached my driveway, the quiet, little voice had won the argument. I resolved to go through with being a Diva, no matter how terrifying it seemed.

Onstage the night of the concert, it was exciting to see a sold-out audience of four hundred and fifty people but also scary for me, the reluctant Diva.

As we ran through our songs, I watched the teleprompter nervously as the song list rolled over one by one. I was dreading the moment "The Shoop Shoop Song" title would appear.

There it was! The band struck up the introductory notes to "The Shoop Shoop Song," and we eleven Divas streamed down the steps and took our places on the floor about five feet in front of the audience. My knees were trembling, and I gained new insight into that old saying "knees made of jelly." I prayed that I wouldn't stumble and fall over.

The opening notes for the first line began. Showtime! I forcibly overrode my anxiety and, taking a deep breath, smiled widely at a stranger in the audience and began to sing, "Does he love me? I want to know!"

I danced with precision, albeit with feigned confidence. I threw my whole being into the rhythm of the song. And I did not fall.

It was one of the most thrilling experiences I have ever had. I exceeded the limits I had imposed on myself. I proved to myself that I *can* do just about anything that my inner self guides me to do, as long as I ignore the voice that says, "I can't."

— Christine Clarke-Johnsen —

92

Captain Mom

As you move outside of your comfort zone,
what was once the unknown and
frightening becomes your new normal.
~Robin S. Sharma

My sixteen-year-old daughter, Leah, burst through the front door, bringing frigid February air. "I'm home!"

"How was your gymnastics meeting?" I called.

She dropped her backpack and joined me in the kitchen, where I was preparing dinner. "Coach Brittany told me I should run for junior captain next year. So I had, like, five minutes to come up with a speech."

"Captain?" I repeated. "Wow!"

She saw the look on my face. "Don't worry. I probably won't win."

"No!" I protested, weakly adding, "Really, it's great that she considers you captain material. Good for you."

I returned to slicing carrots, my mind racing. Leah a captain! If that only meant a leadership role for her, it truly would be great. But as Leah and I both knew, her being a captain would mean one other very important thing: I'd be a captain mom.

I'd never been super-involved in Leah's extracurricular activities. As the ultimate introvert and someone who struggles with insecurity, I tried to avoid situations that sapped my energy or required me to make dreaded small talk. But then, as an eighth-grader, Leah joined her high-school gymnastics team. When the inevitable requests for volunteers came, it didn't feel right to dodge them. So, I signed up for things in my comfort zone, like flashing scores at meets or supplying garlic bread for team dinners.

I was always glad I wasn't one of the three captain moms who did the lion's share of the work. They organized and often hosted team dinners. They also ran the parent meeting, ordered apparel, headed up fundraisers, delivered sandwiches to the gym before each meet, and planned the end-of-season banquet. Oh, and they put together twenty-five individualized photo books, a task that reportedly took fifty hours to complete. If Leah became a captain, I'd have to do those things, too. Did I have it in me?

I didn't think so.

A few weeks after her meeting, Leah was indeed named a captain. Over the next six months, every time I thought about the upcoming season, my stomach fluttered with anxiety. I'm embarrassed to say that when Leah experienced leg pain during summer workouts, I entertained hopes of her quitting gymnastics. And when a coach resigned in late October, right before the season started, I fantasized about the entire team folding. Leah, fully aware of my feelings, always acted apologetic about my new role. "I'm sorry you have to do this," she'd often say. "I'll try to make it easy for you so you won't have to do too much."

Then, one day, it hit me. Was I actually hoping Leah would quit something she loved just so I wouldn't have to face my fears? I was forty-seven years old, for crying out loud! It was time to grow up.

First off, I knew I should change how I talked. Most of what I said about being a captain mom was a complaint or something negative — or both. I didn't want to lie about my feelings, but I could still attempt to be positive. So, when the subject came up, I tried to say things like, "I'm going to learn a lot from this," or "This will be a good challenge for me." Being a person of faith, I also started to pray about it, asking God to help me do the job with a good attitude… and to please help me not hate it too much.

My prayers intensified after Deb, the head captain mom, set up a meeting with me and Jody, the third captain mom. My insecurities intensified, too. Would I fit in? What if I had to take on a task I couldn't handle? When meeting day arrived, I felt almost overwhelmed by nervousness. "Help me!" I prayed. "Help me to see this in a different light." And, suddenly, I received a new insight. Yes, I was feeling afraid, but that fear was just an illusion. Behind all the smoke and mirrors, there wasn't really anything to be afraid of. I was a capable person, and I had the ability to do this job.

Clinging to that thought, I went to the meeting. To my surprise, I enjoyed it! Deb and Jody were friendly, and the tasks assigned to me were doable.

As the season progressed, that continued to be true. Each time I encountered a hurdle — the gymnasium set-up, the parent meeting, the first time I delivered sandwiches to the team — I received grace to leap over it. I actually liked being a captain mom in some ways. During previous seasons, I'd felt a little on the outside at meets, having no one in particular to sit with. Now, I often sat with Deb and Jody. Conversation came easily because we had business to discuss, and as I got to know them better, we had other things to chat about, too. Slowly, my confidence increased.

Then, in February, while watching TV with my husband, I got a text from Deb: "Just want to remind you that Senior Night is next Monday. Junior moms have traditionally been in charge of that."

In spite of how far I'd come, I panicked. In three years of gymnastics, I'd only attended one Senior Night. And now I had to plan it all by myself?

I hurriedly typed, "What does that involve?"

Seconds later, I received Deb's reply. "On Senior Night, the team recognizes the senior girls with a reception after the meet. You'll need to get a cake, drinks, decorations, flowers, and a banner."

For the rest of the TV show, I maniacally texted back and forth with Deb, trying to figure out exactly how things had been done last year. I couldn't mess this up! As I waited for Deb to find her banner order from the year before and text me a screenshot of it, I suddenly came to my senses. I didn't have to do this perfectly; I just had to get it done. If I kept the goal in mind — to make the senior girls feel special — everything would work out fine.

And it did. The day after the reception, one of the senior moms even took time to e-mail me, thanking me for the good job I'd done.

A month later, the farewell banquet arrived. As the gymnasts received their ribbons, plaques, and certificates, I felt like I'd earned one, too. I had faced my fears and made it through the season.

But my job wasn't finished. The next year, Leah became a senior, and now I was the head captain mom. Some parts were challenging — leading the planning meeting, trying to get people to volunteer for those team dinners, and putting together those notorious photo books. Overall, though, I'm glad I had the experience. I learned that if I approach something with faith and a positive, can-do attitude, I can accomplish a lot more than I thought I could.

And I can show up — like a grown-up — to support the people I love.

— Sara Matson —

Reach Out and Connect

93

Party-Vous Français?

As I enter a new phase of life and my circle broadens,
I start learning new things.
~Kapil Dev

used to be a wallflower. When I would go to an event, I would only talk to the small group of people I already knew. That was until I went to a party at my niece Brynn's house.

Brynn and her French husband, Franck, lived in Kansas City, Missouri, where Franck taught at Académie Lafayette, a French immersion school. Soon after Brynn and Franck got settled, they invited my husband and me to a barbecue. "Some of our French friends will be there," Brynn said.

At the party, I staked out a corner of the patio near the grill and settled into a comfy lawn chair, enjoying the aroma of hamburgers cooking. I chatted with my husband and a cousin. As others arrived, I greeted acquaintances with a wave but kept to myself.

A pair of strangers burst through the open sliding-glass doors with a flurry and headed straight for me. They introduced themselves. "We met Franck at Académie Lafayette."

"I'm Brynn's aunt," I said.

They greeted all the other guests the same way. The couple was extra friendly, but I must admit I thought they were a little weird. When the next French guests arrived, they, too, circled the crowd, meeting each person. In fact, all of Brynn and Franck's French friends did the same thing.

After the party, I asked Brynn, "Is greeting every person a French party thing?"

She nodded. "At any event, in France, you're expected to acknowledge each person's existence when you arrive."

It sounded like a good idea, but I wondered if I could do it. "I'm going to try it next time," I told Brynn.

She grinned. "You should!"

Armed with the new protocol, I decided to try the "French way" at my friend Maggie's afternoon garden party. I knew her from my writers' group and expected to see lots of other writers there. When I got there, though, dozens of guests with unfamiliar faces mingled in small groups on the lawn and patio. Across the way, I saw some friends from my writers' group.

Normally, I would have headed straight to them. Instead, I started with strangers closest to me. Closing my eyes, I took a deep, calming breath and introduced myself. "How do you know Maggie?" It was a lame question, akin to asking, "What's your major?" in college. But it worked.

"We're relatives," one man said.

"Oh, I'm so glad to meet you! She's in my writers' group, and we all love her."

Two women at a table near some pink hydrangeas told me their names. One shot me a sideways glance. Maybe she thought I was weird. I understood.

My mouth felt dry as I approached a half-dozen women standing under a pear tree.

"How do you know Maggie?" I asked.

"We attended a church retreat together years ago," one said. "We still stay in touch every month."

As I went around the circle, I heard a familiar name. A woman I thought I didn't know was a high school classmate. We hadn't seen each other for decades.

"I didn't recognize you!" I said. I fluffed my bottle-blond hair. "I'm sure you don't recognize me, either. I used to be a brunette."

We laughed.

After the brief reunion, I felt more comfortable. *I can do this,* I thought.

I moved on to my writers' group friends and relaxed. "I'm trying the French way to party," I said and explained the custom. "I'll come back when I finish my rounds."

A man sat alone near two rose of Sharon bushes in a far corner of the yard. My stomach fluttered a little as I walked toward him. "Do you want to be alone?"

He smiled and shook his head. "I just like to watch the crowd." He was a professor who worked with Maggie on research for her doctoral thesis. I learned she was renowned in her field of special education. I knew her only as a poet.

A few more guests joined us in the corner. We introduced ourselves. One of the women was my little sister's best friend growing up. "I remember you!" she said.

We hugged.

I headed to the patio with a little more confidence.

The next group sat in a circle. "How do you know Maggie?" I asked.

"She's in our writers' group," one man said.

Maggie had another writers' group? Who knew? I always love to meet other writers and thought about introducing them to the friends from my group. I glanced toward where they'd been standing, but they'd already left.

"What genres do you write?" I asked. As we discussed our writing interests, I settled in. This group felt like family, and we chatted happily.

I realized that partying the French way is fun. While I thought I was simply acknowledging others' existence, I was really learning more about my friend Maggie, reuniting with guests I wouldn't have noticed, and turning strangers into friends. And I changed myself from a wallflower to a party girl, the French way.

— Mary-Lane Kamberg —

94

The Bare Truth

To be comfortable in your own skin
is the beginning of strength.
~Charles Handy

"That is the most beautiful Boxer I have ever seen." My husband, who knows that Boxers are my favorite breed of dog, looked at me with an incredulous shake of his head.

"Really, that's what you notice?"

We both started to laugh — loud enough to attract the attention of the man walking the Boxer. He smiled, waved at us, and continued down the street. Oh, did I mention that both the dog and the man walking it were completely naked?

Tom and I were, for the first time in our lives, visiting a nudist resort.

Let me back up a little.

I can't remember a time when I didn't find nudity a comfortable and natural way to live. I used to clean my second-floor apartment in the nude. No one could see in the windows, so I could work up a sweat, cleaning like a demon, and pop right into the shower (the last thing I cleaned). It seemed more than free-spirited; it was efficient. Deep down, I was sure that I would like to try spending time at a nudist park, but I didn't know what I would find there. Well, yes, I knew some of the things I would find there. That is surely no surprise. It was the unknown, not the obvious, that made me hesitate.

I did some research, which made me a bit more comfortable

about going to a nudist resort. But knowing something intellectually and knowing it through experience are two different forms of awareness. Trying nudism, even with an armload of data, didn't keep me from having some misgivings. What if I got there, and it wasn't what I expected? What if it was more than I wanted? What if the people were interested in more than wine, a game of bridge, and light banter? I have been wrong before.

I was placing myself at risk and felt vulnerable. But the best way to face a fear is to talk it out. My husband and I did just that, and we both agreed that if we were not comfortable, we would leave, lesson learned. With that commitment, I had the confidence to take a chance. We booked a weekend at a nudist park in Michigan while on our vacation.

It was after we checked in that we met the Boxer. It was clear that if the first thing I noticed was the dog, then nudity and I were comfortable with one another. There was no "easing" into the concept with us. We settled into our room, tossed off our clothes and set off on an exploration of the park. Within five minutes, I felt completely at home. I was, in fact, more relaxed than I had been in years. The tensions of my high-stress life evaporated in the sun. The people we met were welcoming, and nudism has become a regular part of our lives.

There are some 180 clubs affiliated with the American Association for Nude Recreation across the United States and Canada. Tom and I have visited many of them. These clubs vary in size, cost, and locale. Some are rustic; some are sophisticated. Some are highly social with lots of planned activities, and some are almost contemplative. Some are family-oriented, and others are retirement communities. But they are alike in several important ways. They all want to provide a place where people who appreciate nudism can relax in a guarded environment. They believe in body acceptance, not body perfection. They judge people by what is in their hearts and their minds, not by their threads. It is hard to tell the butcher, baker, and candlestick maker apart when they are all naked.

Nudists truly are comfortable in our own skin. We are not perfect specimens. The minute someone tells me I wouldn't want them at our nudist resort because they are too old (overweight, out-of-shape, scarred from surgery... the list goes on), I know they have fallen into the trap of equating nudism with sexual allure. Nudists know the best-kept secret in the Western world: Sexuality exists from the neck up, not the other way around.

We are old, wrinkled, and suffering the slings and arrows of a life well lived. It doesn't matter. It goes unnoticed. We are people with a mind, a story, and a life, and we are living it with fewer cares than most.

Some questions always come up when friends find out we are nudists. Here are the top five:

1. Is there hanky-panky going on? No, the fastest way to get booted out of a nudist park is to behave in a lewd manner.
2. What do you do when it gets cold? We wear clothes!
3. What about hygiene? You always carry and sit on your own towel. This is nudist protocol 101.
4. Why do you like nudism? It is calming. When you are nude, you are totally vulnerable. To be accepted at that moment means you are totally accepted. Such self-affirmation is rare.
5. Where do you keep the second ball when you are playing tennis? At the net.

Taking a chance on nudism has led us to a retirement community in the lower Rio Grande Valley of Texas. The social schedule is exciting, the people are pure joy, and the friends we have made are the best in my life. Besides, doing mahjong, book club and karaoke in the nude means you are spending much less time doing laundry.

Oh, and by the way, that really was a great-looking Boxer. I found out that it was an AKC champion. You learn the most interesting things at a nudist resort.

— Louise Butler —

95

Take a Hike

The great thing about new friends is that
they bring new energy to your soul.
~Shanna Rodriguez

"Jen, do you hike?" Was she talking to me? There was another Jennifer in the group who went by Jen, and I thought I'd distinguished myself from her earlier.

I tried again. "Me? Oh, I go by Jennifer. And, yes, yeah, I hike," I told Karen, whose trim physique and sun-kissed cheeks suggested she was a regular.

"Great, do you want to come with us tomorrow? We meet in front of Bobbie's house at 6:30, before it's too hot, and we go over to Thunderbird Mountain. It's about three miles total. Does that sound okay?"

Three miles. I wasn't sure how long that was, partly because I didn't actually hike. I was somewhat familiar with the area where they planned to go, but our family had just moved from Oregon to Arizona. I walked our dog around the neighborhood all the time, but I wasn't sure if we went three miles or even one. I wondered if hiking could be much different from walking. Being new to town, and excited about an invitation from women I wanted to befriend, I accepted.

"Sure, yes, that sounds great. I'm, uh, I'm unpacking still, so I'm thinking I'll just wear..." It was, and always is, for me, a little about what I'm wearing.

Thank goodness the actual Jen added her comment in the enthusiastic and warm way I've come to love about her. "Just wear what's comfortable! Hiking shoes if you have them. Otherwise, tennis shoes with good treads, and thick socks, so you don't blister. Bring water, too."

When this hiking conversation among my new friends occurred, I was at a monthly dinner for moms in my new neighborhood. I was delighted to have been invited to substitute for a woman who couldn't attend. The group was eight women in their forties, all with high-school kids, jobs, a fondness for reading and music, and tricks for simplifying work-life balance via laundry secrets and bargain shopping. So, they were my kind of women, and I was giddy to have found them in my new life, even though I was uncertain about whether I could hike with them.

I was flattered to be invited since making friends in your forties in a new town is not easy. After this re-location for my husband's career, making friends was not as simple for me as it was for him. He came to the community for a full-time position at a busy university. Our teenaged son and daughter immediately plugged in to school and social groups through sports and clubs. I was enormously grateful for the ease of the transition for my family, but nervous for myself. I wondered if and when I would also feel a sense of belonging. So, while at the monthly ladies' gathering, when hiking came up, I just played along.

The next day, I got up early, showered, washed and styled my hair. I left it a little messy, so it didn't look like I had tried too hard. I also applied sunscreen and a scant amount of make-up, again trying to look like some natural version of my usually-made-up self. I took time to select comfortable yet coordinated "hiking clothes" — a light-blue shirt with sleeves to hide my less-than-perfect upper arms and black, stretchy bike shorts with a pocket. I put some honey-scented lotion on my neck, wanting to smell honest and clean, like someone who was going to be a good hiker. I wore my tennis shoes with good treads, and thick socks, and I took along a bottle of water. When I arrived at the designated friend's driveway a little early, one of the other three women was standing there waiting.

"Hey, Jennifer, I'm glad you came to hike," she said cheerfully and hugged me. I was already sweaty. She offered me a lightweight backpack for my water and had brought me an extra bottled water. When the others joined us, we started walking to the park. We naturally broke into two groups of two and walked rapidly along the sidewalk to the base of the mountain in North Glendale. I was a little out of breath before we even started going uphill.

"So, where did you hike in Oregon?" one of them asked.

"Well, uh, I mainly walked a lot. We lived in the suburbs, so we were in a neighborhood in southwest Portland with sidewalks, and — "

Again, the real Jen saved me by saying, "There are all kinds of hikes around here. Hey, let's do this one today…." And she led us on a trail that I guess was about three miles. I later learned it was one of the easier paths in terms of elevation. We hiked and talked about our families, jobs, and dogs. We shared concerns about our kids in school with sports, grades, or significant others.

That day, I became a hiker, and I gained new friends. They continued to invite me to hike on Saturday mornings and to join them for birthday lunches and couples' nights. We all even landed in the same mother-daughter group, volunteering in our community alongside each other. Over the years, we continued to share stories about our husbands, parents, and kids. We hugged and laughed over broken-down cars, broken hearts, and even the complexities of a worldwide pandemic affecting graduations, weddings, and funerals in our immediate families.

Recently, nine years after that first hike, my husband and daughter put together a surprise birthday dinner for me. My "hiking friends," as I've come to call them, were among the first invited. At the party, they sat close to me, and we joked and visited all evening, even though we'd been together twice in the previous week, on a hike and at another event.

By accepting the invitation to hike, I stretched myself, both literally and figuratively, and made amazing new friends. I still enjoy hiking with them, and I imagine I will always remain connected to these lovely women who enveloped me in their circle and continue to do so. I also feel confident that there are some other hikers, more great friends I've yet to meet, but who I'll come to love simply by agreeing to try something new.

— Jennifer Priest Mitchell —

96

Divine Direction to Diversity

*Diversity is about all of us, and about us having to
figure out how to walk through this world together.*
~Jacqueline Woodson

caught sight of my daughter as she walked out of the bathroom one morning. A white film of lotion masked her face like cream just poured into coffee. She averted her eyes. I was about to scold her when a thought occurred to me: *She wants to look white.*

"Honey, are you trying to make your skin white?" I asked softly.

She nodded and looked up. "I want to be white like you, Mama," she whispered.

I wept inside.

Why does she want to be white? Why does a seven-year-old from Liberia, Africa, and my daughter for only a year, want to change her skin color?

My inner voice asked, *What have you done to show her that brown skin is just as beloved?*

My husband and I had taught our daughters over and over that God makes all people in His image and loves all those He creates. But our daily lives undermined our words. People of color were infrequent in our lives. There wasn't much diversity at the grocery store, library, or park. Half of the students attending the girls' school were children of color, but adult role models of similar appearance were scarce. Then, there was our church. Our adopted daughters saw few people who bore any resemblance to themselves when they attended services.

I began to grasp the message all of this whiteness sent to my daughter: being white is preferred.

For most of my life, I inhabited a comfortable, white-centric bubble. I believed there was no serious racism in the northern U.S., certainly not in Minnesota. But after police killed Jamar Clark in 2015, protests at the police department's 4th precinct in Minneapolis near our home went on for weeks. I began to realize things were not as I believed them to be.

At that time, one daughter with brown skin called me "Mama." I wondered what discrimination and mistreatment she would face outside the wings of our white privilege.

In 2018, we adopted our second daughter. At age six, she was quick to observe differences in skin color, hairstyles, and other features of people she knew in Liberia and met in her new home. As racial tensions simmered in Minnesota, I attended workshops for transracial adoptive families. I listened as adult adoptees described what it was like to be raised by white parents. They emphasized how important it is for my children to know other children like them: adopted into a white family. As they spoke, I asked myself, "What are my girls going to say about how they were raised when they're adults?"

We were thrust out of our inaction by the nine minutes of video captured on Memorial Day 2020 when a white police officer knelt on George Floyd's neck, resulting in his death. We realized that we could no longer turn a blind eye to racism. We could no longer just hope that, by the time our girls became adults, the inequities and injustices would be gone. We couldn't deprive them of a community that included all people.

We felt an urgency to look for a new church, but it was hard to leave what was familiar. My husband had lived his whole life firmly anchored in one faith tradition because his father was a pastor. We had many friends there and enjoyed activities like packing food for the hungry. Our wedding service was held in the chapel. Unmoved by resistance, my inner voice directed, "You need to go to a Black church."

My husband agreed and typed "churches" into the map app on his phone. "There's a church on Broadway near 94," he said. It was a little over two miles away in a predominantly Black neighborhood.

We attended virtually the next Sunday. As the music started, a woman vocalist took the stage.

My younger daughter, now eight, turned her head away from the TV to look at us. "She's brown?"

She flashed a smile as she danced to the upbeat music. She didn't say anything when the Black male pastor began the sermon, but my husband and I exchanged a glance. I felt like we had taken a baby step in the right direction.

The pastor made a statement that felt like an affirmation to me: Sacrificial love leads us to places that are out of our comfort zone, places we wouldn't go on our own. I knew that God was telling me we were in the right place, and He would provide for us.

As the pandemic months wore on, we continued to gather in front of the TV in our pajamas for church. Through these streamed messages, my husband and I heard far more about biblical values specifically involving those who have been marginalized in our society — the widow, the orphan, and the stranger. We heard many different voices of color. They preached from the same Bible we'd always read, but from their perspective. We began to see the world through a different lens. We questioned the power differential that exists in our society and observed that Jesus spent his time on Earth with those viewed as lowly in His time.

A full year after we began tuning in online, the church opened its doors again to in-person worship. That morning, we threw off our pajamas and dressed up. I made a hearty breakfast. It felt like a holiday or birthday celebration. Though their faces were covered with masks, my girls were all smiles as we walked through the doors of the modern building. We checked in, wrote our names on nametags, and found seats. During the first song, tears clouded my vision as I took in the diversity of those gathered. Families that appeared to be transracial through adoption like ours, interracial couples, white families, Black families, and Asian families all worshiped together.

For several months, it was hard to feel connected. On Sundays, everyone wore masks and dispersed soon after the service was over. We volunteered a couple of times to refill the hand-sanitizer dispensers and decorate trees for Christmas, meeting a few people along the way. When there were cultural references during the service that my husband and I didn't understand, we'd glance at each other. Being outside the inside joke was good for me. It gave me a glimpse at what it feels like to be marginalized.

As my husband and I took steps that we thought were about finding a more diverse community for our daughters, I found that God had a deeper plan for me as well. I found a faith community that is more aligned with my beliefs than any I've experienced in the past. It works for justice and reconciliation, values all people, and honors Jesus's command to love each other. God has shown me the beauty of being part of a community of people with a diversity of skin colors. I'm challenged each week to think a little differently about our world and my role in making it a better place for all people. Best of all, my daughters will know the steps our family took to be part of a community that includes all God's beloved people.

— Becky Hofstad —

97

The Reluctant Volunteer

Each new day is a blank page in the diary of your life.
The secret of success is in turning that diary
into the best story you possibly can.
~Douglas Pagels

July 1971. I am taking a summer class in Black-American literature on the campus of SUNY Oneonta in upstate New York. Professor James walks into the classroom and announces that he has invited a special guest to class, but his guest has been delayed. The class stirs with curiosity and anticipation.

"Who's coming?" someone asks.

"All I will tell you is that he is the author of one of the books you have read for this class," he says. "I need a volunteer to meet him in the lobby of the administration building and escort him here."

To my amazement, my right hand shoots up as though it has a mind of its own. *What am I doing?* I think. I never volunteer for anything. I am introverted, shy, and uncomfortable meeting new people. In fact, I am absolutely the wrong person for this job. Realizing my mistake, I pull my hand down quickly, but it is too late.

"Thank you, David," Professor James says. "You'd better leave now. He'll be arriving any minute."

Seeing no way to back out, I reluctantly get out of my seat and head for the classroom door. When I reach it, I stop.

"Umm," I say. "If I don't know who this person is, how will I recognize him? I'd hate to bring back the wrong guy."

Professor James laughs. "Good point," he says. He pulls me aside and whispers a name in my ear. "Alex Haley," he says.

"Really?" I say. I give a thumbs-up to the class and leave the room.

As I enter the empty hallway, I chastise myself for volunteering. *You dumb, dumb dummy! Why didn't you let someone else do this?* Alex Haley is the author of *The Autobiography of Malcolm X*. He is also famous for his probing *Playboy* interviews with the likes of Miles Davis, Martin Luther King, Jr., and Muhammed Ali (then Cassius Clay).

As I walk across campus, I am dimly aware that it is a bright, sunny afternoon. My anxiety grows as the massive administration building looms ahead. I fear that I am about to embarrass myself in front of this famous gentleman by asking stupid questions, or worse, by clamming up and escorting him in painful silence. I reach the front steps and climb them slowly.

As I pull open the heavy glass door, I realize why I instinctively raised my hand to volunteer for this job. This man is what I want to be: a writer. He is living my dream. I can learn from him.

The lobby is empty except for two students waiting for the elevator. Alex Haley is nowhere to be seen. I pace back and forth across the polished lobby floor until a Black man with a briefcase enters the building. He stops and scans the lobby. His gaze falls on me.

"Mr. Haley?" I say.

"Yes," he says.

"I'm from Professor James's class. Welcome."

"Thank you," he says. He extends his hand, and we shake. He is a man in his forties, medium height, wearing a sports jacket over an open-collared dress shirt.

"Alex," he says.

"Dave," I say. "The classroom building is this way." I hold the door for him as he passes through.

"How was your trip?" I say.

"It was a pleasant drive through the countryside," he says. "I'm currently Writer in Residence at Hamilton College in Clinton."

"Oh, I am from that area," I say. "I grew up on a farm ten miles east of Clinton."

"Beautiful country," he says. "You're lucky."

As we begin our trek across campus, I am struck by how approachable this man is. My fear is replaced by curiosity and purpose. A few students pass by, but they fail to recognize Mr. Haley. I am not surprised as he could easily be mistaken for a professor.

"Do you mind if I ask you a question?" I say.

"No. Not at all," he says.

"I'd like to become a writer, but I don't know if I have the talent," I say. "How did you discover that you had a gift for writing?"

Mr. Haley laughs.

"I didn't," he says. "And I don't."

"I don't understand," I say. "You've accomplished so much."

He stops and looks me in the eyes as though he is no longer in a hurry to get to class, and I'm the only person who matters.

"Writing is a craft," he says. "I learned to write through practice and sheer persistence."

He explains that when he entered the Coast Guard in 1939, he was assigned mess duty. He became so bored that he bought a portable typewriter. He began to write letters for sailors who wanted to correspond with their girlfriends and others back home, but they lacked writing skills. He wrote every day. As his writing skills improved, he eventually became a journalist for the Coast Guard.

"If you want to become a writer," he says, "don't worry about whether you have some magical gift. Put in the work. Write every day, and don't give up until you succeed."

This is not the answer I expect. I thank him for his advice. We arrive at the classroom all too quickly. My personal time with him is over.

For the next two hours, Alex Haley holds our class spellbound as he describes his quest to track his ancestors through seven generations from Africa to present-day America. This is the research he used in writing his book, *Roots*, published five years later, and turned into a TV miniseries.

After my conversation with Alex Haley, I no longer obsess over whether I have the "gift" or talent to become a writer. Instead, I start writing every day. Within two years, I publish three stories in national children's magazines. I have been writing and publishing ever since. Had I not volunteered to meet this extraordinary man, I never would have received the benefit of his wise advice and the rewards that followed.

—D.E. Brigham—

98

A Reformed Introvert

A friend may be waiting behind a stranger's face.
~Maya Angelou, Letter to My Daughter

I marched into the darkened restaurant and looked around the room. Businesswomen stood around in clusters. I glanced into each face. I didn't know one person.

The room started to blur, but I shook it off. I was here to talk to people, and I would. I let my eyes focus on one group at a time, trying not to stare. It seemed to me that they all knew each other. They stood in tight circles, focused inward. I had read in a networking book that if someone left the circle open, it was okay to drift into it and listen. Most of these circles were closed. I considered backing out the door and going home.

Then I saw a woman standing alone, her back to the wall, gazing at the floor. I stepped up to her and said, "Hello." She looked startled. I improvised. "Have you been here before?"

She said, "No, I usually work too late for these meetings."

"Where do you work?"

"I work at the Better Business Bureau."

"That sounds interesting."

Now, we were off and running.

When I moved from Massachusetts to Ohio, I knew I would have to move out of my comfort zone. Here, I knew no one. I would have to make a real effort.

I began to network — ah, the chill in that word. The fear of confident strangers when you are trying to break into their already established group. It was like middle school all over again. And not in a pleasant way. I tried the fake-it-until-you-make-it method. I tried to pretend I was an extrovert and was used to wiggling my way into groups of strangers.

It wasn't easy. Sometimes, it seemed that all the people I met had gone to school together and I was from a different planet, which wasn't that far from the truth. Little by little, however, I met friendly and helpful people, who slowly welcomed me.

Someone once told my daughter in grade school to be nice to the new kid because, when she was the new kid someday, someone would be nice to her. It was the old what-goes-around-comes-around theory. It worked for her, and it was working for me.

When I approached new groups or attended meetings, I looked for the people who looked more scared than I was, more isolated and out of place, and I moved toward them. When I spoke, they initially looked shocked and then relieved. Sometimes, it worked, and we had a conversation. Sometimes, they were too tongue-tied, and the conversation bombed. Then, I'd try to look around and find a person who looked like they would like to be anywhere else. I would challenge myself to stay an hour.

Sometimes people responded; sometimes they didn't. If they didn't, then, oh well. It turned out that I didn't die from embarrassment, it didn't ruin my life, and the floor didn't open up and swallow me. It was just awkward and uncomfortable, but I made it through.

If they did respond, it meant a potentially awkward conversation. All meetings end eventually, and I could pick myself up and get going, and then try to figure out what worked and what didn't work. And I found that, each time, my heart raced a little less, and I was more and more able to catch my breath. The weak feeling in my knees began to disappear, too.

My favorite people were the experienced networkers. They were used to doing this and could move through the crowd with ease and confidence. I watched them and tried to learn how to do what they did.

If I knew then what I know now, I would have gone to a successful hairstylist or manicurist and jotted down their lines.

"What did you do this weekend?"

"What are you doing after this?"

"How was your summer?"

They are innocuous open-ended statements, fishing for a conversation.

There were times when I met a truly nice, interesting or friendly person who I wanted to meet again and again, and we did. I met Ann, and Linda, and Robin. We met for breakfast, lunch or coffee every month and caught up. That would never have happened if I hadn't risked my neck by walking into a room where I knew no one.

Now, I am a reformed introvert — or an introvert who can act like an extrovert. I make it a habit to chat with cashiers, salespeople, mail carriers, dog-walkers and neighbors. It makes life interesting and pleasant. Today, I met three people at the mall who were friendly and helpful.

And it came in handy when I moved to another state again where I knew no one. I am starting to develop some, dare I say it, friends. Faked it till I made it.

— Laurie Neveau —

99

A Cartoonist's Tale

Great opportunities to help others seldom come,
but small ones surround us every day.
~Sally Koch

When I heard my friend Samantha had fallen from her balcony and broken her arm, I immediately set pen to paper and rushed over to bring her a special cartoon. I've been cartooning since the age of eight. That was not new. Seeing the impact my cartoon would have on her, however, would prove to be a game changer.

When her partner answered the door, he explained that she didn't want any visitors. When I offered to merely hand her a cartoon and leave, he let me in. She was not happy about that, to say the least. Her eyes shot daggers at both of us. Undeterred, I handed her the cartoon.

I had designed a business card showing her in a free-fall position about to impact the ground at terminal velocity with a knapsack on her back instead of a parachute. The card read SAMANTHA'S SKYDIVING SCHOOL. I watched her instantly transform from angry and in pain to a person doubled over in laughter.

Not long after that, I attended a lecture by Dr. Patch Adams about his life-long commitment to the marriage of humor and healing. I was definitely inspired. Then I met a nurse who told me that our local hospital had a Mirth Department. A Mirth Department? It was staffed by nurses doing off-duty clowning. I lost no time in getting on the phone with the head nurse. I informed her I was a Clinical Cartoonist.

She said, "I've never heard of that."

I replied, "That's because I just made it up."

The life of a cartoonist can be lonely. I've spent untold hours in my studio bent over a drafting table, producing work to be seen elsewhere by someone at some time. The idea of grabbing a pad and pen and marching into hospitals to draw stuff on the spot… Let's just say the thought of it was both exciting and mildly terrifying. It was certainly something I'd never done before.

It would take some time to complete the required paperwork, be TB-tested, and buy a white doctor's coat embroidered in red thread with the letters: Brian Narelle, Cartoonist. Then came the day to take the plunge into this new endeavor. I met with the head nurse while she was on duty in the ICU. As soon as I received my hospital badge, I was thrown right into the deep end.

Family members in the ICU were astounded to see that the hospital had a cartoonist on staff (albeit voluntary). One patient I met was about to be transferred to a rehab facility called North Coast. I whipped out my pad and drew him abandoned on a stretcher along Highway One, overlooking the crashing waves near Mendocino. As an ambulance is seen driving away, one of the EMTs says, "Are you sure that's what he meant by 'north coast'?" And thus I left my first critically ill patient laughing. He would not be my last.

Working hospital wards alone proved awkward because I must retreat into my drawing temporarily while with the patient. I would soon remedy that by hooking up with therapy dogs as they did their rounds. Hannah, a Golden Retriever, and Tigger, a shaggy mutt, would become my sidekicks, engaging patients as I stood quietly by, doing my thing. By the time the dogs departed, each patient would have a cartoon of their very own in a room filled with laughter.

Regular wards were one thing. It took another leap of faith to plunge into dementia wards. One day, a Patch Adams visit had drawn clowns from all over the world for a seminar in San Francisco. The following day, I joined a few of them at Laguna Honda Hospital. We gathered in a small conference room… twelve clowns and me… then twenty-five clowns and me… then thirty… thirty-five… forty-five…

all in this small room. It was like a clown car in reverse.

I stayed behind in Laguna Honda on one of three five-person teams. That meant the remaining thirty clowns, bound for other SF hospitals, all marched to the nearest bus stop and boarded a municipal bus. I so wish I could have seen the inside of that bus.

I soon found myself in the day room of a dementia ward. One patient pointed to a large painting on the wall, featuring a lake nestled at the base of a mountain. He told me, "I bet there's a lot of fish in there." In turn, I drew a cartoon of him holding a fishing pole with a line running off the bottom of the paper. I suggested he stick it in the bottom of the frame of the painting with the idea he might catch some fish. He was thrilled at the prospect.

From there, it was a natural progression to psych wards. In one dayroom, a woman enjoying Tigger's licks was asked if she'd like a drawing. "Oh, no," she replied, "I don't have my new teeth." I assured her that was no problem and proceeded to draw her being licked by Tigger as she grinned from ear to ear, sporting a mouthful of new dentures. When I gave her the cartoon, she was so excited that she jumped to her feet and showed it to everyone else in the dayroom, announcing over and over, "Look at my teeth! Look at my teeth!"

My next psych ward visit was at the VA in San Francisco. There, a bearded man of Vietnam War vintage sat alone in a hospital gown. He made it abundantly clear that he did not want anyone coming near him, including the dogs. I kept my distance and began drawing. He noticed me and inquired, "Are you drawing?"

"Uh-huh," I answered.

"Are you drawing me?"

"Uh-huh," once again. End of conversation.

I drew him just the way he was, slouched on a sofa in his gown. At the end of the couch, I drew both dogs looking at him adoringly with little hearts floating off them.

Without coming too close, I slowly leaned over and stretched out my arm in order to give him the cartoon. He examined it closely.

"Is that me?" he asked.

One last "Uh-huh."

His scowl turned into a little smile. I can still see it now.

And so it went for several years until both Hannah and Tigger made their way to that Big Dog Park in the sky.

At first, it was scary and presumptuous to declare myself a Clinical Cartoonist, but I'm so glad I did. I've drawn a lot of cartoons over the years. The paying work takes care of the bills, but stepping out of the comfort and security of my studio into hospitals and psych wards has filled my heart like no paying job ever could.

— Brian Narelle —

Hiking with My Sister

Our feelings are our most genuine paths to knowledge.
~Audre Lorde

"Supermarket girl." That wasn't her name, but that's how I'd saved her in my phone. It was the way I'd always saved the numbers of random people who weren't friends or family. "Plantain guy" for the African man I met on my evening walk. He'd offered me green plantains. "Go-go girl" for my co-worker, who took pole-dancing classes on a Saturday. "Man on the train" for the Caucasian gentleman I'd exchanged phone numbers with because I was reading a book by his favorite author.

I met "supermarket girl" in 2018 while shopping for groceries. When two Black women meet anywhere else in the world, they nod and move on. But two Black women in the same supermarket in Japan? We stopped to talk. I learned she lived a station away and had been in Japan for almost twenty years. I told her I'd been here for three. We exchanged numbers and promised to meet up.

I walked away knowing we probably never would. This is Japan. The intense work culture dictates that I leave my day job at 5:00 P.M. and head to my evening and weekend part-time job by 6:00 P.M. Sparing time to meet and greet was a concept I'd given up on from year one. My off day was used to replenish, rejuvenate, and rest.

In April 2020, the coronavirus pandemic upended life as we knew it. Seemingly overnight, the entire world slowed down. My day-to-day existence shifted from the hustle and bustle of Tokyo to adjusting to a daily routine of sitting in front of my computer screen, learning how to navigate online teaching software, Google Classroom, and Zoom. My personal space became a virtual public space.

That, coupled with being confined to my tiny apartment, did something to my psyche — or maybe it was the stress of online teaching. Sitting in front of a computer for six hours each day, learning as my students learned, thinking on my feet and trying to be innovative, were taking their toll. After week one, I noticed a drastic shift in my mood, as well as chronic pain in my back and neck.

In week two, time started playing tricks on me. Some days were moving too fast. Some were moving too slow. Each day began morphing into the other without a specific end or a defined beginning. Every day felt like a fresh eternity. The supermarket became my escape. I'd go there during my lunch break, even when I didn't need to purchase anything, just to walk the aisles.

That's where I ran into her again: supermarket girl. This time, I learned her name: Julia. She explained that the pandemic had her feeling anxious and isolated, and working from home was beginning to take a toll on her, too. We immediately recognized our need for sun, solidarity and sisterhood, so we made a date to go for a Saturday morning walk together. That's how it started.

Ten kilometers to the nearest recycle shop.

We talked about the stress that comes with trying to flourish in a foreign land: the differences in culture, the language barrier, the difficulty of building meaningful relationships. We talked about moving away from friends, family, foods we love, and hair products we need to settle in a country where we always feel like the odd one out. Oftentimes, we felt certain that we didn't belong.

Eight kilometers to Costco.

This time, we bonded over the main thing we had in common: struggles that come with being a woman. She shared that the world expected her to have her life together. Although it appeared that way on the surface, there were many insecurities poking through her wall of confidence, which made her feel perpetually overwhelmed and unproductive in her professional life. Her insecurities made her pessimistic about what she had to offer to the world. They kept layers of sadness beneath her mask of happiness.

I gave her a glimpse into what was happening behind my surface as well. I allowed her to see me in the same authentic way she had shown herself to me. I opened up about my emotional exhaustion. I talked about feeling like there was a rush on my biological clock to find romance and have children by a certain age. I didn't always feel in alignment with myself or as if I were walking in my truth and integrity.

Five kilometers to the ocean.

This time, we went to pray. Our talks had revealed us to each other, and we came to the realization that we were not okay. Tears ran down both our cheeks as we made a commitment to rediscover ourselves, rediscover our strength, and find value in self-love.

Every single Saturday, rain or sun, we were devoted. Soon, we switched to better shoes and authentic hiking gear, and our walks became hiking different trails in Kanagawa Prefecture.

Three kilometers along the Kamakura Hiromachi Ryokuchi Loop. Four kilometers through the forest, historic shrines and temples on the Kuzuharaoka-Daibutsu Hiking Course. Eight kilometers on the Ten-en Hiking Course with views overlooking Kamakura. We exhausted them all.

It wasn't long before we both noticed the changes. We'd begun to lose weight. We were sleeping better, and the anxiety of living in a pandemic, though it didn't diminish, wasn't at the forefront of our minds. By the end of July, I'd also started to notice that there was a drastic reduction in my back and neck pain.

Walking outdoors had not only provided a connection with nature, but it had also given us the beautiful simplicity of human connection. I was able to open up to someone who looked just like me. Someone who could relate to my Black experience as well as the experience of navigating the world as a woman. It was something I didn't even know I needed.

I'm proud of us. Instead of isolating ourselves, drowning in despair and allowing the pandemic to become the bane of our existence, we took control. We decided to walk, talk and pray. We decided to lace up our sneakers, lean into our pain, and focus on existing in a whole space again.

Through sisterhood, solidarity, and sunshine, we used our walks to truly change our lives.

— Keisha-Bree Brissette —

IRL

Trust the still, small voice that says,
"this might work and I'll try it."
~Diane Mariechild

First, let me tell you my age: seventy-three. Then, let me tell you my name: Geistfrau. At least, that's been my gaming name since I began playing as a mere child of sixty-one.

I never thought I'd like gaming, especially a game where players try to kill each other. I'd watched my boys play for years, and I'd never once had any desire to play myself. I was more of a crossword-puzzle girl.

Then, my husband, Bill, got sick.

I tried to keep up our spirits, but his road to wellness was fraught with obstacles: the late diagnosis, his allergy to the treatments, the distances we traveled. In my quiet moments, I experienced a nauseating fear that wouldn't abate.

Our son, Billy — the most dedicated gamer in the house — had been one of the original beta testers of a game he said I'd enjoy. I knew he was wrong. It was expensive and "not me."

But Billy didn't relent, and I had to admit that a game where you could "meet" people from all over the world was intriguing.

Still, I had real-life things to worry about. I had no time for games. He insisted I needed distraction from the fear, so, mostly to please him, I bought the game and subscribed.

Everyone thought it hilarious that a sixty-one-year-old woman was playing World of Warcraft. Not only was that kind of gaming seemingly reserved for the young, but it didn't fit my personality at all. I was no fighter in my daily life, not really capable of the type of aggression or strategic thinking required to prevail in a PVP — player vs. player — environment.

But at night, when the work was done and Bill slept, I played. I got into many silly situations and laughed again, something I never expected to do. Sometimes, in my dark office, I fell asleep at my keyboard, chatting with newfound friends.

I learned a whole new language: mob, aggro, boss, zerg, turtle, twink, squishy, pown. When my son and I talked to each other, no one understood a word we said. We had a form of communication just between the two of us. It was fun, and, even at my age, I learned a lot from the game.

I learned that people are the same in-game as they are "IRL" — in real life — and my own approach to the game proved it. I love pets in real life, so I play a class where I can have many. I love to fish in real life, so I fish in-game to feed my pets. I love going new places in real life, so I leveled my character exploring a vast world, which you travel in real time.

But, also in real life, I do *not* like to fight. Therefore, the class I chose was Hunter. They fight from a distance with a ranged weapon. If I get too close and get scared, I can run. And run I did, early and often.

That was the most important thing I learned about myself in Azeroth.

The game changed me. It taught me that sometimes you have to stop and face the fear. You have to stop and calm down so you can defend yourself and others. I had to get over the shame of being "killed" by a nine-year-old boy. In short, I had to learn to be a fighter, not a runner.

In my free time, I put my heart into learning those things, and I took out my anger over what was happening to Bill on every unsuspecting Alliance player I could dredge up. They invariably killed me, but I found myself calming down and finding the courage I was going to need to help Bill get well again. I wasn't running anymore. I was turning around and fighting.

At home, I redoubled my efforts: cheerleading, sanitizing to prevent infections, washing down the tables if we ate out, and adding made-from-scratch nutrition to his program. And Bill, with my help, modern medicine, and his own iron will, recovered.

Slowly, all my friends left World of Warcraft as newer games were developed, and I soon found myself alone in Azeroth. I still think about it sometimes because I miss the landscape that gave me hope and peace during a difficult time. But I mostly stopped playing.

Then, three years ago, Bill developed Parkinson's disease. Although I was right back in that horrible place of fear, I saw myself repeating the patterns that WoW taught me. I turned around and fought immediately—cleaning, cooking, and finding the best doctors I could.

But fear is a lonely place, so when I was at my most fearful, I went back to Azeroth, the place that had given me courage. There I made new friends: Dragon, Convoke and Grumbles. They keep me laughing and when an old woman "aggros" every mob in a dungeon, they laugh it off and ask me to play again the next time they go. When they see me online, they always ask how Bill is. Then they ask how I am and I say, "Fighting the good fight."

—Leslie C. Schneider—

Meet Our Contributors

Julie Angeli writes for both children and adults. Her children's stories have appeared in *Spider* and *Cricket* magazines. She has also co-authored two picture books. Her adult credits include *Sterling Script 2022* and *Once Upon a Time* magazine. She enjoys traveling with her family, paddleboarding, and playing with cats.

Tandy Balson lives with her husband in Southern Alberta. Tandy's greatest joy is spending time with her children and seven grandchildren. Other times you will find her on nature walks, reading, writing, and baking gluten-free treats. She has published four books of short inspirational stories and can be found at timewithtandy.com.

Fran Baxter-Guigli grew up in Seattle, WA and graduated from the University of Washington with a B.A. in English. She received a master's degree from the University of California, Berkeley, where she worked for more than twenty years. She and her mystery-writer husband live near Sacramento, CA with their spoiled dogs.

Karen Ambro Bernatis lives in the Bay Area with her husband. She loves to walk in nature and dance at night! Karen worked with children with autism for ten years when she prayerfully asked to make a bigger difference with her life. This led to her greatest passion, seeing lives being changed through nutritional epigenetics.

Monique Bloomfield lives in Tokyo, Japan with her husband. She moved from her hometown of New York City in 2019 to teach at a private Japanese university. Monique enjoys writing personal essays and short stories and has recently gotten into poetry. You can find inspirational blog posts on her website composedbymonique.com.

Jan Bono has completed a six-book cozy mystery series set on the

SW Washington coast. She's also published five collections of humorous personal experiences, three poetry chapbooks, nine one-act plays, a collection of 12 murderous short stories, and one quiet series novel. Learn more at www.JanBonoBooks.com.

Trish Bonsall lives in Mint Hill, NC. She is a wife, mother, and nanny. Her passions (other than writing) are cooking, entertaining and most recently, travel. Her ultimate goal is to put pencil to paper and finish that book she's been working on for most of her adult life.

Helen Boulos received her Master's in Education from the University of Virginia. She has three teenagers, five cats, two dogs, seven chickens and a tortoise. She has been published in the *Chicken Soup for the Soul* series, *Scary Mommy*, *Mamapedia* and wrote for *Greenville Neighbors* for three years. Helen is working on her first novel.

Natalie Bradish is a nature fanatic, which led her to complete her bachelor's in biology, traveling from Guatemala to South Africa and many places in between while doing so. Her pursuit of "The Land of the Uns" pushed her into the Midwest-to-Colorado pipeline, where she works as a yoga teacher and marketing manager.

Cynthia Briggs embraces her love of cooking and writing through her nostalgic tales and recipes. She enjoys reading, reviewing books, speaking to women's groups, writing for the *Chicken Soup for the Soul* series, and coaching budding authors. E-mail her at cynthiabriggsbooks @yahoo.com.

D.E. Brigham lives and writes in Tellico Village in eastern Texas. He enjoys pickleball, kayaking, hiking, bicycling, gardening, and traveling. E-mail him at davidbrigham@gmail.com.

Keisha-Bree Brissette is a Jamaican educator and writer. Her fiction has been published with the Jamaican Library Service as a part of their 2016 writers showcase. She enjoys reading, writing, hiking, and working with children. Currently, she works as an ESL educator in Tokyo, Japan.

Karla Brown is currently pursuing her TEFL certification. She has a lovely family, especially her grandkids. She enjoys swimming, reading, movies and gardening. She has one romantic-comedy novel published and is working on a series.

S.L Brunner was born in the Philippines and raised in the small northern California town of Placerville. She now resides in Southern California with her husband and two children. She works in events and marketing for a technology company, loves to travel, write, dance, and spend quality time with her family.

Jill Burns lives in the mountains of West Virginia with her wonderful family. She's a retired piano teacher and performer. She enjoys writing, music, gardening, nature, and spending time with her grandchildren.

Louise Butler is a retired educator with advanced degrees in administration and economics. She was a speaker at the Global Summit on Science and Science Education. She now enjoys the life of a writer. Louise is active in her community where she enjoys good books, bad golf, and great friends.

Caroline Caine has worked in animal rescue in Sri Lanka, Thailand, and Vietnam. She started writing as a hobby and then took a course in creative writing at the Open University. She has written a novel that she hopes to publish soon. She has a diploma in health science from Reading University. Caroline lives in the UK.

Donna Cameron is author of *A Year of Living Kindly: Choices That Will Change Your Life and the World Around You.* Her career has been spent working with non-profit organizations and causes, where she saw kindness in action on a daily basis. Her articles and essays have been published in numerous publications.

Barbara Sue Canale, award winning author of *Prayers, Papers, & Play: Devotions for Every College Student,* is also the author of *To Have and To Hold: A Daily Marriage Devotional,* and *Hope and a Whole Lotta Prayer: Devotions for Parents of Teenagers* by Liguori Publications. She is a frequent contributor to the *Chicken Soup for the Soul* series.

Lorraine Cannistra's first book, *More the Same than Different: What I Wish People Knew About Respecting and Including People with Disabilities,* is available on Amazon. She loves cooking, writing, wheelchair ballroom dancing, laughing out loud and her dog, Levi. Learn more at lorrainecannistra.com or on TikTok at Lorraine_can.

Danielle Cappolla received her Bachelor of Arts in English from Fordham University, where she graduated *magna cum laude*. She has a Master of Science in Education and Special Education from Touro College. She teaches second grade in Manhattan. Danielle enjoys reading, writing, dancing, and working with children.

Hannah Castelli is a freelance writer from Wollongong, Australia. She loves exploring her world locally but also hopping on a plane and exploring everywhere else as well. When she's not out exploring, she's probably snuggled up on the couch with her cat.

Brittany Cernic is a mother, an avid reader, a dreamer, a painter, a writer, and a lover of all things Irish. At eight, she learned the poem "Sick" by Shel Silverstein and can still recite it by heart. Brittany co-reads with her daughter every night, hoping to instill a lifelong love of reading in her.

Debbie Chase is a writer, strategy consultant, restaurant cook, drummer and mother of two young adult children. Her work has appeared in *Jacobin* magazine, *Under the Gum Tree*, *The Cincinnati Review*, and *Five Minutes*. She lives in St. Louis, MO.

Christine Clarke-Johnsen lives in Nanaimo, BC, Canada. She enjoys singing in choirs, hiking in forests, and walking the many local beaches. At home she enjoys writing short stories, playing guitar and gardening. She has been a storyteller since 2016 and is a regular contributor to the *Chicken Soup for the Soul* series.

Christina Ryan Claypool is an award-winning journalist who has been featured on *Joyce Meyer Ministries* and CBN's *700 Club*. She is a graduate of both Bluffton University and Mt. Vernon Nazarene University. She enjoys time with family, an inspiring film or book, and good coffee. Learn more at www.christinaryanclaypool.com.

Kelly Close lives in North Royalton, OH with her family, where she works in library services and loves to see customers (especially young readers) connect with stories. She enjoys being outdoors — especially near beautiful Lake Erie! Kelly is thrilled to be a repeat contributor to the *Chicken Soup for the Soul* series.

Courtney Conover will never stop trying to nudge herself out of her comfort zone. A self-professed creature of habit, Courtney has learned, however, that good things can come when we least expect them. A University of Michigan graduate, she lives in suburban Detroit with her husband and their two children.

Barbara Davey is a graduate of Seton Hall University where she received her bachelor's and master's degrees in English and journalism. A recently retired writer from the corporate world, she now enjoys writing short stories and essays, rather than annual reports and strategic plans. She and her husband live in Verona, NJ.

Lindsay (L.A.) Detwiler is a *USA Today* bestselling author of *The Widow Next Door* and twenty other novels. She is a former high school English teacher and currently a communications specialist. She lives in Pennsylvania with her husband, Chad, their Great Dane, Edmund, and their rescue cats.

A native of Cleveland, OH, **Joan Donnelly-Emery** now resides with husband Alan, dog Dottie, and birds Carl and Ellie in Franklin, TN. She performed in regional theater, national tours, and theme parks, but now thoroughly enjoys her role as caregiver for the local elementary school's childcare program. She gardens on weekends!

Glenda Ferguson got out of her comfort zone and into Mammoth Cave. She graduated from College of the Ozarks and Indiana University, contributes devotions to *All God's Creatures*, and writes with Dr. Burton's writers forum. Glenda, Tim, and Speckles the cat live in southern Indiana, a region with many caves.

Rebecca Franklyn writes from British Columbia, Canada. Her short fiction has won Writer's Digest Short Story awards. She is currently working on a poetry collection, short stories, and a YA fantasy novel. She can also be found storytelling through photos @onelife2write.

Gina Lee Guilford was born and raised in Miami, FL. She earned her Master's in Screenwriting at University of Miami and now works as a freelance writer. Gina enjoys spending time with her grandchildren, taking OLLI classes, cooking, gardening, tennis and traveling. She's working on a mystery novel, *Murder in the Mangroves*.

Lila W. Guzman is the author of middle-grade and young adult novels. *Lorenzo's Revolutionary Quest* (Arte Publico Press) tells the story of the first cattle drive in U.S. history. E-mail Lila at lorenzo1776@ yahoo.com for information about school visits and author visits or learn more at lilawguzman.com.

Dawn L. Hauter and her husband live in rural Ohio, and they have two adult children. Her career has focused on marketing, fundraising, and human resources, and she continues to take healthy risks.

Carol Goodman Heizer lives in Granbury, TX, and is an eight-time published author. Her work has appeared in several editions of the *Chicken Soup for the Soul* series. Her latest books include *Losing Your Child–Finding Your Way*, *Seasons of a Woman's Life*, and *Snapshots of Life from a Writer's View*.

Linda Loegel Hemby is an award-winning author who has authored eight historical fiction novels and four nonfiction books. She's a member of the NC Scribes read and critique group. She was interviewed on television for a local show, *The Tar Heel Traveler*, as well as being interviewed for the *Speak Up Talk Radio* Firebird Book Award.

Dr. Tory Wegner Hendrix grew up in Wisconsin and went on to earn her Doctorate in Acupuncture and Chinese Medicine from Pacific College of Health and Science in San Diego, CA. She owns a successful holistic clinic in North Carolina and enjoys life with her husband, two girls, and goofy rescued yellow Lab.

Kristen Herrington has called Halifax, Nova Scotia home for more than a decade where she lives with her husband and revolving door of foster animals. She works as a full-time artist with emphasis on abstract painting and furniture design. She published her first co-authored book in 2021 and launched a podcast in 2022.

Tracy Chamberlain Higginbotham is a thirty-year award-winning woman entrepreneur promoting and uniting other women in business, sports, and equality events around New York State. She is an avid lover and participant in sports with a life goal of trying every sport once. She invites other women to enjoy this passion with her.

Becky Hofstad writes about faith and special needs, adoption, and transracial family parenting. Her work has been published in *Life Repurposed: Stories of Grace, Hope and Restored Faith* and in several *Guideposts* publications. Becky also enjoys cooking and active adventures of all sorts with her family in Minnesota.

Mary-Lane Kamberg is a professional writer/editor/speaker in Olathe, KS, and author of *The "I Don't Know How to Cook" Book* and more than thirty nonfiction books for school libraries. She is a former swimming coach for the KC Blazers. She studies Tai Chi, has swum with dolphins, ridden an elephant and been kissed by a camel.

Lisa Kanarek is a freelance writer based in Texas. Her articles and essays cover topics including family, co-parenting, relationships, and health. Her work has been published in *The New York Times*, *The Washington Post*, *The Independent*, *Huffington Post*, *WIRED*, *The Saturday Evening Post*, and *PBS Next Avenue*.

Jennifer Kennedy is a writer and storyteller who lives in the Philadelphia suburbs with her family. As a features writer for *Guide Monthly* magazine, she enjoys telling the stories of the people of Gainesville and Tampa Bay. This is her eighth story published in the *Chicken Soup for the Soul* series. Follow her on Twitter @Jenkennedy2.

Steve Krysak is a Canadian radio personality based in Alberta. He's married with three children. Steve nearly failed high school English but discovered a love for reading and writing later in life. He's working on memoir and fiction projects.

Dana Lamb-Schaubroeck is an award-winning music educator, author, music theater writer, and songwriter. She is so honored to be a writer in this collection of wonderful stories. She is currently a doctoral candidate in Instructional Technology and Design at American College of Education and is a high school chorus teacher.

Lynne Leichtfuss is published in *Decision* and *California Climber* magazines, and the books *Mammoth Bouldering* and *Tuoloumne Meadows Bouldering*. When Lynne's adventure husband of thirty-nine years died she chose to sell their corporation and return to the outdoors, working in the High Sierra — climbing, kayaking and backpacking.

Kimberly Taybron Lucas is an alumna of ECU, LU, and UNCG. She is a full-time educator but spends her free time writing and making memories with loved ones. She's published several works that span multiple genres, intent on exploring several avenues of the writing craft. Her goal is to inspire others through varied art forms.

Nancy J. Lucas discovered her love of writing in college. She enjoys short stories, romance, and cozy mysteries. She finds her own story ideas in the funny, complex situations of life. In her free time, she enjoys traveling to see her daughters and her grandchildren.

Allison Lynn is drawn to the power of story to grow hearts and communities. Singer, songwriter and worship leader, Allison and her husband, Gerald Flemming, form the award-winning duo, Infinitely More. Publications include *Guideposts*, *The Upper Room* and four titles in the *Chicken Soup for the Soul* series. Learn more at www.InfinitelyMore.ca.

Diana Lynn is a mother, small business owner, and twelve-time contributor to the *Chicken Soup for the Soul* series.

Mary Beth Magee has been writing for as long as she can remember: news, reviews and feature articles for print and online publications, cozy Christian fiction, poetry, and devotions, as well as recollections in several anthologies. She is a member of several writing organizations. Learn more at www.LOL4.net.

Molly Magid is a freelance science communicator and journalist. In first grade, she skipped recess every day to write stories. She grew up in Denver, CO, but now lives in Christchurch, New Zealand, and loves running, hiking, and biking. Her work has been published in *Hobart*, *Ravishly*, and *The Refresh*.

Brenda Mahler is a retired teacher who loves to share her passion for words. She writes nonfiction stories about simple life experiences that provide inspiration and excitement for adventures that grow from the ordinary moments. She has published three books that are available on Amazon.

Norbert F. Markiewicz is a freelance writer with two published novels, articles and poetry. He has a B.A. in Journalism and works in health care. He lives with his wife Angie and their two grown children on the Florida Space Coast. Norbert is a member of Word Weavers International — a writing critique group.

Sara Matson lives in Minnesota with her husband. Her daughter Leah (and Leah's twin) recently graduated from college and will soon leave home for good, so Sara will be trying some new experiences as an empty-nester. She's ready! Learn more at www.saramatson.com.

Christine Powell McClintock received her Bachelor of Arts degree from Winthrop University in 1994. Currently she is the drama director at her church, and a married mother of two cats. She enjoys spending time with family and friends, comedy, and games. She is always quick with a joke and the life of every party.

Brian Michael's passion for writing was nurtured at the Allegany County Public Library. Despite possessing limited financial means, Brian's mother always managed to find both the time and the resources to enable bi-weekly visits. Brian feels that reading success at a young age often translates to success later in life.

Mark Miller has been a journalist, copywriter, *Los Angeles Times* humor columnist, joke writer for Jay Leno, Garry Shandling, Joan Rivers, and Rodney Dangerfield, and a stand-up comic who's written on numerous sitcom staffs. His humor essay collection is *500 Dates: Dispatches from the Front Lines of the Online Dating Wars.*

Jennifer Priest Mitchell, a native of Ohio, holds a bachelor's degree from Capital University, and a master's degree from Arizona State University. Jennifer writes essays, fiction, and poetry and loves spending time with her favorite inspirations — her family, friends, and dogs — out on the hiking trails.

Linda Morel has published stories about her life in previous *Chicken Soup for the Soul* anthologies, among many other publications. She writes a monthly food column for the *Jewish Exponent*. She has a master's in creative writing from The New School. Linda is a proud grandmother who loves to cook. She is writing a memoir.

Sandra Nachlinger enjoys reading, quilting, writing, lunching, spending time with her granddaughter, and hiking in the beautiful Pacific Northwest. She has written two novels (so far!), and her short stories have appeared in *Northwest PrimeTime*, *Woman's World*, and several titles in the *Chicken Soup for the Soul* series.

Brian Narelle, a graduate of USC Cinema, has been cartooning his entire life. He started out writing and animating for *Sesame Street* and wound up co-starring in the children's TV series *Bingo & Molly*. Along the way he created the San Diego Chicken, originally a cartoon, as well as starring in John Carpenter's *Dark Star*.

Susana Nevarez-Marquez is a lifelong writer. Long ago, she developed the habit of writing every day. She regularly participates in open mics and poetry readings. Another story, "Blue Bug Angel," was published in *Chicken Soup for the Soul: Angels Among Us*. E-mail her at nevmarwrite@gmail.com or on Twitter at @SusanNevarezMar.

Laurie Neveau is a wife, mother, grandmother, sister, daughter, and friend. She received a B.A. in Languages and a Master's in Business Administration. She has networked in four states and aims to encourage others with her writing.

Jeanne Nott is an actor, playwright, published author and stand-up comedian. Last year, she was crowned Ms. Colorado Senior America 2022. After participating in the Ms. Senior America pageant, she was awarded the title of Ms. Congeniality Senior America 2022.

Carole Olsen is an author and freelance writer. She is an outdoor enthusiast who loves to hike and kayak. She volunteers at an animal rescue. She resides outside of Richmond, VA with her husband, Eric, and her rescue dogs, Zoey and Dobby.

Mary Oves is a college English professor in New Jersey. When not working on her novel, she keeps busy with adventure travel and can be most often found on a horse, on her boat, on the water (or under it), or traipsing around caves, deserts and mountains. Her three grown sons, John, Dustin and Tommy, are her best work.

Marie T. Palecek loves discovering profound insights in simple, everyday things. She shares these nuggets in her transformational devotional book, *Listen for His Voice*. Visit www.marietpalecek.com for information or a sneak peek inside. Marie lives in Minnesota and enjoys all four seasons outdoors with her family and dogs.

Laura Niebauer Palmer has always been fascinated by the power of words, which led her to receive her graduate degree in English from DePaul University. She escaped the cold weather and now resides in Austin, TX with her husband and son. This is her fourth story published in the *Chicken Soup for the Soul* series.

Kim Patton is a wife and adoptive mama living in north Georgia with her husband Kevin and two daughters. She has written for *Shaunti Feldhahn, Her View from Home*, and *Waiting in Hope* infertility ministry. She published her first memoir in 2018, will publish her second in 2023 and hosts the "Book Therapy" podcast.

Nicole Perrigo was born and raised in Upstate New York. She received a bachelor's in international relations, forensic science, and sociology from Syracuse University in December of 2021, and is currently pursuing a master's degree. In her free time, Nicole enjoys traveling, hiking, and sports.

Andree Philpot is from Cincinnati, where she lives with her husband and daughter. She previously lived in Nepal where she worked alongside organizations fighting against human trafficking. She enjoys travel, motorcycling, reading, and spending time with family and friends. E-mail her at andreephilpot@gmail.com.

Vicki Pinkerton is known as a child of God, mother, wife, teacher, writer and yaya to her grandchildren. After retiring from teaching in public schools, she continues her love of teaching part-time in a private school. She enjoys playing in the dirt, otherwise known as gardening, and watching her grandkids play sports.

Connie Kaseweter Pullen lives in rural Sandy, OR near her five children and several grandchildren. She earned a B.A., with honors, at the University of Portland in 2006, with a double major in Psychology and Sociology. Connie enjoys writing, photography and exploring nature. E-mail her at MyGrandmaPullen@aol.com.

Shirlene Raymann is Dutch American and lives in Germany. She has a master's in psychology and has a private practice where she works with American military families stationed in Germany. She has two sons and is committed to living her best life and empowering others to do the same. E-mail her at Psychotherapy.oduber@gmail.com.

Jamie A. Richardson is a freelance writer and nonprofit leader. She is living proof that it's never too late to rekindle your fire, find your purpose, and pursue your dreams. Connect with her on Facebook @ JamieA.Richardson, her website www.jamiearichardson.com, or LinkedIn @freelance-writer-and-editor.

Kathleen Cox Richardson has published two books: *Taking Life Back* and *Canal Zone Brats Forever*.

Mark Rickerby is an owner and lead writer at Temple Gate Films. He has written over thirty stories for the *Chicken Soup for the Soul* series. He can be found on YouTube at "Mark Rickerby's Tales of Mystery and Adventure". He says, "No matter what I accomplish in this world, my daughters, Emma and Marli, will always bring me the most pride and joy."

Kate Ristau is an author, folklorist, and the Executive Director of Willamette Writers. She is the author of two middle-grade series, *Clockbreakers* and *Wylde Wings*, and the young adult series, *Shadow Girl*. You can read her essays in *The New York Times* and *The Washington Post*.

Carolyn Roberts received a Bachelor of Science in Accounting and subsequent Massachusetts CPA license in 1985. She recently retired from working in nonprofit for twenty-seven years. She is now looking to travel and support local animal shelters any way she can.

Emily Ruth Rusch is a wellness advocate, health coach and fitness instructor. She received her BSA in Health Science from Brenau University. The mother of three boys, Emily believes a life full of learning, laughter and movement is the happiest kind of life. She lives with her family in Turkiye.

Sue Harris Sanders has been an English teacher and high school administrator. Her children's stories have been published in magazines. Sue is an avid reader and traveler and enjoys experiencing new cultures and meeting interesting people. She loves spending time with her grandchildren, as well as taking long walks in the sunshine.

Vanessa Schaefer is an Irish writer, director, and actor. She graduated with a First Class Honours M.A. in Screenwriting from IADT in 2023 and has written various screenplays and directed two short films. You can find her acting in the movie *Dive* on Amazon Prime.

Tanya McClure Schleiden is grandmother to two little girls who enjoy adventures as much as their grandma. Her next adventure is a river cruise in France with her husband. She writes as T.R. McClure and is currently working on a women's fiction novel.

Leslie C. Schneider started writing with chalk on the sidewalk and has been going at it ever since. In addition to writing, she loves to read, knit, and make Ukrainian eggs. She and her husband of fifty-three years, Bill, are Montanans by birth but now live in Colorado where they enjoy their friends and, of course, the Rockies.

Abby Alten Schwartz is a Philadelphia writer whose essays, reported stories, humor and creative nonfiction explore a range of topics like parenting, health and wellness, mental health, chronic illness and Gen X culture. She works as a healthcare writer, designer and marketing consultant for hospitals and is writing a memoir.

Jane Seskin is a clinical social worker and writer. Her essays and poetry have appeared in numerous national magazines and journals. Her new collection of poetry is *Older Wiser Shorter: An Emotional Road Trip to Membership in the Senior Class*. She enjoys listening to jazz, reading mysteries and visiting with friends.

Mandy Shunnarah is an Alabama-born writer who now calls Columbus, OH home. Mandy's essays, poetry, and short stories have been published in *The New York Times*, *Electric Literature*, *The Rumpus*, and more. Mandy's first book, *Midwest Shreds*, is forthcoming from Belt Publishing. Learn more at mandyshunnarah.com.

Christine M. Smith lives in Oklahoma with her husband of fifty-four years. Her life revolves around her family. She has three children, fourteen grandchildren, and fourteen great-grandchildren. Storytelling, in both verbal and written form, is her favorite pastime. E-mail her at iluvmyfamilyxxx000@yahoo.com.

Eleanore R. Steinle has experienced being a caregiver and advocate for her daughter through cancer treatment and terminal lung disease. She shares her writings hoping to encourage and inspire others. She lives in New York with her husband, son, and their many pets. E-mail her at EleanoreRSteinle@gmail.com.

Amy Stros is a nurse practitioner living in Metro Detroit. She received her undergraduate degree from Western Michigan University and her master's in nursing from University of Michigan-Flint. She is a busy mom of two little girls. She enjoys traveling with her husband and kids, reading, gardening, and staying active.

Sue Sussman freelanced articles for Chicago papers for many years before shifting to books. Now a Florida resident, she writes for all ages, children through adults. Married to her husband for almost sixty years, she still has the mitt she used when she first dared to play ball all those years ago.

Sara Todd-Stone left a successful career in insurance to follow God's calling on her life. She is dedicated to serving His purpose through encouraging others to take risks, go farther and live a life without regrets by learning to trust in Him; something she's still working on herself! Learn more at LivinginHisGrace.com.

Michele Vagge has been writing since she was a young girl. She studied at William Paterson University where she wrote for the student newspaper and graduated with a bachelor's degree in journalism in 2006. She enjoys traveling, concerts and spending time with her wonderful fiancé, family, and friends. E-mail her at michelevagge@gmail.com.

Denise Valuk lives and writes in San Antonio, TX. Her writing experiences include *Guideposts* and *Mysterious Ways* magazines, several titles in the *Chicken Soup for the Soul* series and other inspirational publications. Denise spends her spare time hiking through Texas with her boys. E-mail her at denisemarievaluk@gmail.com.

Marcia Wells taught English and history to middle and high school students before changing directions. Now she enjoys writing, gardening, kayaking, snorkeling and spending time with family. Currently she is working on finishing her young adult book series.

Cristin Wenninger graduated from Texas Wesleyan University with a B.A. in Art. She taught art for two years. Cristin is an avid photographer who also enjoys traveling and gardening. She currently resides in Texas.

Alisa Tapia, writing as **N.L. Zuniga** is a freelance writer and an administrative law judge. She enjoys writing and fine wine. Her inspiration to write comes from her late mother, N.L. Zuniga. She has been published in *The Federal Lawyer* magazine and her story, "A Special Place," was published in *Chicken Soup for the Soul: Believe in Angels*.

Meet Amy Newmark

Amy Newmark is the bestselling author, editor-in-chief, and publisher of the *Chicken Soup for the Soul* book series. Since 2008, she has published 193 new books, most of them national bestsellers in the U.S. and Canada, more than doubling the number of Chicken Soup for the Soul titles in print today. She is also the author of *Simply Happy*, a crash course in Chicken Soup for the Soul advice and wisdom that is filled with easy-to-implement, practical tips for enjoying a better life.

Amy is credited with revitalizing the Chicken Soup for the Soul brand, which has been a publishing industry phenomenon since the first book came out in 1993. By compiling inspirational and aspirational true stories curated from ordinary people who have had extraordinary experiences, Amy has kept the thirty-year-old Chicken Soup for the Soul brand fresh and relevant.

Amy graduated *magna cum laude* from Harvard University where she majored in Portuguese and minored in French. She then embarked on a three-decade career as a Wall Street analyst, a hedge fund manager, and a corporate executive in the technology field. She is a Chartered Financial Analyst.

Her return to literary pursuits was inevitable, as her honors thesis in college involved traveling throughout Brazil's impoverished northeast region, collecting stories from regular people. She is delighted to have come full circle in her writing career — from collecting stories "from the people" in Brazil as a twenty-year-old to, three decades later, collecting stories "from the people" for Chicken Soup for the Soul.

When Amy and her husband Bill, the CEO of Chicken Soup for the Soul, are not working, they are visiting their four grown children and their spouses, and their five grandchildren.

Follow Amy on Twitter @amynewmark. Listen to her free podcast — Chicken Soup for the Soul with Amy Newmark — on Apple, Google, or by using your favorite podcast app on your phone.

Thank You

We owe huge thanks to all our contributors and fans. We received thousands of submissions for this popular topic, and we spent months reading all of them. Laura Dean, Maureen Peltier, Susan Heim and D'ette Corona read all of them and narrowed down the selection for Associate Publisher D'ette Corona and Publisher and Editor-in-Chief Amy Newmark. Susan Heim did the first round of editing, and then D'ette chose the perfect quotations to put at the beginning of each story and Amy edited the stories and shaped the final manuscript.

As we finished our work, D'ette continued to be Amy's right-hand woman in working with all our wonderful writers. Barbara LoMonaco, Kristiana Pastir and Elaine Kimbler jumped in to proof, proof, proof. And yes, there will always be typos anyway, so please feel free to let us know about them at webmaster@chickensoupforthesoul.com, and we will correct them in future printings.

The whole publishing team deserves a hand, including our Vice President of Marketing Maureen Peltier, our Vice President of Production Victor Cataldo, and our graphic designer Daniel Zaccari, who turned our manuscript into this beautiful, inspirational book.

Sharing Happiness,
Inspiration, and Hope

Real people sharing real stories, every day, all over the world. In 2007, *USA Today* named *Chicken Soup for the Soul* one of the five most memorable books in the last quarter-century. With over 110 million books sold to date in the U.S. and Canada alone, more than 300 titles in print, and translations into nearly fifty languages, "chicken soup for the soul®" is one of the world's best-known phrases.

Today, thirty years after we first began sharing happiness, inspiration and hope through our books, we continue to delight our readers with new titles, but have also evolved beyond the bookshelves with super premium pet food, television shows, a podcast, licensed products, and free movies and TV shows on our Crackle, Redbox, Popcornflix and Chicken Soup for the Soul streaming apps. We are busy "changing your life one story at a time®." Thanks for reading!

Share with Us

We have all had Chicken Soup for the Soul moments in our lives. If you would like to share your story, go to chickensoup .com and click on Books and then Submit Your Story. You will find our writing guidelines there, along with a list of topics we're working on.

You may be able to help another reader and become a published author at the same time! Some of our past contributors have even launched writing and speaking careers from the publication of their stories in our books.

We only accept story submissions via our website. They are no longer accepted via postal mail or fax. And they are not accepted via e-mail.

To contact us regarding other matters, please send an e-mail to webmaster@chickensoupforthesoul.com, or write us at:

Chicken Soup for the Soul
P.O. Box 700
Cos Cob, CT 06807-0700

One more note from your friends at Chicken Soup for the Soul: Occasionally, we receive an unsolicited book manuscript from one of our readers, and we would like to respectfully inform you that we do not accept unsolicited manuscripts, and we must discard the ones that are sent to us.

Changing your world one story at a time®
www.chickensoup.com